100 European Horror Films

100 EUROPEAN HORROR FILMS

BFI SCREEN GUIDES

edited by Steven Jay Schneider

Published in 2007 by the
British Film Institute
21 Stephen Street, London W1T 1LN

The British Film Institute's purpose is to champion moving image culture in all its
richness and diversity across the UK, for the benefit of as wide an audience as
possible, and to create and encourage debate.

Series cover design: Paul Wright
Cover image: *Suspiria* (Dario Argento, 1977, Seda Spettacoli S.p.A)
Series design: Ketchup/couch

Set by Fakenham Photosetting Limited, Fakenham, Norfolk
Printed in the UK by The Cromwell Press, Trowbridge, Wiltshire

British Library Cataloguing-in-Publication Data
A catalogue record for this book is available from the British Library

ISBN 978–1–84457–164–2 (pbk)
ISBN 978–1–84457–163–5 (hbk)

Contents

Acknowledgments

My sincerest thanks goes to Andrew Lockett, Rebecca Barden, Sarah Watt and all the contributors for their support, generosity and patience as this collection was conceived, developed and came to fruition. This book is dedicated to the love of my life, Katheryn.

Notes on Contributors

Linda Badley is a Professor of English at Middle Tennessee State University. The author of *Film, Horror, and the Body Fantastic* (1995) and *Writing Horror and the Body* (1996) and co-editor of *Traditions in World Cinema* (2006), she is currently at work on books on Lars von Trier and American commercial-independent film.

Colette Balmain is the founder of the Asian Studies Research Group at Buckinghamshire Chilterns University College, where she teaches Film and Media. Her doctorate was on the *gialli* of Dario Argento. She has published articles on European and East Asian horror and is currently writing a book on Japanese horror.

Linnie Blake is Senior Lecturer in Film Studies in the Department of English at Manchester Metropolitan University. She has published widely on cult and genre cinema and has recently completed a book on trauma studies and the politics of national identity in the horror cinema of Germany, Japan, the United Kingdom and the United States for Manchester University Press.

Curtis Bowman received his PhD in Philosophy from the University of Pennsylvania in 1993 and taught in the Philadelphia area for a decade. He is now an independent scholar living in Texas. Besides horror film, his research interests include the history of German philosophy, aesthetics and contemporary continental thought.

Frank Burke is Professor of Film at Queen's University (Canada). He has published three books on Fellini and provided the commentary (with Peter Brunette) for the 2006 Criterion DVD of *Amarcord*. He is currently writing a book for Edinburgh University Press on the Italian sword-and-sandal film of the 1950s and 1960s.

Jodey Castricano is Associate Professor in the Department of Critical Studies at the University of British Columbia in Kelowna and the author of *Cryptomimesis: The Gothic and Jacques Derrida's Ghost Writing* (2001). She is currently working on *Occult Subjects: Literature, Film and Psychoanalysis*, a book-length study of the nineteenth-century debates on spiritualism and the rise and practice of psychoanalysis.

Garrett Chaffin-Quiray was educated at the USC Film School and now teaches writing and media history. Most recently his story 'Service Advisory' was included in the book *The Subway Chronicles*. His work has also appeared in publications like the *San Francisco Chronicle, Writer's Journal* and *PopMatters*, and he's contributed to several books on cinema, including *1001 Movies You Must See before You Die* (2003).

Brigid Cherry runs the Film and Television programme at St Mary's College, University of Surrey. Her research is in the area of horror film audiences and fan cultures, and she is currently writing a book on feminine forms of horror. Other recent work is in the area of gender, nationality and identity in science-fiction fandoms, in both online and face-to-face fan communities. She has also written on vampire cinema and Gothic horror.

Ian Conrich is Senior Lecturer in Film Studies at Roehampton University. The author of the forthcoming book *New Zealand Cinema*, he is an editor or co-editor of eleven books, including *The Technique of Terror: The Cinema of John Carpenter* (2004), *Film's Musical Moments* (2006) and the forthcoming *Horror Zone: The Cultural Experience of Contemporary Horror Cinema*.

Travis Crawford is the Associate Program Director of the Philadelphia Film Festival, and the creator of this event's acclaimed 'Danger after Dark' forum devoted to international genre cinema. He is also a contributing writer to such publications as *Film Comment, MovieMaker, Fangoria, Film-maker* and the *Village Voice*. He began his career by interviewing Dario Argento for the fanzine *European Trash Cinema*.

Ruth Goldberg teaches Cinema Studies, Screenwriting and Cultural Studies at SUNY/Empire State College and the Escuela Internacional de Cine y Television in San Antonio de los Baños, Cuba. Her work has been included in the volumes *Planks of Reason: Essays on the Horror Film* (2004), *Japanese Horror Cinema* (2005), *Fear without Frontiers: Horror Cinema across the Globe* (2003) and *From Hobbits to Hollywood: Essays on Peter Jackson's* Lord of the Rings (2006), among others. She has also contributed to the journals *Limen, Kinoeye* and *Miradas*.

Ken Hanke is the author of several books on film – *Ken Russell's Films* (1984), *Charlie Chan at the Movies* (1989), *Tim Burton* (1999), etc. – and has written extensively for *Films in Review, Filmax, Video Watchdog* and *Scarlet Street* (for which he is also associate editor). He is the movie critic for the *Mountain Xpress* in Asheville, NC, associate critic for the *City Paper* in Charleston, SC, and a member of the Southeastern Film Critics Association.

Steffen Hantke has published essays and reviews on contemporary literature, film and culture in *Paradox, College Literature, Post Script, Scope, Science Fiction Studies* and other journals, as well as in anthologies in Germany and the US. He is author of *Conspiracy and Paranoia in Contemporary Literature* (1994) and editor of *Horror*, a special topics issue of *Paradoxa* (2002), as well as *Horror: Creating and Marketing Fear* (2004). He currently serves on the editorial board of *Paradoxa* and is chair for the 'Horror' area at the Southwest/Texas Popular Culture and American Culture Association. He teaches at Sogang University in Seoul.

Matt Hills is a Senior Lecturer in the Cardiff School of Journalism, Media and Cultural Studies, Cardiff University. He is the author of *Fan Cultures* (2002), *The Pleasures of Horror* (2005) and *How to Do Things with Cultural Theory* (2005). Among other projects, Hills is currently researching and writing a book about the BBC Wales TV series *Doctor Who.*

Reynold Humphries is Professor of Film Studies at the University of Lille 3. The author of *The American Horror Film: An Introduction* (2003) and *The Hollywood Horror Film, 1931–1941: Madness in a Social Landscape* (2006), he has contributed a study of Mario Bava to the collective volume *Monstrous Adaptations.*

Peter Hutchings is a Reader in Film Studies at Northumbria University, Newcastle upon Tyne. He has published widely on film genres and national cinemas. His most recent books are *Dracula* (2003) and *The Horror Film* (2004) and he is currently completing a dictionary of Horror Cinema.

James Iaccino is Professor in Psychology and faculty member in the Film Studies programme at Benedictine University in Lisle, Illinois. He has written several texts on Jungian archetypes in film, including *Psychological Reflections on Cinematic Terror* (1994), and has published numerous articles on film in *Kinoeye* and Popular *Culture Review.*

Neil Jackson obtained his PhD from the University of Westminster, UK. He has contributed to the *Critical Guides to Contemporary North American Directors* (2001) and *British and Irish Directors* (2001) and the Robert De Niro and Christopher Walken *Movie Top Tens.* He has also contributed to *Post Script, Video Watchdog* and is a regular columnist on the website <kamera.co.uk>.

David Kalat is a film historian and DVD producer living in Alexandria, VA, with his wife and two children. He has written several books on movies, including *J-Horror* (2007) and *The Strange Case of Dr Mabuse* (2001), and presides over the specialist DVD label All Day Entertainment.

Mikel J. Koven is Lecturer in Film and Television Studies at the University of Wales, Aberystwyth. He has published extensively in the area of folklore and film in such journals as *Ethnologies, Culture & Tradition, Contemporary Legend, Journal of American Folklore, Literature/Film Quarterly* and *Scope*. He is co-editor of a special issue of *Western Folklore* on folklore and film, co-editor of *Filmic Folklore* (2007) and author of *La Dolce Morte: Vernacular Cinema and the Italian Giallo Film* (2006).

Tanya Krzywinska is a Professor of Screen Studies in the School of Arts at Brunel University, UK. Publications include *A Skin for Dancing In: Possession, Witchcraft and Voodoo in Film* (2002), *Sex and the Cinema* (2006) and *Tomb Raiders and Space Invaders: Videogames, Forms and Contexts* (2006). Her interests coalesce around fantasy and the occult across a range of screen-based media.

Frank Lafond teaches Film Studies at Lille (France). He has written on the horror genre and film noir for several journals and in various collections. He has edited a book on the modern American horror film and is the editor of a journal called *Rendez-vous avec la peur*.

Tarja Laine is Assistant Professor at the Media and Culture Department of the University of Amsterdam. She has published a range of articles on the emotional and sensual experience of the film spectator in various film magazines and edited collections. She is currently preparing a manuscript on emotions and intersubjectivity in contemporary European cinema, to be published at the end of 2006.

Mirek Lipinski is the webmaster and chief writer for *Latarnia: Fantastique International* <www.latarnia.com> and *The Mark of Naschy* <www.naschy.com>. His writings on international horror cinema have appeared in magazines, books and DVD liner notes. A translator from Polish, he has introduced to English-speaking readers, to significant acclaim, the short fiction of Poland's supreme fantasist, Stefan Grabinski (1887–1936).

Adam Lowenstein is Associate Professor of English and Film Studies at the University of Pittsburgh. He is the author of *Shocking Representation: Historical Trauma, National Cinema, and the Modern Horror Film* (2005).

Lauri Löytökoski is a Finnish film writer specialising in the horror genre. After researching the works of the South African film-maker Richard Stanley, he wrote a text on Finnish horror films, which is slated to appear in the upcoming compilation book, *Fear without Frontiers, Volume 2*.

Patricia MacCormack is Senior Lecturer in Communication and Film at Anglia Ruskin University, Cambridge. Her PhD was awarded the Mollie Holman doctorate medal for best thesis. She has published on perversion, Continental philosophy, feminism and Italian horror film. Her most recent work is on *Cinesexuality, Masochism, Necrophilia and Becoming-Monster in Alternative Europe.* She has contributed to *Women: A Cultural Review, Thirdspace, Rhizomes* and *Theory Culture and Society.* She is currently writing on Blanchot, Bataille and Cinecstasy.

Ernest Mathijs is Assistant Professor of Film and Theatre Studies at the University of British Columbia, Canada. He researches alternative and cult cinema, and film performance. His work has appeared in *Screen and Cinema Journal*. He has edited several collections and written a book on David Cronenberg. He co-coordinates the series *Contemporary Cinema* and *Cultographies*.

Jay McRoy is an Associate Professor of English and Film Studies at the University of Wisconsin – Parkside. His books include the edited volume, *Japanese Horror Cinema* (2005), a monograph, *Nightmare Japan:*

Contemporary Japanese Horror Cinema (forthcoming) and his second anthology, *Monstrous Adaptations: Generic and Thematic Mutations in Horror Film* (co-edited with Richard Hand, also forthcoming).

Philippe Met teaches at the University of Pennsylvania. He has published widely in various areas, including modern French poetry, horror literature and film, and French noir. Several new projects in film are in progress, including a book-length study of representations of childhood in international horror cinema.

Gary Needham teaches Film and Television Studies in the School of Arts, Communication and Culture, Nottingham Trent University. He is the co-editor of *Asian Cinemas: A Reader and Guide* (2006).

Kim Newman is a novelist, critic and broadcaster. His fiction includes *Anno Dracula* (1993), *Life's Lottery* and *The Man from the Diogenes Club* (2006). His non-fiction includes *Nightmare Movies* (1988), *Horror: 100 Best Books* (1988) and the BFI Classics studies of *Cat People* (1999) and *Doctor Who* (2005). He is a contributing editor to *Sight and Sound* and *Empire*. He wrote and directed a short film, *Missing Girl* (2001).

Dejan Ognjanovic lives in Nis, Serbia. He has published literary and film essays in Serbian magazines. His reviews in English can be found at <www.kfccinema.com> and <www.unrated.co.uk>. His essay on Serbian horror films is forthcoming in the second edition of Steven Jay Schneider's collection, *Fear without Frontiers: Horror Cinema across the Globe*. He has written books on the devil in cinema and on Serbian horror films.

David Sanjek has written on film for *PopMatters, Senses of Cinema, Bad Subjects* and *Quarterly Review of Film and Video*. He will publish *Always on My Mind; Music, Memory and Money* and *Stories We Could Tell: Putting Words to American Popular Music* in 2007. He is the Director of the BMI Archives.

Steven Jay Schneider has an MA in Philosophy from Harvard University and an MA in Cinema Studies from New York University's Tisch School of the Arts. He is the editor of numerous books on various areas of film, including *1001 Movies You Must See before You Die* (2003), *New Hollywood Violence* (2004), *Fear without Frontiers: Horror Cinema across the Globe* (2003) and *Horror International*.

Linda Schulte-Sasse is Professor of German Studies at Macalester College, St Paul, MN. In 1996, Duke University Press published her book *Entertaining the Third Reich: Illusions of Wholeness in Nazi Cinema* (1996). Besides German cinema, her research interests include American political discourses and horror. She is completing a monograph on Dario Argento.

Michael Sevastakis completed his BA at the Catholic University of America in Washington DC and his MA at Manhattan College in New York in English Literature specialising in the Victorian Age. He received a second MA and PhD in Cinema Studies from New York University. He has written extensively in film journals and authored the books *Songs of Love and Death: The Classical American Horror Film of the 1930s* (1993) *and Narrative Voices in Russ Meyer's Films: A Cacophony of Carnality* (2006). He is currently a Professor in the Communication Department at the College of Mt St Vincent in Riverdale, NY.

Philip L. Simpson received his BA and MA degrees in English from Eastern Illinois University in 1986 and 1989, respectively, and his doctorate in American Literature from Southern Illinois University in 1996. He serves as Academic Dean of Humanities/Fine Arts and Behavioral/Social Sciences at Brevard Community College in Melbourne, Florida. He also serves as Vice President of the Popular Culture Association and Area Chair of Horror for the Association. His book, *Psycho Paths: Tracking the Serial Killer through Contemporary American Film and Fiction*, was published in 2000. He is the author of numerous other essays on film, literature, popular culture and horror.

Marcus Stiglegger received a PhD in Film Studies at the University of Mainz, Germany. He has published books and articles on film aesthetics, history and theory. He is the editor of the cultural magazine *:Ikonen:*<www.ikonenmagazin.de> and contributes to such journals as *Filmdienst, Splatting Image* and *Eyeball*.

Andrew Syder is a doctoral student in the School of Cinema-Television at the University of Southern California. His dissertation focuses on issues of visual culture and psychotronic film from the 1960s and 1970s.

Nathaniel Thompson is the editor of the three-volume *DVD Delirium* series for Fab Press and is a contributing writer for Turner Classic Movies. He lives in Los Angeles, where he coordinates and produces cult and horror releases on DVD for Image Entertainment.

Donato Totaro is the editor of the online film journal *Offscreen* <www.offscreen.com>. Totaro received his PhD in Film and Television from the University of Warwick (UK) and is a part-time lecturer in Film Studies at Concordia University (Montreal). He is currently preparing a manuscript entitled *Time and the Long Take in Narrative Cinema*.

Rebecca and **Sam Umland** are Professors of English and Film Studies at the University of Nebraska at Kearney. The have co-authored two books, including the biographical study *Donald Cammell: A Life on the Wild Side* (2006). They have spoken and published widely on topics ranging from world cinema and postmodernism to the emerging cyberculture, and their work has been published in numerous countries, including the United States, the United Kingdom, France, Germany, Australia and Hong Kong.

Cosimo Urbano holds a PhD in Cinema Studies from New York University where he has recently taught the modern horror film. His essays on the genre have appeared in *CineAction!, Psychoanalytic Review* and the collection *Horror Film and Psychoanalysis: Freud's Worst Nightmares* (2004). He divides his time between New York and Rome.

Darryl Wiggers is currently Director of Programming for SCREAM, a Canadian digital TV channel dedicated to airing thrillers, suspense and horror films. He previously worked at Showcase Television and History Television. Born and raised in Whitby, Ontario, he graduated from York University in Canada in 1988 with a Bachelor of Fine Arts, Film Theory and Screenwriting.

Andrew Willis teaches Film and Media Studies at the University of Salford. He is the co-author, with Peter Buse and Nuria Triana Toribio, of *The Cinema of Álex de la Iglesia*. He has also edited *Film Stars: Hollywood and Beyond* (2004), co-edited, with Antonio Lazaro Reboll, *Spanish Popular Cinema* (2004) and *Defining Cult Movies* (2003), with Mark Jancovich, Antonio Lazaro Reboll and Julian Stringer.

William S. Wilson earned a degree in Literary and Cultural Studies from the College of William & Mary in Williamsburg, VA. When he isn't watching good movies, he is usually watching really bad ones.

Rick Worland received his PhD in Motion Picture/Television Critical Studies from UCLA. He is Associate Professor and Chair of the Division of Cinema-Television at Southern Methodist University, Dallas. His research has been published in *Cinema Journal, Journal of Film and Video, Journal of Popular Film and Television* and *Historical Journal of Film, Radio and Television* among others. His book, *The Horror Film: An Introduction* was published in 2006.

Introduction

'Eurohorror' is a term that has been used primarily by reviewers and fans
– and fans who are reviewers – to refer to post-1960 horror cinema
emanating from Italy, Spain, France and, to a lesser extent, Belgium,
Germany and other European nations. The reason for the post-1960
dating has largely to do with the fact that it was during this period that
on-screen sex (including nudity and lesbianism), violence (both
psychological and physical, including sadism, torture and gore) and what
might be generally termed 'alternative imagery' (where the sex is often
combined with the violence) became a great deal more explicit in the
European commercial film industry. This opening up of the restraints on
what could be shown on screen, along with the thematic and stylistic
influence of several groundbreaking American horror films of the same
period, from *Psycho* (1960) to *Night of the Living Dead* (1968) and *The
Exorcist* (1973), resulted in a new, more graphic, sensational,
transgressive type of European horror cinema.

The long tradition of horror film-making in Europe means that it is
necessary to include certain pre-1960 films in the Eurohorror category. In
fact, relatively clear precursors can be found in Riccardo Freda and Mario
Bava's *I Vampiri* (1957) and Georges Franju's *Eyes Without a Face* (1960);
and one could certainly argue for a line of descent extending as far back
as, say, Benjamin Christensen's *Häxan* (1922), with its shockingly
surrealistic, graphic and frightening imagery. While it is very interesting
and valuable to discuss such ancestors and precursors in the larger context
of Eurohorror cinema, this should not be taken to imply that 'Eurohorror'
was an identifiable category in its own right prior to the 1960s.

A similar line of thinking motivates the inclusion of predominantly Western European films in the Eurohorror tradition. With the sorts of censorship restrictions endemic to most Eastern and Central European cinemas during the period in question, horror films of any kind were much more difficult to make or watch, to say nothing of the hyper-violent and transgressive horror films qualifying as 'Eurohorror'. Once again, there are several fascinating and important exceptions to this general rule, and this Screen Guide will make a clear effort to be inclusive and discuss horror films from outside Western Europe that at the very least bear interesting connections to the more obvious and straightforward examples of Eurohorror cinema.

Interestingly, subgeneric distinctions do *not* seem particularly important for Eurohorror classification. Thus, one finds gore, *giallo*, stalker, slasher, splatter, cannibalism, zombie, serial killer, body horror and (of course) lesbian vampire films included for discussion, regardless of these films' numerous and immediately recognisable differences at the levels of convention, narrative, iconography, atmosphere and setting. What matters most are that the films in question – whatever their subgenre – showcase a greater degree of explicit violence, sexuality and trasnsgressive, alternative imagery than earlier examples of their form.

With the recent opening up of academic film studies to such previously undesirable and neglected cinematic categories as 'trash', 'psychotronic', 'exploitation' and 'cult', film scholars in North America and Great Britain have started giving the notion of Eurohorror a wider currency. Critical attention to and interest in Eurohorror continues to grow today, just as it does with respect to the horror film output in so many other countries. This refreshing change has as much to do with the increased availability of the films in question to English-speaking scholars – primarily via paracinema mail-order companies and internet websites – as with any unfounded critical bias towards British and North American productions.

For distributors, promoters and, of course, fans, the Eurohorror tag is something of a badge of honour, implying membership in a fairly exclusive club of horror films that manage to be simultaneously artistic *and* generic, innovative and derivative, highbrow *and* lowbrow. The cultural value and prominence of Eurohorror has risen dramatically in recent years with the advent of DVD technology and what Raiford Guins, discussing the promotion and consumption of Italian horror films in the United States, identifies as processes of 'remediation'. According to Guins, 'The companies promoting the likes of [Dario] Argento, [Mario] Bava, and even [Lucio] Fulci on DVD, selling a title as part of a "collection", place their directors on the market as auteurs in order to invoke value statements that valourise the director's work as an art-object, an "authored original", and a masterpiece of Italian horror cinema'.[1]

At this still-early stage in the cultural and critical reappraisal and 'opening up' of Eurohorror cinema, the scholar's main task should be to identify a canon of key directors, actors, films and cycles. The BFI Screen Guide you hold in your hands endeavours to do just that, offering a personal but broadly representative summary of 100 recommended Eurohorror titles, along with credits for each movie, an accessible introductory essay and useful information on where to obtain the films in question on VHS and DVD. The essays – composed by an assortment of experts in the field – are informed, colourful and engaging, written with the non-expert and probably quite curious reader in mind. It is hoped and intended that the authors' collective enthusiasm for this topic will stimulate new interest and discussion, as well as provide a guided tour through an otherwise messy and frequently frightening (in a good way!) area of film.

Anatomy (*Anatomie*)
Germany, 2000 – 110 mins
Stefan Ruzowitzky

Produced by the German branch of Columbia Pictures, Stefan
Ruzowitzky's medical horror movie *Anatomy* is somewhat of an oddity in
post-war German horror cinema. With its technical competence and
stylistic sleekness, the film stands out in a production landscape of small-
scale and underground horror efforts. Featuring an ensemble cast of
attractive young stars – first among them Franka Potente, a star in
Germany and elsewhere since the success of Tom Tykwer's *Run Lola Run*
(1998) – *Anatomy* belongs to a wave of European horror films that, since
the 1990s, marks the emulation of American mainstream cinema in
production and financing as well as in visual and narrative aesthetics.

The film tells the story of an elite programme for medical students
that serves as a cover for a conspiratorial cell of the 'Anti-Hippocrates'.
Devoted to pure science over the humanitarian mandate to ease human
suffering, this secret organisation conducts dubious medical experiments
and recruits star pupils to further its agenda. Paula Henning (Potente), one
of the students chosen for the programme, begins to suspect that some of
the cadavers used for a pioneering preservation technique called
'plastination' have not died of natural causes (the film draws on the
controversial 'body art' exhibition 'Koerperwelten' and its creator, Gunther
von Hagens, which had toured Germany at that time, before going
international shortly thereafter). When not only a casual acquaintance but
also a fellow student turn up on the operating table as 'plastinated'
corpses, Paula's enquiries make her the target of the group's attempts to
keep its existence secret. Its self-appointed henchman, another student in
the programme, goes after her, and though she manages to kill him, the
group itself continues to exist, carrying its nefarious activities into the
sequel, *Anatomy 2*, also directed by Ruzowitzky (2003).

The film falls into the loose subgenre of medical horror, harking back
to pictures like *Eyes Without a Face* (1960) and *Coma* (1978). A young

man waking up on an operating table to discover that his body has been partly opened up and dismantled – this is the iconic image of medical horror, exploiting the sense of helplessness we all experience when faced with the stern authority of medical science.

Though this subgenre determines the paranoid theme and graphic imagery in *Anatomy*, Ruzowitzky's script ties the film in with two specific aspects of post-war German history. First, a reference to the Anti-Hippocrates flourishing during the Third Reich suggests that *Anatomy* draws on anxieties about unacknowledged continuities between Nazi Germany and post-war Germany – anxieties which were all the more poignant because of the political resurgence of rightwing groups in the wake of so-called German reunification. Second, the film's critique of the consequences of professional and social elitism refers to the neo-liberal dismantling of the welfare state, and with it the erosion of the ideal of civic and social equality, which many Germans began to notice under the conservative government of Helmut Kohl during the 1990s. Since these psychological fears and social trends are by no means limited to post-reunification Germany, however, *Anatomy* has had an easy time finding appreciative audiences elsewhere as well.   SH

Dir: Stefan Ruzowitzky; **Prod**: Jakob Claussen, Norbert Preuss, Andrea Willson, Thomas Wöbke; **Original Music**: Marius Ruhland, Fatboy Slim; **Wr**: Stefan Ruzowitzky; **Art**: Annette Ingerl, Jochen Proske; **Cinematography**: Peter von Haller; **Editing**: Ueli Christen.

Angst (aka *Fear*)
Austria/West Germany, 1983 – 82 mins
Gerald Kargl

The unnamed antagonist played by Erwin Leder in *Angst* – based on the real-life case of Salzburg-born triple murderer Werner Kniesek – seems to have missed out on recent cinema's various efforts to popularise, romanticise and above all commercialise the figure of the serial killer (see, for example, *Manhunter* [1986], *Se7en* [1995], *Kalifornia* [1993], *The Silence of the Lambs* [1991], *Natural Born Killers* [1994]). For Götz's character is neither charismatic nor creative, neither imaginative nor attractive . . . not even in a rough, uncultured sort of way.

While he succeeds in slaughtering a bourgeois family of three – a young woman, her retarded, wheelchair-bound brother and their elderly mother – most viewers are apt to view him as a complete and utter failure, even when it comes to his chosen 'profession'. Early in the film, voiceover narration spoken by the killer while he is still in jail for an earlier crime tells of a mysterious and malevolent plan that he has spent years perfecting, and that he promises to put into effect immediately upon his release. But this carefully laid plan goes up in smoke every time he gets a chance to put it into effect.

For example, shortly after his release from prison he bolts from a cab when the increasingly suspicious female driver suddenly stops the car. This scene thwarts our expectations by having the killer lose his nerve, panic and make a break for it rather than enter a test of strength and will against his potential victim. Running through the woods at random, he stumbles upon an isolated house and his spirits rise once again. Hiding while the family who resides there returns home that evening, he quickly springs into action: knocking the son out of his wheelchair, he ties up the daughter and sets to work killing the mother by strangling her and stuffing paper down her throat. In one of the most disturbing – because so disturbingly realistic – fictional murder scenes ever committed to celluloid, we watch him struggle to kill the woman, who, despite her advanced age and apparent infirmity, puts up an amazing fight. Biting, scratching, clawing and butting heads, the two wage distinctly unromantic battle before the woman, false teeth popping out of her mouth, finally loses consciousness.

Kargl's 'genius' here is to show everything in real time, with numerous close-ups and diegetic sound. Viewers get to experience none of the pleasure (whether guilty or gleefully acknowledged) that comes from watching stylised, aestheticised killing replete with slow-motion camerawork, overlapping edits and a meticulously composed *mise en scène*. Instead, writer-cinematographer Zbigniew Rybczynski alternates close-up point-of-view shots of the victim and her attacker, constantly altering our relationship to the action. We have no one to identify with, or rather, no one person with whom to identify, experiencing not only the old woman's terror but the killer's increasing excitement and determination as well.

Refusing to accept the fact that the woman has died, the killer stands her up and drags her across the room in a grotesque *danse macabre*; he even goes so far as to stuff pills down her throat, a desperate attempt to revive her in order that he might kill her again, only more slowly this time. His rampage culminates in the stabbing death of the daughter that evening, after which he has sex with the corpse, practically covering himself in her blood. The utter lack of suspense in this latter scene, the director's refusal to gratify viewers by placing the young woman's body on display and the emphasis on revealing the utterly compulsive, animalistic nature of the murderer's behaviour – all of this places *Angst* squarely at odds with mainstream American (and American-influenced) serial killer movies.

What makes *Angst* so interesting, even important, is the fact that the film's numerous 'failures' are precisely what constitute its success. Not only the failures of the killer, whose grand scheme amounts to nothing more than three chaotic and wholly undignified murders, but also the failures of the director, who satisfies none of the genre's conventions, and who eschews the popular tradition of romanticising the serial killer, of turning him into a sort of neo-Gothic anti-hero. Even more than Michael Rooker in John McNaughton's infamous 1986 film, *Henry: Portrait of a Serial Killer*, Leder's sociopath comes frighteningly close to providing us with a true 'portrait' of a serial killer. And if we find that portrait less than appealing, this only speaks to the film's haunting power and strikingly original construction.   SJS

Dir: Gerald Kargl; **Writer**: Gerald Kargl, Zbigniew Rybczynski; **Original Music**: Klaus Schulze; **Cinematography**: Zbigniew Rybczynski.

Anguish (Angustia)
Spain, 1987 – 89 mins
Bigas Luna

An intricately constructed Chinese puzzle-box of shifting reality layers
and explorations of ocular trauma, both literal and allegorical, *Anguish* is
almost so po-mo it hurts, and at times, the film's gimmicky self-reflexivity
threatens to overwhelm an already complexly interlocked dual narrative.
Yet the film remains one of the most alarmingly neglected titles of the
Eurohorror lean years of the 1980s (its inability to secure a larger
international audience upon theatrical release is notably lamentable, in
that it is conceptually designed for theatre viewing), and even when its
meta-cinematic commentaries on voyeurism and sadism become so
obvious that subtext towers over story, eclectic director Bigas Luna's
literally hypnotic thriller is so skilfully manipulative that it could give both
Brian De Palma and William Castle a run for their collective money.

Anguish is impossible to discuss without revealing a critical story
twist, so just as the film's opening advises members of the audience to
leave the auditorium if they feel dizzy (the fact that the narrator's
comments differ slightly from the on-screen warning should offer a sly
indication of the structural shift that awaits), one should avoid reading
further if one wishes to approach this – highly recommended – movie.
Beginning as a broad *Psycho (*1960*)* homage with portly ophthalmologist
orderly Michael Lerner carving out 'the eyes of the city' under the
instructions of his diminutive mother (*Poltergeist* clairvoyant Zelda
Rubenstein), *Anguish* memorably morphs into a different film at the
twenty-two-minute mark, as a swirling montage of spirals, snails and
stroboscopic effects reveals that the entire opening of the movie – Luna
deserves credit for having the *huevos de oro* (to cite another of his films)
to carry the joke on for as long as he does – is actually 'The Mommy', a
horror movie being viewed in a bland suburban theatre by a group of
increasingly traumatised spectators. Two patrons are a bit more affected
by the on-screen mayhem than most – a hollow-eyed psychopath with a

silencer-equipped pistol begins to believe the drama and initiates a maternally driven shooting spree, while a terrified teenage girl attempts to convince her irritated friend that something sinister is occurring off-screen as well. Meanwhile, Luna intercuts between the banal brutality of the movie-mad maniac and the more traditional Gothic suspense of 'The Mommy' as it continues to unfold in front of the oblivious audience; as the cinephiliac's body count peaks, the film-within-a-film's eye-hunter's escapades culminate in a similarly secretive mass slaughter in – you guessed it – a movie theatre.

Anguish could have easily succumbed to the temptation of lazily lapsing into a purely cerebral conceptual prank, but Luna succeeds by keeping the grisly proceedings fundamentally visceral: the hypnosis sequences of 'The Mommy' are genuinely powerful and, indeed, the film is quite skilful in keeping both storylines suspenseful even after the cinematic hoax has been unveiled. While Luna's ambitious thriller suffers from some comparatively minor flaws – the film quickly begins to feel strangely redundant once it settles into a rhythm of precision cross-cutting between the two simultaneous theatre massacres, and occasionally Luna hits the metaphorical nail a little too firmly on the head (the climactic police sniper shot emanates from the projection booth window, for example) – it remains a bravura stylistic exercise that is also every bit as disturbing a meditation on film viewing as Michael Powell's *Peeping Tom* (1960).   TC

Dir: Bigas Luna; **Prod**: Pepón Coromina, Andreu Coromina, George Ayoub, Xavier Visa; **Original Music**: José Manuel Pagán; **Wr**: Bigas Luna, Michael Berlin; **Art**: Felipe de Paco; **Editing**: Tom Sabin; **Cinematography**: Josep M. Civit.

The Awful Dr Orloff (aka *Cries in the Night, The Diabolical Dr Satan/Gritos en la noche*)
Spain/France, 1962 – 86 mins
Jesús Franco

Before Jesús Franco's *The Awful Dr Orloff*, Spanish cinema primarily produced socially serviceable films and simple entertainments, and did not have a horror tradition. Only Edgar Neville's *La torre de los siete jorobados* (literally, 'The Tower of the Seven Hunchbacks', 1944) could lay claim to being part of the genre, though it was at heart a macabre fantasy whose frequent light touches generate nothing more than a delightful and safe frisson.

Based on a fictitious novel by 'David Khune' (a frequent Franco pseudonym), *Orloff*'s story of a surgeon seeking to reconstruct the face of his scarred daughter seemed to tie in with the plastic surgery nightmares in vogue after the success of Georges Franju's *Eyes Without a Face* (1960). Franco denies a connection, claiming he never saw Franju's picture at the time of its release. Rather, the impetus for his film arose when he viewed Terence Fisher's *Brides of Dracula* (1960) and thought he could make a better and more shocking movie.

Franco was born into a large family in Madrid in 1930. Seduced by jazz and its improvisational freedom, he spent time in France and, after a return to Spain, began working for and learning from such noted directors as Juan Antonio Bardem and Luis Garcia Berlanga. He made his directorial debut with the comedy *Tenemos 18 años* (1959), but it was with *Orloff* – his fifth film – that he began acquiring his credentials as a horror auteur.

An eager cinephile with an appreciation of American B-movies, Franco suffused his chiaroscuro nightmare with the kinetic camera angles he so admired in films noirs like Robert Siodmak's *Phantom Lady* (1944). Shadows and music halls threatened ravishment and rape; capture meant bondage and, afterward, mutilation. The French co-production company, Eurocine, mandated the addition of a couple of nude shots that further accented the film's darkly sexual tone, though the showing of these scenes was limited to French playdates.

The film introduced one of Spain's iconic horror figures, Dr Orlof/Dr Orloff. Played by Howard Vernon, this medical man inhabited a self-contained world of quiet madness and stubborn visions, and, despite his demise here, he would return in numerous films thereafter, as would his servant, Morpho (Ricardo Valle).

On release, typically on the lower half of exploitation double bills, *Orloff* was either critically ignored or savaged, as many critics, protective of societal laws of decency, bristled at its Sadean elements and moments of unrepentant sleaze. In this regard, and considering that *Orloff* took time to be disseminated, the film was not uniquely influential, but rather a notable benchmark in the history of perverse cinema.

After *Orloff*, Spanish film-makers began to see possibilities in the horror genre, particularly when coupled with foreign investment, and a steady – albeit slow – stream of Spanish horror movies followed, leading up to Spain's horror boom of the 1970s that was initiated by the impressive national success of Léon Klimovsky's *Shadow of the Werewolf* (1971), a Paul Naschy classic.

As for Franco, his other early horror films, such as *The Secret of Dr Orloff* (1964) and *The Diabolical Dr Z* (1965), seemed to herald an impeccable craftsman of the genre, but that promise devolved with his voracious acceptance of making too many films at a quick pace for devious producers with problematic finances. His filmography of over 175 pictures, which comprises subject matter ranging from women-in-prison to pornography, and which grows to this day, has alternately fascinated, annoyed, impressed and exasperated both his followers and detractors, making him the most controversial figure in Spanish *fantastique*.   ML

Dir: Jesús Franco; **Prod**: Leo Lax, Marius Lesoeur, Serge Newman; **Original Music**: Antonio Ramírez Ángel, José Pagán; **Wr**: Jesús Franco (as David Khune); **Cinematography**: Godofredo Pacheco; **Editing**: Alfonso Santacana.

The Beast (*La Bête*)
France, 1975 – 102 mins
Walerian Borowczyk

Part costume drama, part schlock and part softcore pornography
channelled through a black comedy of manners, writer–editor–director
Walerian Borowczyk's *The Beast*, an adaptation of the short story 'Lokis'
by Prosper Merimée, is a revision of old fables concerned with storybook
romance. Further complicating this loose play on *Romeo and Juliet*,
Beauty and the Beast and *Little Red Riding Hood* are numerous bared
breasts, a gigantic lupine phallus, truly copious ejaculant and sensually
executed bestiality, altogether resulting in a sex-crazed and often
uproariously funny freak show masquerading in the guise of a horror
movie.

Action begins when the head of a declining French family, Pierre de
l'Espérance (Guy Tréjan), matches his socially inept son Mathurin (Pierre
Benedetti) with the wealthy American heiress Lucy Broadhurst (Lisbeth
Hummel). Travelling under the watchful eye of her Aunt Virginia
(Elisabeth Kaza), Lucy arrives at the Chateau de l'Espérance and quickly
uncovers the founding family myth; that a former lady of the house,
Romilda (Sirpa Lane), was once ravished by a lupine creature lurking in
the nearby woods and corrupted her family line, making all offspring
half-man, half-animal. Local clergy therefore take exception to the family,
making the search for Mathurin's match difficult since no priest will
perform the ceremony because it would be considered heretical.
Regardless, Lucy accepts her betrothed and dreams of suffering – or
enjoying – Romilda's fate, which coincides with Mathurin's gradual
decline before their marriage can be consummated. Exit Lucy and
Virginia for simpler American shores; exit Mathurin and Pierre via alcohol
poisoning and suicide, respectively.

While horror cinema has always been fascinated by the similarity
between animals and humans – like an instinct for survival in the most
pedestrian sense, but leading all the way up to interspecies love – *The*

An unnatural sight: Walerian Borowczyk's *The Beast*

Beast literalises these often implicit connections. In so doing, it makes perverse the straightforward romance of finding a good family heir, or even of educating the naive foreign dame about heartier, older European charms. Yet in its execution *The Beast* is a work of such vulgar titillation that its social critique is necessarily muted by successive money shots.

What remains most memorable, however, is the way staid dramatic sequences are punctuated with truly unexpected sensual events, as if the point of montage was turned away from dogma towards narrative, and the reason (aside from naked women masturbating) that makes Borowczyk's film a keynote for both art house and grind house. There's an erect stallion mounting a mare in the midst of oestrus-related excitation at the beginning, and there's a surreal nightmare flashback of Romilda's ravishment at the claws, snout, penis and tongue of the monster eventually revealed as Mathurin's sire at the end. A constantly interrupted servant's coupling carves up the niceties of preparing for an unholy wedding. And then there's the skewering of the priesthood – and Catholicism at large – through the characterisation of clergy as homosexual paedophiles. Nowhere is *The Beast* more effective, though, than when Romilda is attacked by the monster, first with comic resistance and then with complete rapture, until she turns the trick on him, literally fucking him to death.   GCQ

Dir: Walerian Borowczyk; **Prod**: Anatole Dauman; **Non-Original Music**: Domenico Scarlatti; **Wr**: Walerian Borowczyk; **Cinematography**: Bernard Daillencourt, Marcel Grignon; **Editing**: Walerian Borowczyk.

A Bell of Hell (La campana del infierno)
Spain/France, 1973 – 106 mins
Claudio Guerín, Juan Antonio Bardem [uncredited]

This ambiguous 1973 study of the more nightmarish aspects of arrested development charts the perverse journey of John (Renaud Verley), an institutionalised prankster who is released into the care of his Aunt Marta (Viveca Lindfors) and her three daughters. The ladies' suspicious motives in his committal provoke the young man into an increasingly perverse and dangerous series of macabre practical jokes: a re-enactment of Saki's 'The Open Window', a vicious bee attack and even a harrowing recreation of a slaughterhouse involving human victims. When Marta arranges to have John put out of the way permanently during a church service, the gamesmanship ultimately turns fatal for more than one of the parties involved.

The previous decade had seen a marked shift in the treatment of youth on film, with war protests, counterculture movements and drug-friendly behaviour characterising most cinematic efforts. One typical response was 1966's *King of Hearts*, which posited that the most natural response to an insane system is to simply go mad and retreat into blissful isolation at an asylum with fellow-minded lunatics. However, this vision from director Claudio Guerín offers a somewhat more sinister take, providing a dark sequel to that film as our hero is released into 'normality' only to unleash chaos on the scheming, utterly corrupt elders around him. John finds that insanity is indeed the most sensible response to a diseased environment controlled by avarice, but his madness is far more malicious (and justified) than the sunny flights of fancy endorsed in the late 60s.

The film's perverse, much discussed sense of devilish humour is obviously its strongest and most memorable component, with the audience often the butt of the jokes as much as the characters. The talented Guerín (who fell to his death from the film's bell tower at the end of shooting under mysterious circumstances) steadfastly refuses to openly deliver the gory and sexy thrills audiences were demanding at the time; a gory eye-gouging turns out to be a crafty make-up jest, the numerous set-ups for seduction sequences end in frustration and the eventual nudity of the three young women is only delivered with them hanging like sides of beef in the most anti-erotic manner possible. In fact, the only overt bloodshed comes courtesy of an early scene in a real slaughterhouse (often deleted from prints), where John's observation of this daily routine inspires his third-act scheme. Guerín's strongest moments come from the dreadful anticipation of violence, particularly the magnificent climax which finds Marta in church hovering in anticipation as she awaits the fateful tolling of the bell above her. However, Guerín still isn't satisfied, administering another last-minute jolt that manages to deliver retribution and additional mystery in equal measures.

Inspired more by classic horror practitioners like Poe, Rampo and Le Fanu than by his cinematic contemporaries, the film makes use of the simplest, most childlike pleasures to yield chills, as in the refraining chant of 'Alouette' and the wicked mirth on John's face when he sends a guest running in horror from the house with the power of mere words. Though Guerín would never again entrance viewers with his uniquely haunting powers, he managed to leave behind a masterpiece of the genre which still lingers in the memory with the same ghostly but firm grasp as the eerie organ notes of the film's final musical passages.   NJ

Dir: Claudio Guerín, Juan Antonio Bardem (uncredited); **Prod**: Robert Ausnit, Claudio Guerín, Luis Laso; **Original Music**: Adolfo Waitzman; **Wr**: Santiago Moncada; **Cinematography**: Manuel Rojas; **Editing**: Magdalena Pulido.

The Beyond (aka *E tu vivrai nel terrore – L'aldilà* [*And You Will Live in Terror: The Afterlife*])
Italy, 1981 – 88 mins
Lucio Fulci

The years between 1979 and 1981 saw Lucio Fulci at his creative peak. During this period, Fulci produced some of his most remarkable films – *Zombie* (1979), *City of the Living Dead* (1980), *The Black Cat* (1981), *The House by the Cemetery* (1981) and *The Beyond*. What demarcates these years as especially significant for Fulci's film-making was his increasing interest in creating graphically gory set pieces, often at the expense of narrative coherency; while his visual sensibility became more baroque and complicated, his stories (along with frequent screenplay collaborator Dardano Sacchetti) became less logical and more impressionistic. Early Fulci, like his *giallo* films, were entirely dependent upon narrative, and within the narrative the director would look for moments to include his grotesque and over-the-top set pieces. A decade later, Fulci learned no one was really paying attention to his stories anyway, and so his films became more loosely linked set pieces than horror stories.

The Beyond's quasi-plot centres on Liza Merril (Katherine MacColl), a New Yorker who inherits a dilapidated hotel in rural Louisiana which was built upon one of the 'Seven Gates of Hell', according to an apocryphal book. Hunky local doctor, John McCabe (David Warbeck), becomes involved as various mysterious incidents, deaths and disappearances occur while the hotel is renovated. As this gate to hell is opened, the dead rise, zombie-like, menacing the living. But the film's story, such as it is, is secondary to its overall effect – an outline which connects various horror set pieces. We watch *The Beyond* not for any kind of cinematic storytelling, but to see someone whipped with chains and then crucified in the hotel; to see another have his mouth and tongue torn apart by the worst-looking fake spiders in cinema history; to see a blind girl have her throat ripped out by her beloved guide dog; and, of course, the finale of the film, Dr McCabe and Liza fighting their way out of the hospital's morgue through an army of zombies.

In the end, *The Beyond* offers little else but these jaw-dropping horror set pieces. What makes the film so noteworthy is that, by refusing to drive it with narrative, Fulci brings horror cinema back to its nightmare-like origins. *The Beyond* works as a nightmare; these graphic images of horror and violence are aesthetic moments which feel almost completely independent of one another. Like a dream, Fulci and Sacchetti thinly link the images together so that the power and visceral impact of the set piece is not subsumed within the overall narrative. There is no 'logic' behind the gore, nothing to 'justify' its inclusion. The violence ultimately needs no justification as it is part of the film's oneiric flow. One could argue that, by returning *The Beyond* to its essence as dark dream, Fulci returns to a more ontological question for cinema itself. The nightmare-like picture reminds us that cinema, as a medium, is rooted within the alogical experiences of the subconscious.

Ever a playful film-maker, Fulci invites a psychological reading of his film while denying simplistic analysis. The oneiric flow of *The Beyond* refuses any imposition of meaning on it. As a psychoanalytic film, or rather, a film which invites an orthodox psychoanalytic interpretation, Fulci has the final laugh at our expense: *The Beyond* doesn't *mean* anything, for it was just a dream.   MJK

Dir: Lucio Fulci; **Prod**: Fabrizio De Angelis; **Original Music**: Fabio Frizzi; **Wr**: Dardano Sacchetti, Giorgio Mariuzzo, Lucio Fulci; **Cinematography**: Sergio Salvati; **Editing**: Vincenzo Tomassi.

Beyond the Darkness (aka *Blue Holocaust* [*Buio omega*])
Italy, 1979 – 85 mins
Aristede Massaccesi [aka Joe D'Amato]

The most prevalent representation of necrophilia on screen involves aggressive violence, violation and misogyny. While gory necrophilia is typically met with outrage, violent but 'clean' deaths can seem less offensive despite their 'kill-'em-and-fuck-'em' mentality. Films such as *Nekromantik* (1987), *The Necro-Files* (1997), *August Underground* (2001) and *Lucker the Necrophagous* (1986) offer cinematic representations of clinical associations between criminality, murder and necrophilia, but the necrophilia in *Beyond the Darkness* is as tender as it is perverse.

Francesco (Kieran Canter) is a taxidermist. His girlfriend Anna (Cinzia Monreale, Emily in Lucio Fulci's *The Beyond* [1981]) dies after Francesco's housekeeper places a curse on her. Francesco is not particularly saddened by his loss and does not cry; instead, he disinters Anna, preserves her corpse and places it at his side in bed. Francesco attempts to substitute his love for animated versions of Emily, but fails and ends up murdering two women. After being scratched on the neck by a hitchhiker he removes her nails and, when bitten by a lover, he fatally bites her back. These causal responses somewhat nullify allegations of misogyny.

Beyond the Darkness has been criticised as offensively gory and excessively visceral. Examples include the melting down of one of Francesco's victims and particularly the scene of Francesco preserving Anna. The latter plays unflinchingly in loving close-up and includes the extraction of entrails and eyes, as well as body fluid extravasation and preservation. Francesco clearly indulges his appetite for the love of his girlfriend by cunnilingually eating her heart. The scene is extreme and gory because the heart fails to remain simply metaphorical. The inside of the body, the internal organs, lose their metaphoric signification when the thorax is opened because in so doing they become the property of medicine rather than desire; the corpse is typically viewed as the domain of forensic medicine and religious ideology. Like Jane Baker (Bernice Stegers) in *Macabre* (1980), Francesco is not delusional in that he is aware of the necessary practicalities involved in maintaining such a lover, prone as she is to decomposition. In spite of their functional purpose, the use of surgical tools along with tools of embalming, adds a surgical fetishism to the connection between Anna and Francesco.

'Surgical fetishism' is somewhat of a misnomer here as *Beyond the Darkness* does not deal with psychoanalytic fetishism so much as with forming new and different connections between bodies, organs and tools. While the films of David Cronenberg, particularly *Dead Ringers* (1988), would seem appropriate benchmarks here, the uncanny doubling and particularly the use of investigative and explicitly gender-specific surgical tools to interrogate the female interior prevents Cronenberg's work from truly challenging psychoanalytic relations of desire. More interesting examples of surgical fetishism can be found in Antonio Margheriti's *Castle of Blood* (1964) and Paul Morrissey's *Flesh for Frankenstein* (1973). PMacC

Dir: Aristede Massaccesi; **Prod**: Marco Rossetti; **Original Music**: Goblin, Maurizio Guarini, Agostino Marangolo, Carlo Pennisi, Fabio Pignatelli; **Wr**: Ottavio Fabbri, Giacomo Guerrini; **Cinematography**: Aristede Massaccesi; **Editing**: Ornella Micheli.

The Bird with the Crystal Plumage (*L'uccello dalle piume di cristallo*, aka *The Gallery Murders*)
Italy/West Germany, 1970 – 98 mins
Dario Argento

While in Rome, American writer Sam Dalmas (Tony Musante) witnesses the apparent attempted homicide in an art gallery of the beautiful Monica Ranieri (Eva Renzi). The assault is followed by several violent crimes against women, the investigation of which absorbs Sam. He and the police consider everything resolved with the confession of Monica's dying husband Alberto (Umberto Raho). However, searching for his missing girlfriend Julia (Suzy Kendall), Sam discovers that the true killer has been Monica, with some copycatting by her husband, and their motivation is explained by a psychologist at the film's close.

Though not the first *giallo*, *The Bird with the Crystal Plumage* may have been the first to gain international credibility for this Italian mystery/crime (and often horror) genre that emerged in the 1960s. It is beautifully shot by Vittorio Storaro and scored by Ennio Morricone and recalls, on the purely horror/*giallo* side, the work of Riccardo Freda and Mario Bava. Its tight, clue-centred script recalls Alfred Hitchcock (note the bird motif and the *post facto* psychologist), and its strong aesthetics and undertones of ennui evoke Michelangelo Antonioni. The film may have influenced the visuals of Alan Pakula's *Klute* (1971), sound in Francis Ford Coppola's *The Conversation* (1974) and the look and horror/suspense devices of Brian De Palma's *Dressed to Kill* (1980). Though Argento has influenced numerous other film-makers as well, including John Carpenter, Wes Craven, Quentin Tarantino, Clive Barker, Lamberto Bava and Michele Soavi, it is more by his later, more purely horror films, such as *Suspiria* (1977). His relationship with George Romero, with whom he has worked as producer and collaborator, is one of mutual admiration more than direct influence.

Bird is noteworthy not only for its aesthetics, scripting and technical competence, but for its very 1960s', though still relevant, themes: the domination of nature, material accumulation, colonisation and, linked to all three, male domination and violence against women. Though Argento's work often seems open to the charge of misogyny, the grounding of Monica's rage in abuse allows for a reading of this film that is not only highly sympathetic to women but in keeping with the contemporary female-centred work of Italian directors such as Antonioni, Federico Fellini and Antonio Pietrangeli; the building of the Italian women's movement; and perhaps most strikingly, the early films of Marco Ferreri, whom Argento had interviewed shortly before embarking on *Bird*, and whose work is an explicit attack on what he himself called in the interview 'a male society [in which] women are the last colony'.

The film may well be most impressive for its strategic deception, introducing not just Hitchcockian 'MacGuffins' but implausible or partial interpretations, foremost the psychologist's, that incite viewers to their own readings of key issues including gender, and lead to an existential questioning of meaning itself.   FB

Dir: Dario Argento; **Prod**: Salvatore Argento, Artur Brauner (uncredited); **Original Music**: Ennio Morricone; **Wr**: Dario Argento, Fredric Brown (novel *The Screaming Mimi*, uncredited); **Cinematography**: Vittorio Storaro; **Editing**: Franco Fraticelli.

Blood and Black Lace (aka *Sei donne per l'assassino* [*Six Women for the Murderer*], aka *Fashion House of Death*)
Italy, 1964 – 86 mins
Mario Bava

With *Blood and Black Lace*, Mario Bava established a template which would later serve at least two brands of Italian *giallo* and heavily influence the American slasher movie. In his black-and-white *The Girl Who Knew Too Much* (1963), the director had already experimented with some ideas which came to the fore in this highly coloured work. He was drawing on the efforts of others – Alfred Hitchcock's lighter suspense films (*The Girl Who Knew Too Much* is a reference to one of Hitch's favourite titles), the stylised 'krimis' made in Germany in the early 1960s (usually adapted from books by Edgar Wallace), the 'body count' plot

Of models and murders: Mario Bava's *Blood and Black Lace*

structure of Agatha Christie's *Ten Little Indians* and the shivery mix of black wit and Sadean poetry found in Georges Franju's films – but *Blood and Black Lace* synthesised these elements, along with Bava's own personal style, into a new form of horror-thriller.

The credits sequence of the Italian version (altered for the English-dubbed release) establishes a delicate, self-aware tone that is otherwise easy to miss: the director introduces his cast posed like mannequins in compositions that include wicker dummies, indicating that they are puppets rather than characters (in his 1970 *Five Dolls for an August Moon*, the victims are 'dolls'), and then pulls them on strings through a plot so complex it is impossible to take seriously. The killer (actually, as is often the case in Christie, two killers with one disguise between them) is a masked, slouch-hatted, black-gloved figure who murders beautiful models in a variety of horrid, disfiguring ways, and the bland cop on the case theorises he's dealing with a sexual psychopath who loses control at the sight of beauty. But actually, as in many *gialli* to come, the villains are only *pretending* to be insane serial killers, and are actually murdering for profit and to avoid blackmail. If there's a compulsion to destroy beauty, it is on the part of the director and, by extension, the audience.

Whereas a Hitchcockian thriller depends on audience identification, even with characters who turn out to be more dangerous than endangered, Bava presents a cast of folks no one could possibly care about – the murdered women are uniformly catty, immoral, greedy and hard-faced, while the men are a line-up of red herring suspects (an impotent designer, a bankrupt marquis, a drug-addict antique dealer, a neurotic epileptic, a callous heel). Bava's camera winds through multilayered sets, accompanied by a playfully sinister mambo score (by Carlo Rustichelli), and scenes of murder, intrigue or just plain standing around are framed gorgeously, with rich deep red and blue lighting gels.

In the 1930s, Italian cinema saw a cycle of smart society comedies which became known as the 'telefono bianco' style after the white telephones which were the height of chic. Critic Tom Milne has noted that Bava hit on the 'telefono rosso' style here, and indeed the last image of the film is a dangling red telephone receiver.   KN

Dir: Mario Bava; Prod: Alfredo Mirabile, Massimo Patrizi; Original Music: Carlo Rustichelli; Wr: Giuseppe Barilla, Mario Bava, Marcello Fondato; Cinematography: Ubaldo Terzano, Mario Bava (uncredited); Editing: Mario Serandrei.

Blood and Roses (... *Et mourir de plaisir*)
France/Italy, 1960 – 87 mins
Roger Vadim

A vampire love story set in modern Italy, *Blood and Roses* features the stunning Carmilla de Karnstein (Annette Vadim), whose passion for her first cousin and childhood playmate, Leopoldo (Mel Ferrer), gives way to a jealous obsession when he announces his engagement to Georgia Monteverdi (Elsa Martinelli).

Like Leopoldo, Carmilla is a descendent of an ancient, European family with an unusual history. Two hundred years earlier, in 1765, local peasants revolted because the Karnsteins — a family of vampires — had been victimising them. One night, led by their local priest, the peasant mob invaded the Karnsteins' ancestral cemetery, located on the nearby abbey grounds, drove stakes through the hearts of the vampires and burned the corpses, all in order to avoid becoming prey. However, Carmilla insists, one family member escaped this fate: a beautiful woman, Mircalla (an anagram of Carmilla's own name). Mircalla was in love with her cousin, Ludwig, but she died in his arms before they wed. Ludwig, who had pledged his eternal love, preceded the peasants to the cemetery; when they opened Mircalla's tomb, it was empty. Carmilla narrates her story while standing next to a large painting of Mircalla, with whom she shares an uncanny likeness. After a fireworks celebration in honour of Leopoldo's engagement accidentally sets off some unexploded wartime bombs near the abbey, Carmilla finds herself drawn, hypnotically, to the abbey – and Mircalla's disturbed tomb. Mircalla's soul takes possession of Carmilla's body, allowing for a modern re-enactment of the old love triangle. Indeed, both Georgia and Leopoldo find Carmilla/Mircalla irresistible, resulting in an emotional *ménage à trois* and lending new meaning to the term 'eternal triangle'. As the wedding approaches, Mircalla, in her latest incarnation, plots to subsume Georgia in order to possess her beloved Ludwig/Leopoldo.

Atmospheric horror in Roger Vadim's *Blood and Roses*

Blood and Roses is loosely based on the 1872 novella *Carmilla*, by
the Irish writer Joseph Sheridan Le Fanu, which also served as the source
for Hammer's more faithful but less effective version, *The Vampire Lovers*
(1970). Yet with its emphasis on transmigration and incestuous love,
Blood and Roses also owes a decided debt to Edgar Allan Poe's short
stories from the 1840s, especially 'Ligeia' and 'Morella'. Although not
overtly based on these works, *Blood and Roses* anticipates Roger
Corman's group of films made in the early 1960s explicitly based on Poe,
the first of which, *The Fall of the House of Usher*, was also released in
1960. *Blood and Roses'* main innovation is that vampires not only suck
the blood of their victims but also draw the colour from flowers (hence
the film's alternate title). The film's artful approach to horror is reflected

in its exploration of the theme of eros and death, as it explored rather daring sexual territory (at the time) by its erotic portrayal of the *ménage* and the under-stated lesbian attraction between Carmilla and Georgia (Carmilla/Mircalla's other victim is female as well). *Blood and Roses* is thus a precursor to later vampire films with homoerotic themes, such as *The Hunger* (1983) and *Interview with the Vampire* (1994).   RU and SU

Dir: Roger Vadim; **Prod**: Raymond Eger; **Original Music**: Jean Prodromidés; **Wr**: Claude Brulé, Claude Martin, Roger Vadim, Roger Vailland, Joseph Sheridan Le Fanu (novella *Carmilla*); **Cinematography**: Claude Renoir; **Editing**: Maurizio Lucidi, Victoria Mercanton.

The Blood Spattered Bride
(*La novia ensangrentada*, aka *Blood Castle*)
Spain, 1972 – 102 mins
Vicente Aranda

A key film in the Spanish horror cycle of the early 1970s, *The Blood Spattered Bride* is yet another reworking of Sheridan Le Fanu's vampire novella, *Carmilla*. Here, a young bride (Maribel Martin) is whisked away to her new husband's (Simón Andreu) country manor. On the way, the pair stop at a hotel where the young woman dreams of being attacked by a masked man. Understandably this unsettles her. Once the couple are ensconced in their traditional style, the husband begins to behave towards his wife in a manner that is both macho and cruel. She slowly begins to immerse herself in her dreams in which she is visited by the strange Carmilla (Alexandra Bastedo) and which involve moments of extremely violent revenge. The film blurs the distinction between dream and reality as its female characters begin to seek revenge on the male-dominated micro-society that surrounds them.

In its representation of Spanish machismo, *The Blood Spattered Bride* is one of a group of horror films of the era, alongside Claudio Guerín's *A Bell of Hell* (1973), Eloy de la Iglesia's *Cannibal Man* (1972) and Juan Antonio Bardem's *The Corruption of Chris Miller* (1973), that uses the codes and conventions of the genre to critique the dominant ideologies of Franco's Spain. The film is also available in a number of different versions. These reveal the practice, common at the time, of shooting more explicit and more violent sequences for different markets. For example, the early attack in the hotel can be seen in both clothed and naked versions in Spanish and British prints. And the dream sequence when Susan kills her husband can be found in various extensions, some containing much more gore than others.

Bastedo is perhaps best known internationally for her work on the popular British TV series, *The Champions* (1968), although she did make a number of other films in Spain for directors associated with the horror boom, such as León Klimovsky and José Larraz. Andreu, meanwhile, has since gone on to become something of a genre film stalwart in Spain, appearing in a range of works, including most recently Agustí Villaronga's *99.9* (1997) and Brian Yuzna's *Beyond Re-Animator* (2003).

Director Vicente Aranda first came to critical notice in the mid-1960s as a member of the loosely linked 'Barcelona School' of film-makers, which included maverick Gonzalo Suarez among others. Their aim was to move away from the social realist films that had become associated with the 'New Spanish Cinema' of the period. Aranda had made *The Cruel Women* (1969) and *Fata morgana* (1965), establishing his own company and producing this blood-soaked vampire tale. *The Blood Spattered Bride*'s dreamlike qualities represent perhaps the clearest link to those non-realist aspirations. While never really venturing into the horror genre again, Aranda would become a key figure in the post-Franco Spanish cinema, making such acclaimed pictures as *Change of Sex* (1977) and *Lovers* (1991). Almost eighty, he is still a very active film-maker with over twenty-five credits to his name.   AW

Dir: Vicente Aranda; **Prod**: Jaime Fernández-Cid, José López Moreno; **Original Music**: Antonio Pérez Olea; **Wr**: Vicente Aranda, Joseph Sheridan Le Fanu (novella *Carmilla*), Matthew Lewis; **Cinematography**: Fernando Arribas; **Editing**: Pablo González del Amo.

Bloody Pit of Horror (*Il boia scarlatto*)
Italy/USA, 1965 – 80 mins
Massimo Pupillo

Massimo Pupillo's *Bloody Pit of Horror* merits special attention for its unique pop culture blending of peplum ('sword-and-sandal' movies), *fumeti* (Italian comic books) and Gothic horror film. It is also one of the first genre films to feature a character espousing a neo-Fascist aesthetic ideology of physical perfection as a reflection of a moral ideal.

The picture begins with a 1648 pre-credit prologue, indebted in content if not in style to Mario Bava's *The Mask of Satan* (1960), where a cloaked man named the 'Crimson Executioner' is executed by a tribunal for crimes of torture, sadism and murder. We then cut to the present, where a crew of ten men and women trespass into the same castle seen in the prologue to shoot photographs for horror/*giallo* novel covers. Once inside they discover that the castle is home to a strange recluse named Travis Anderson (Mickey Hargitay), who lives with a bevy of beefy, moustached manservants, all dressed in identical tight white pants and striped T-shirts. Travis becomes 'possessed' by the spirit of the Crimson Executioner, and begins torturing his house guests for their wanton ways.

Dressed in *Kriminal*/*Diabolik*-like red hood and tights, black eyemask and leather belt, and gold medallion chain, the muscular Hargitay – Mr Universe in 1955 – makes an imposing and highly sexualised figure. It is hardly a stretch to suggest that Hargitay's tanned, sculpted body, alternating between fully erect postures and frantic up/down movements, is symbolically transformed into a human-sized penis. These 'body gestures' are especially evident while he is torturing his victims, and since only the women are sexualised during these scenes, one can read Travis's Sadean violence as a perverse symptom of his repressed homosexuality (which has led some critics to label the film homophobic, as well as misogynistic).

The defining moment of *Bloody Pit of Horror* is the scene in which Travis tells Edith (Luisa Barrato), his former lover, why he had to leave her for a life of seclusion. The camera is fixed at a distance on Travis's multiple reflected mirror image, the perfectly centred ornate mirror flanked by phallic candles. As he speaks to Edith, positioned off-screen, he sensually rubs oil across his muscular, hairless chest, while reciting his neo-Fascist philosophy:

> Mankind is made up of inferior creatures, spiritually and physically deformed, who would have corrupted the harmony of my perfect body. I came to the isolation of this castle to avoid the contagion of human sentiment . . . and a woman's love . . . would have destroyed me . . . It is because of that, I abandoned you.

Travis's fear of being 'destroyed' by a woman becomes a reality, symbolically, at the conclusion when he impales himself on one of his own torture concoctions, a spiked mannequin referenced earlier as male but feminised by a long, blond wig. Looking down at his bloodied chest, Travis theatrically proclaims his tragic demise: 'My perfect body . . . in the poisonous clutches of the "Lover of Death".' Thanks to such lines, and Hargitay's delirious performance as a Nietzschean 'Overman', this cultural potpourri has rightly attained the status of a 'queer/camp' cult classic.   DT

Dir: Massimo Pupillo; **Prod**: Francesco Merli, Ralph Zucker; **Original Music**: Gino Peguri; **Wr**: Romano Migliorini, Roberto Natale; **Cinematography**: Luciano Trasatti; **Editing**: Mariano Arditi.

Brotherhood of the Wolf (*Le Pacte des loups*)
France/Canada, 2001 – 142 mins
Christophe Gans

Christophe Gans's *Brotherhood of the Wolf* stems from the mythical beast of Gévaudan that plagued the French countryside in the late eighteenth century, during the rule of Louis XV. The King assigns the royal biologist Grégoire de Fronsac (Samuel Le Bihan) and his Iroquois-Indian companion Mani (Mark Dacascos) to hunt down and capture the beast. War hero de Fronsac is a stern supporter of Enlightenment ideals, refusing to believe the beast to be of supernatural origin. Mani shares his respect for Nature, while seeking answers to the mysterious killings from the spiritual world.

However, in Gévaudan, superstition has vanquished reason among the tormented locals. De Fronsac's superiors settle for outright bloodshed, including the slaying of hundreds of common wolves by hunting parties of local aristocrats. Ultimately, the royal court grows tired of the unsuccessful hunts, ordering the beast to be presented to them. Thus, de Fronsac reluctantly participates in an elaborate ruse, after which a large common wolf is unveiled to the King as the fallen beast.

At this point, the royal advisor notes to de Fronsac: 'The truth is a complicated matter'. The narrator agrees, stating that de Fronsac's return to Gévaudan and the ultimate source of the carnage are not found in history books. The narrator is the sole living witness to the events, an old man in the midst of the French Revolution, a generation after the Gévaudan events in the 1760s. His dim recollection serves the film-maker's decision to inject the story with martial arts sequences, political intrigue and a larger-than-life monster. Gans establishes himself not as a reciter of history, but as a creator of a myth.

Thematically, *Brotherhood of the Wolf* is a clash of different cultures. While de Fronsac is a typical French hero (a lover as much as he is a fighter), his companion Mani serves as a guide to the Native American spirit world, as well as to martial arts. Thus, Gans manages to merge

Hong Kong action films with Westerns, both of which influences are passed on to the Frenchman. Such growth also reflects the story's historical climate. The French were soon to retire monarchy, with the Catholic Church facing a crisis with the rise of Enlightenment ideals.

De Fronsac's logic defies the ruling superstition, but as the story progresses, both will ultimately make way for a more overpowering force: the legend. Gans's film shifts from a supernatural murder mystery into historical drama, increasing the already exhaustive pace with eye-pleasing combat scenes. Horror has its strongest point in the early part of the story. The unstoppable monster preying on lone women and children is a suitably enthralling notion, with the killings shot by going back and forth between slow-motion and high-speed cinematography. This helps to give the gruesome events an almost graceful appearance.

While *Brotherhood of the Wolf* is not solely a horror film, Gans's dreamlike and firm directing keeps the story borderlining the otherworldly throughout. A box-office hit in its native country, *Brotherhood of the Wolf* did succeed in delivering the French an epic tale, with a framework recognisable enough for them to embrace it as their own.   LL

Dir: Christophe Gans; **Prod**: Emmanuel Gateau, Richard Grandpierre, Samuel Hadida; **Original Music**: Joseph LoDuca; **Wr**: Stéphane Cabel, Christophe Gans; **Cinematography**: Dan Laustsen; **Editing**: Xavier Loutreuil, Sébastien Prangère, David Wu.

(*Opposite page*) A spiritual moment in Christophe Gans's *Brotherhood of the Wolf*

The Cabinet of Dr Caligari (Das Cabinet des Dr. Caligari)
Germany, 1919 – 81 mins
Robert Wiene

Cinema is a plastic art with many stylistic approaches. At one extreme is an impulse to document everyday experience. At the other is wholesale manipulation of cinematic form and content so that all relations with the Real are thrown into question.

Somewhere between these poles lies Robert Wiene's 1919 classic, *The Cabinet of Dr Caligari*. Through production design and costumes by Walter Reimann, Hermann Warm and Walter Röhrig, and as framed by cinematographer Willy Hameister, Wiene's movie is a nightmare that has influenced virtually every other film movement and genre in the eight decades since its original release. Moreover, the picture centres on this nightmare state and presents an expression of outright madness as both theme and content of the work. *The Cabinet of Dr Caligari* is therefore a psychologically realist film shot through the prism of a highly impressionistic style.

Historians use the shorthand 'German Expressionism' to distinguish the format. But what appears to be an artistic response to German defeat following World War I – and that country's subsequent socio-economic collapse – is also a first-rate recognition of cinema's plasticity: that individual film frames can be combined to form new meanings through editing; that actors can enliven character and psychological states through posture, gesture, voice and presence; that the medium can be manipulated within the frame by transformation of pro-filmic space, including production design, lighting and cinematographic technique.

Written by Hans Janowitz and Carl Mayer, *The Cabinet of Dr Caligari* involves the many criteria of Expressionism and focuses on the story of Dr Caligari (Werner Krauss) and his somnambulist, Cesare (Conrad Veidt), as related by a man named Francis (Friedrich Fehér). And it is Francis who tells us about how Alan (Hans Heinrich von Twardowski) and Alan's

Expressionist horror in full effect: *The Cabinet of Dr Caligari*

fiancée, Jane (Lil Dagover), visit a carnival where Caligari offers the
attraction of Cesare, a man who can predict the future. Engaging these
services, Alan learns he won't live through the night and is quickly
murdered by Cesare who desires Jane, with whom he's fallen in love.
Cesare then kidnaps Jane and is chased to his death by the police,
whereupon we learn that Caligari is either the director of an insane
asylum or else one of its inmates.

    Throughout, characterisation is histrionic, the pace uneven and the
look and feel deliberately distancing and unsympathetic to our

sensibilities that are more attuned to entertainments that insinuate us into the action through processes of identification. Given these tendencies, modern audiences often dislike Wiene's creation due to the performance style and the unrealistic production design, while aficionados recognise these choices and celebrate the film's attempt to terrorise us with scenes of madness, chiaroscuro lighting, an absent vanishing point, schematic make-up and fashion, a simplistic melodrama and the unpleasant proposition that we are all characters in a madman's dream. In the end, this single allegory persists. For Caligari may orchestrate all action but, like God, he is unable to escape the consequences of the scene he's set, precisely because it is a dream state bordering on nightmare. GCQ

Dir: Robert Wiene; **Prod**: Rudolf Meinert, Erich Pommer; **Original Music**: Guiseppe Becce; **Wr**: Hans Janowitz, Carl Mayer; **Cinematography**: Willy Hameister.

Cannibal Ferox (aka *Make Them Die Slowly*)
Italy, 1980 – 91 mins
Umberto Lenzi

While researching her doctoral thesis, Gloria Davis (Lorraine del Selle) visits a village in Paraguay in an attempt to prove that 'cannibalism, as an organised practice of human society, does not exist and historically, has never existed'. Along with companions Rudy (Bryan Redford) and Pat (Zora Kerowa), she encounters not only local jungle natives but a New York drug dealer, Mike (Giovanni Lombardo Radice), who claims to be fleeing from a flesh-eating tribe, a story that seems to dismantle the foundation of Gloria's work.

Having reached its zenith in 1979 with Ruggero Deodato's *Cannibal Holocaust*, the subcultural cachet of the Italian cannibal subgenre was swiftly eroded in the hands of Umberto Lenzi, whose *Eaten Alive* (1980) and *Cannibal Ferox* effectively marked the end of the cycle. Nevertheless, Lenzi can lay claim to launching the Italian cannibal film with *Man from Deep River* (1972). As a direct genre descendant of the so-called 'mondo' documentary, the cannibal cycle drew explicitly on morbid Western fascination with the customs of ancient tribal communities in the Third World. Furthermore, as in the mondo film, the cannibal cycle is replete with imagery of the actual slaughter of jungle wildlife, an element foregrounded in *Cannibal Ferox* at several junctures.

While paying lip service to themes of colonialism and exploitation, the film wallows in the excess it professes to condemn. This charge is often levelled at *Cannibal Holocaust* but, while Deodato's film is equally excessive, it presents its atrocities within a self-reflexive framework that always serves as a legitimate commentary on the appalling violence depicted. There is no such level of formal or thematic sophistication at work in *Cannibal Ferox*, where the commentary on colonialism seems arbitrary and opportunistic. Cannibalism itself is posited by Gloria as a myth reaching back to the conquistador expeditions. As her convictions are gradually unravelled, the film allows itself the luxury of remaining critical of colonial expansion while indulging every fear or suspicion a 'civilised' audience may hold about the natives. The retribution visited upon the American characters provides a convenient narrative 'justice', but only serves further to characterise the natives as vengeful, fearsome savages.

The film's distinction stems chiefly from its brazen use of graphic mutilation and bloodshed, often in a highly sexualised form. It could be said that the energy of *Cannibal Ferox* is derived chiefly from isolated moments of crude sado-erotica, not least when Pat is suspended by hooks that have bloodily penetrated her breasts, and in the castration and dismemberment of Mike. Coupled with the gloating nature of the animal deaths (the demise of one jungle mammal in the grip of a snake is particularly repulsive), the violence meted out to the human cast betrays a general misanthropy that only achieves any real force in the film's cynical conclusion, in which Gloria presents a complete fabrication of her jungle experience to ensure academic and professional advancement.

As a point of trivia, 'ferox' is a Latin term meaning wild, bold, fierce or savage. The film was notable as a central 'video nasty' in the UK in the early 1980s, where it is distributed in a heavily censored form even now. Finally, the film's US release became infamous for its lurid advertising campaign, not least the dubious claim that it was 'banned in 31 countries!'. Given its centrality at all levels of discourse, this is an exploitation film in every sense of the word.   NJ

Dir: Umberto Lenzi; **Prod**: Antonio Crescenzi, Mino Loy (uncredited), Luciano Martino (uncredited); **Original Music**: Roberto Donati, Fiamma Maglione; **Wr**: Umberto Lenzi; **Cinematography**: Giovanni Bergamini; **Editing**: Enzo Meniconi.

Cannibal Holocaust
Italy, 1979 – 95 mins
Ruggero Deodato

One of cinema's most frequently banned and censored films, Ruggero Deodato's *Cannibal Holocaust* weaves two interconnected narratives. The first focuses on a New York-based anthropologist, Professor Monroe (Robert Kernan), and his quest to discover what happened to a celebrated crew of four documentary film-makers who mysteriously vanished in the Amazonian jungle. Travelling from Manhattan's towering skyscrapers and crowded sidewalks to a tangled expanse of South American rainforest ominously dubbed 'The Green Inferno', Monroe encounters members of several indigenous tribes, including the hut-dwelling Yacumo and the arboreally inclined Yamamonos, or 'Tree People'. After careful negotiations with the Yamamonos, a tense exchange that ultimately requires him to earn the tribe's trust by dining on chunks of human flesh, Monroe retrieves multiple unopened canisters of film shot by the missing film-makers, who he believes may be little more than skeletal remains. Upon his return to New York, Monroe screens the recovered films in the presence of television executives eager to construct a critically and commercially successful documentary from the rescued footage.

Throughout these screenings, however, a second narrative unfolds in which we discover that the documentary crew purposefully manipulated the events they recorded for the sake of sensationalism, raping and murdering members of the very population they purported to be studying. *Cannibal Holocaust* culminates with the documentary film-makers' gruesome deaths at the hands of the Yamamonos, who dismember and devour the crew before the camera's unflinching gaze. Disgusted, Monroe demands the recovered film be destroyed so that no one will ever see it. Of course, for those spectators consuming Deodato's infamous work, Monroe's injunction ironically serves to stigmatise and exploit further the horrific representations we have already devoured.

Filmed largely on the border between Columbia and Brazil, *Cannibal Holocaust* combines tropes from popular Italian horror cinema traditions, such as zombie and cannibal films, with aesthetic and narrative motifs from the pseudo- or mock-documentary genre. In its deployment of 'found footage', including archival newsreel depictions of executions by African dictators, as well as in its non-simulated killing of animals, Deodato's film likewise conforms to the parameters of 'mondo' cinema, recalling the content of anthologies like *Mondo cane* (1961), and anticipating both the iconography of 'pseudo-snuff' informing the infamous *Faces of Death* series (1979–96), and the faux vérité aesthetic mobilised in recent popular entertainments like *The Blair Witch Project* (1999) and 'reality TV' programmes like *Survivor* (2000).

Cannibal Holocaust is particularly compelling, however, in its deconstruction of authenticity, a practice that posits so-called 'verist' or 'documentary' film-making as every bit as constructed and manipulative as any other cinematic tradition. Perhaps no sequence better illustrates this dynamic than the scene during which the documentary film-makers manufacture spectacle by hustling members of the peaceful Yacumo community into a tiny hut before setting the structure ablaze to simulate an attack by a neighbouring tribe. Reminiscent of mass media images from Vietnam, Africa and other sites of brutal colonialist aggression, *Cannibal Holocaust*'s most unsettling moments reveal Western culture as virulently imperialistic. Paradoxically, Deodato's film is very much a product of a European entertainment industry; as such, in both its representation of the indigenous population of South America as cannibalistic, and in its actual extermination of animal life for entertainment, the picture ultimately risks perpetuating the very ideologies it pretends to critique.

'I wonder who the real cannibals are?', Monroe asks in *Cannibal Holocaust*'s closing moments. It is a fitting question indeed. JMcR

Dir: Ruggero Deodato; **Prod**: Franco Di Nunzio, Franco Palaggi; **Original Music**: Riz Ortolani; **Wr**: Gianfranco Clerici; **Cinematography**: Sergio D'Offizi; **Editing**: Vincenzo Tomassi.

Cannibal Man (*La semana del asesino* [*The Week of the Killer*])
Spain, 1972 – 118 mins
Eloy de la Iglesia

Riding home with his girlfriend, slaughterhouse worker Marcos (Vicente Parra) gets into a fight with an irate cab driver and clobbers him with a rock. With news of the driver's death surfacing the next day, Marcos tries to convince his girlfriend that going to the police is not an option. When she insists, he murders her in a fit of rage. The desperate killer then confesses to his brother, who is justifiably shocked and suggests going to the police as well. Again, this solution doesn't sit well with Marcos and he kills him too. As the days progress, a bevy of visitors who threaten to unearth Marcos's secret all end up dead in his bedroom. Witness to all of these murders from a distance is Nestor (Eusebio Poncela), a young, affluent gay man who cautiously befriends Marcos. As the bodies begin to pile up at home, Marcos can think of only one way to dispose of them – in the slaughterhouse!

Dismissed as violent trash upon its initial release, Eloy de la Iglesia's *Cannibal Man* is actually an engaging horror film that potently serves up shocks right alongside some concise political and social commentary. Iglesia portrays his two main characters as societal outcasts as both men are criminals. Nestor is a homosexual, something that was officially ruled criminal in Spain in 1954. Marcos is part of the lower class that has resorted to murder because the police 'listen to the rich only'. In this context, Marcos's killing spree is presented as a reaction to societal changes around him. To reinforce this isolation, Iglesia fills the *mise en scène* with images such as Marcos's tiny house dwarfed by new high-rise buildings and Marcos himself being lost in a crowded subway.

Interestingly, the person Marcos does not kill is Nestor, the only one to impose conscience on him in a relationship permeated by a gay subtext. It is this association that allows Iglesia to use the horror genre as a vessel to confront Spain's attitudes to homosexuality. This also makes

Cannibal Man notable as it is one of the earliest (and few) horror films to comment on this issue. This is not to say that *Cannibal Man* is an entirely solemn experience. Iglesia balances out the seriousness with dark comedy, including scenes such as Marcos shooing away a pack of hungry dogs outside his door or hoodlums tossing around Marcos's gym bag of human remains.

In addition to the subtext, *Cannibal Man* succeeds as a horror movie. The film opens with real footage of cows being slaughtered, shocking and preparing the audience for the gory murders ahead. The film sets a standard for modern 'humans-as-meat' horror, a category started with H. G. Lewis's *Blood Feast* (1964) that saw quick additions with *The Texas Chainsaw Massacre* and *Deranged* (both 1974) ten years later. Strangely, the English title by which the film is best known is a bit of a misnomer as Marcos eats no one. The literal translation, *The Week of the Killer*, is much more apt.   ww

Dir: Eloy de la Iglesia; **Prod**: Vicente Parra, José Truchado; **Original Music**: Fernando García Morcillo; **Wr**: Anthony Fos, Eloy de la Iglesia, Robert Oliver; **Cinematography**: Raúl Artigot; **Editing**: José Luis Matesanz.

The Castle of Terror (aka *The Virgin of Nuremberg* [*La Vergine di Norimberga*])
Italy, 1963 – 85 mins
Antonio Margheriti

The Castle of Terror is a garishly coloured film with a jazz score by Riz
Ortolani, set in modern times. Far from detracting from the Gothic
sensibility, however, this is perhaps Antonio Margheriti's most
accomplished picture, elegantly combining the atmosphere of his early
Italian Gothics (*Long Hair of Death* and *Castle of Blood*, both 1964) with
the gruesome acts and seductive pathos of cruelty seen in his later gore
films (for example, *Cannibal Apocalypse*, 1980).

The story concerns a castle with a torture chamber museum which
reverts to its original use after 300 years under the The Punisher (Mirko
Valentin), a dreaded ancestor of Max Hunter (Georges Rivière). Max's
wife Mary (Rossana Podesta) spends much of the film seeking the truth
behind the murder of women, the first body being found inside the so-
called Virgin of Nuremberg (the torture apparatus also known as the Iron
Maiden). Mary seems to be the only character interested in the castle's
secrets, an investigative drive usually ascribed in such movies to men. She
is made to bear witness to the fruits of her curiosity but, worse still, the
ending reveals an even more horrifying secret: that The Punisher is
actually Max's Nazi father, thought to have died in the war. His madness
has been brought on as a punishment for his betrayal of his fellow Nazis,
who surgically removed all the skin and soft tissue of his face. Thus, The
Punisher is first the punished, as the adept sadist must always first be the
masochist.

The final scene of The Punisher burning in a fire, cradled by Erich
(Christopher Lee) – his orderly during the war, now Max's chauffeur – is
both homoerotic and intensely poignant. The Punisher has flashbacks,
heartbroken and plagued by the trauma of having to send men to die in
the war, pleading that they may go away and be together like in the old
days, while Erich can only think of his beloved master. Hooded for most

of the film, when The Punisher's visage is first revealed the image is truly stunning: his face is little more than a skull. The Punisher pre-dates Mario Bava's similarly Gothic German-castle-with-a-mad-torturer film *Baron Blood* (1972) by almost a decade, as well as other mask-beneath-actor's-skin inversions like *The Abominable Dr Phibes* (1971) and *The Embalmer* (1965). The roles of master and servant played here by Valentin and Lee would be reversed in the Michael Reeves/Luciano Ricci film of the following year, *Castle of the Living Dead*. The dialectic of these two actors working together is marvellous, and they oscillate their roles beautifully.

In *Castle*'s finale, we flash back to the surgery which peeled away The Punisher's flesh, as Valentin is transformed in loving detail from an elegantly handsome man, resplendent in fetishistic Nazi uniform, into skull face. The Punisher decries his torment and vindicates his own diabolic propensities by pointing out that, while progress has changed the way man expresses evil, suffering and malevolence remain nonetheless.   PMacC

Dir: Antonio Margheriti; **Prod**: Marco Vicario; **Original Music**: Riz Ortolani; **Wr**: Frank Bogart (novel), Ernesto Gastaldi, Edmond T. Gréville, Antonio Margheriti; **Cinematography**: Riccardo Pallottini; **Editing**: Otello Colangeli.

The Church (*La chiesa*, aka *Cathedral of Demons*)
Italy, 1989 – 101 mins
Michele Soavi

The Church was originally conceived as the third film in what would become Lamberto Bava's 'Demons Trilogy', but abandoned when Italian horror auteur, and co-writer of the original script, Dario Argento was unhappy with his protégé's proposed treatment of the material. Instead, the project was given to another Argento protégé, Michele Soavi, whose directorial debut, *Stage Fright* (1987), had become a cult success. *The Church* heralds a return to the golden age of Italian horror of the 1950s and 60s, when Gothic horror was the dominant trend with films such as *I Vampiri* (1957) and *The Mask of Satan* (1960), and before it was displaced in the 1970s and 80s by the Italian version of the psychological horror film, the *giallo*, which would account for the majority of Italian horror from Argento's genre-defining *The Bird with the Crystal Plumage* (1970) onwards.

Containing obvious visual cues to films such as *Rosemary's Baby* (1968) and *The Exorcist* (1973), *The Church* combines the elements of Gothic horror – the cloistered society, the symbols of Catholicism, the revelation of a secret through which the past returns to haunt the present – with the demonic possession film. The picture begins with a horrifying massacre of villagers, believed to be in league with the devil, by a group of Knights Templar. The villagers' bodies are thrown into a large 'death pit' which becomes the site of the present-day cathedral, built to keep supposedly evil spirits of the devil worshippers from returning. While based on the real exploits of the Teutonic Knights in the twelfth century, taking into consideration the Germanic symbolism of Argento's earlier Gothic horror, *Suspiria* (1977), and the fact that the Teutonic Knights have been called the inspiration for the SS, it is possible to interpret this sequence as an indirect reference to the horrors and death pits of Auschwitz. As such, *The Church* is a meditation on the nature of violence, and of the evil that men do in the name of religion and nationhood.

The film's subsequent narrative is loosely divided into two sections based upon revelation and concealment of the Gothic secret that lies behind the cathedral's stone walls. In the first section, historian Evan (Tomas Arana) stumbles upon a hidden manuscript, which tells of a secret, contained within a hidden stone of 'seven eyes'. Unwittingly, Evan unleashes the vengeful spirits of the dead onto the living, when he finds the hidden stone, becoming possessed by the spirits as he does so. In the second section, the cathedral literally becomes a cloister, as a number of people become trapped within its stone walls and die in horrific and inventive ways: a schoolteacher impaled against the cathedral's giant doors; an old man decapitated by his wife; and a beautiful young model who tries to tear the skin of her face when she sees herself as an old hag reflected in a mirror.

It is ultimately left to a priest, Father Gus (Hugh Quarshie), and the young daughter of the sacristan, Lottie (Asia Argento) – the only characters to remain immune to possession by the demonic spirits of the past – to find a way to defeat the vengeful dead. Both characters are highly symbolic and represent the imbrication of the past in the present: Lottie, as the girl who is murdered at the end of the beginning sequence, and Father Gus, as one of the Knights who participated in the horrific massacre. The narrative comes full circle as Father Gus sacrifices himself, and all those in the cathedral, in order to prevent the dead escaping its cloistered walls. Only Lottie escapes, once again bearing witness to the evil that men do.   CB

Dir: Michele Soavi; **Prod**: Dario Argento, Mario Cecchi Gori, Vittorio Cecchi Gori; **Original Music**: Simon Boswell, Keith Emerson, Philip Glass, Goblins, Fabio Pignatelli; **Wr**: Nick Alexander, Dario Argento, Fabrizio Bava (prologue, uncredited), Lamberto Bava (uncredited), Franco Ferrini, M. R. James (story, 'The Treasure of Abbot Thomas', uncredited), Dardano Sacchetti (uncredited), Michele Soavi; **Cinematography**: Renato Tafuri; **Editing**: Franco Fraticelli.

City of the Living Dead (Paura nella città dei morti viventi, aka The Fear)
Italy, 1980 – 93 mins
Lucio Fulci

Lucio Fulci's follow-up film to his internationally successful *Zombie* (1979) was *City of the Living Dead*. The latter represents Fulci's full-blown embrace of the horror genre after many years working in other genres, ranging from musicals to thrillers.

The film's plot is relatively simple to summarise, but its execution is unique to Fulci. *City* opens in Dunwich, Massachusetts, with the suicide of a priest, Father Thomas (Fabrizio Jovine). Simultaneously, a medium named Mary (Catriona MacColl) in New York witnesses the suicide in a vision and collapses, apparently dead. In a harrowing scene, she awakens in her sealed coffin at the cemetery and is rescued by a reporter named Peter Bell (Christopher George). Mary's vision has revealed to her that the priest's suicide opened the Gates of Hell. If the gates are still open in a few days' time on All Saints' Eve, the dead will rise. Mary and Peter travel to Dunwich to close the gates by finding Father Thomas's crypt and destroying him. Meanwhile, Father Thomas and other recently deceased people begin appearing to various Dunwich residents, with horrific and gory results. Peter and Mary team up with a local psychiatrist, Gerry (Carlo De Mejo), to enter the underground crypt and put an end to the demonic manifestations. However, the film's ambiguous last scene suggests that the mission has failed, and that the dead are indeed about to break through the Gates of Hell and overrun mankind.

City is the first of a trilogy of Fulci-directed Italian horror films centred on the incursion of the undead realm upon the living and starring MacColl; the other two films are *The Beyond* (1981), and *House by the Cemetery* (1981). These three films are inspired in part by the early twentieth-century horror fiction of H. P. Lovecraft, with *City of the*

(*Next page*) Don't turn around … just run! Lucio Fulci's *City of the Living Dead*

Living Dead and *House by the Cemetery* specifically referencing Lovecraft's fictional haunted town of Dunwich. Lovecraft found horror and monsters in the archaic and degenerated environment of New England as well as incomprehensible and meaningless gulfs of infinite space. Fulci sets his early 1980s' horror films in a forbidding American landscape that opens its dimensional gates to reveal the fathomless realm of Hell itself.

Fulci's vision of Hell in *City* as a borderless place where time fractures, zombies appear and disappear at will, cause and effect do not align, and bodies open up, turn inside out or rot, is original and genuinely disturbing. Almost as unsettling as the extreme levels of violence depicted (a woman vomiting up her intestines, a man drilled through the head) is the violence Fulci inflicts upon narrative. *City* has a much less coherent storyline than the relatively straightforward *Zombie*, and amply illustrates Fulci's desire to eschew sequential narrative altogether. The film is accused by its detractors of being a series of gore set pieces strung together by the thinnest strand of plot and populated by sketchily drawn characters acting implausibly in reaction to illogical plot developments. Yet the film's champions praise it for much the same elements, and laud Fulci for his radical departure from traditional storytelling conventions. Certainly, in Fulci's cycle of horror films inaugurated by *City*, the director's emphasis on oppressive mood, dark atmospherics, surreal amounts of visceral gore, non-sequential time and claustrophobic interiors dislocates and disorients the film spectator. Fulci asks a lot of his audience, but in return he provides them with a provocative subversion of the essence of storytelling itself.   PLS

Dir: Lucio Fulci; **Prod**: Giovanni Masini, Robert E. Warner; **Original Music**: Fabio Frizzi; **Wr**: Lucio Fulci, H. P. Lovecraft (inspired), Dardano Sacchetti; **Cinematography**: Sergio Salvati; **Editing**: Vincenzo Tomassi.

Curse of the Devil (*El retorno de Walpurgis,* aka *Return of the Werewolf*)
Spain/Mexico, 1973 – 87 mins
Carlos Aured

Curse of the Devil marks the sixth entry in Spanish horror icon Paul Naschy's continuing werewolf saga. Following a prologue set in medieval times that sees one of Daninsky's ancestors cursed after he kills a Satan-worshipping knight and burns his wife as a witch, the action jumps forward to what seems to be the late 1800s, where a mother stands with a child over a grave. We are then introduced to Daninsky (Naschy) in this period. While hunting a wolf he kills a man, a gypsy who turns out to have been part of a local clan. The gypsy's family then dispatch a beautiful maiden to put a curse on Daninsky in revenge, one that makes him a werewolf. Daninsky proceeds to kill without realising it, creating something of a sympathetic monster, until his faithful servant explains all to him. In the end he is dispatched by his lover, but as the film closes we return to her and the child at the graveside. As they walk away we hear the Daninsky curse repeated, and there is a freeze-frame of a rather hairy child's hand. The curse continues.

The content of *Curse of the Devil* manages to be in parts both titillating and bloody, and Carlos Aured's direction, like many European horrors of the period, a little zoom-happy. For all this, the film manages to successfully create a sinister and occasionally dreamlike atmosphere. Naschy's werewolf make-up, however, seems to have advanced little since his idol Lon Chaney Jr essayed the role in *The Wolf Man* (1941).

Aured had previously been an assistant to another of Naschy's regular collaborators, León Klimovsky. From there he went on to make a number of Spanish horror films with Naschy, such as *Horror Rises from the Tomb* (1973), *Blue Eyes of a Broken Doll* (1973) and *The Mummy's Revenge* (1973). As with many of Naschy's films of this period, the action is set outside Spain – here in Eastern Europe – to avoid criticism from the Franco government, which operated a strict censorship policy against anything they deemed un-Spanish, such as an Iberian werewolf.

During the transition to democracy in Spain after the fall of the Franco regime in 1975, censorship was abolished. This meant that producers, distributors and exhibitors began to demand increased sexual content in their horror movies. Aured found himself part of this shift and was drawn into including more and more sex in his films, eventually making such sexually explicit titles as *Sexual Apocalypse* (1982), starring the mysterious Anjita Wilson and Jesús Franco regular Lina Romay. Once the need for such material faded, Aured found himself marked as a director of pornography and struggled to re-establish himself back in the mainstream of cinema production in Spain. Sadly, his remains a talent that was unable to extend itself across a substantial directorial career in mainstream cinema.   AW

Dir: Carlos Aured; **Prod**: Luís Gómez, Ramiro Meléndez; **Wr**: Jacinto Molina; **Cinematography**: Francisco Sánchez; **Editing**: María Luisa Soriano.

Dark Waters
Russia/Italy/UK, 1994 – 94 mins
Mariano Baino

Even by the sometimes bizarre standards of European horror cinema, *Dark Waters* is a curious concoction. A Russian–British co-production, directed by an Italian, shot in English (mainly in the Ukraine), and with a plot featuring self-flagellation, homicidal nuns and crossbreeding between humans and demons, it could hardly be described as restrained. However, it is far from being the wild affair that such a description suggests, instead offering itself as a disciplined, if strange, piece of work.

This strangeness is immediately apparent in the film's cryptic opening sequence, in which a church is flooded and a priest impaled on a large cross while outside a nun is flung off a clifftop by an unseen force. Twenty years later, an Englishwoman named Elizabeth (Louise Salter) arrives at a sinister convent where she spent the first part of her childhood but about which she can remember nothing. The discoveries she makes there explain – in part, at least – events in the opening sequence, and eventually lead to her realisation that she is not fully human. And that is about it as far as the story is concerned.

A common critical assumption about European horror is that it tends to privilege style over plot. While one might want to question this as a general statement, it certainly seems to apply to *Dark Waters,* with the film's director, Mariano Baino, often compared in this respect with arch Euro-stylist Dario Argento. This does not mean that *Dark Waters* is without content, but rather that its story – which owes more than a little to the writings of H. P. Lovecraft – is attenuated and functions primarily as the pretext for a series of atmospheric and visually striking scenes.

The lengthy sequence depicting Elizabeth's journey to the convent is a case in point. For fifteen minutes, a series of encounters between Elizabeth and vaguely menacing locals is intercut with mysterious events at the convent. Other than showing how weird and isolated the convent is, this part of the film serves no obvious narrative function. Rather, it works primarily to build up a brooding atmosphere, with Elizabeth, marked as an outsider through her ultra-modern shiny red raincoat, venturing deeper and deeper into a primitive world. The events that follow involve minimal dialogue and little dramatic interaction. Instead Elizabeth explores the confined and mysterious spaces of the convent while periodically fending off assaults from nuns and experiencing a series of increasingly disturbing flashbacks to her childhood.

It has become something of a cliché to describe a film as being like a dream or nightmare, but *Dark Waters*, with its intensely subjective and obsessive-repetitive quality, lends itself well to such a reading. Perhaps it is the film's rootlessness, the fact that it is hard to place in any specific national genre tradition, which bestows this oneiric quality upon it. In any event, what one takes from the film is less a coherent narrative than images of a claustrophobic and alienating world from which there can be no escape. PH

Dir: Mariano Baino; **Original Music**: Igor Clark; **Wr**: Andy Bark; **Editing**: Mariano Baino.

Daughters of Darkness (aka *Les Lèvres rouges*, aka *Blood on the Lips*)

Belgium/Italy/France/West Germany, 1971 – 96 mins
Harry Kümel

Inspired by accounts of real-life Hungarian 'Blood Countess' Erzabet Bathory, who supposedly bathed in the blood of virgins to maintain her youth, but without the finance or resources to make an historical costume picture, Belgian director Harry Kümel speculated on what might have become of the 'female Dracula' had she lived to the present day. The result is less a horror film (the blood-letting is far subtler here than in most vampire movies) than a portrait of psychic vampirism with a disturbing subtext and unsettling imagery. When newlyweds Stefan (cult star John Karlen from the vampire soap *Dark Shadows*) and Valerie (Danielle Ouimet) are forced to stay in Ostend in the off-season, they find themselves alone in a grand hotel with the Countess Bathory (Delphine

A deadly threesome: Harry Kümel's *Daughters of Darkness*

Seyrig) and her companion, Ilona (Andrea Rau). Bathory sets about
seducing the couple, but when Ilona dies, Valerie gives in to the
Countess and together they murder and feed on Stefan. When Bathory is
killed fleeing from Ostend and the encroaching daylight, Valerie assumes
Bathory's role and sets about a seduction of her own.

Kümel's female vampire film fits neatly into 1970s' cinema, and
particularly the erotic/lesbian themes of the horror genre at this time.
It has been claimed as a feminist text and certainly *Daughters of
Darkness* explores relevant themes: domestic violence, female solidarity
and revenge against the oppressive male. With its opulent *mise en
scène* that mirrors the decadence of Seyrig's Countess – particularly the
hotel setting and colour-coded red, black-and-white costumes – the film
contributes to the development of a feminine aesthetic within the
genre.

Kümel himself acknowledges that the film is an exercise in style –
especially the deep focus and moody lighting with exterior scenes shot
only at dusk and dawn, rather than a horror movie that is intended to
scare. It is one of the last films to use arc lighting (which lends an
incandescent glow to the images), and one of the first to depict male
orgasm (which led to cuts in the version released in the UK – Kümel
deliberately set out to scandalise and blaspheme), boasting a series of
bizarre death sequences (Ilona's death by shower, Stefan's murder by
crystal bowl, Bathory's impaling on a dead tree) along the way.

Despite the film's softcore aesthetic, Kümel's artistic aspirations are
clearly delineated in the style and design. At key points, the director
arranges his actors into tableaux that recreate the works of Flemish and
Renaissance artists (including Mantegna's portrait of a dead Christ), the
casts of bodies from the pumice of Pompeii and homages to Carl Dreyer,
Josef Von Sternberg and Ingmar Bergman. Seyrig's appearance is based
on Marlene Dietrich and Rau's on Pabst's Lulu. These images are
emphasised by the mannered performances and exaggerated gestures,
while Seyrig's casting cannot help but bring to mind her performance in
Last Year in Marienbad (1961).

Daughters of Darkness sits alongside Hammer's lesbian vampire cycle, Roger Vadim's *Blood and Roses* (1960) and the cinema of Jean Rollin, as well as American films such as *The Velvet Vampire* (1971), but the emptiness of the setting and the distanciation that arises from the preponderance of overhead shots, shots through glass, fades to blood red and extreme close-ups lend the entire film a dreamlike quality that verges on the surreal and is ironic-verging-on-camp in tone. Ultimately, it is Kümel's formalist style that marks the film out as something far more than just another vampire shocker.   BC

Dir: Harry Kümel; **Prod**: Paul Collet, Henry Lange, Pierre Drouot, Alain C. Guilleaume, Luggi Waldleitner (uncredited); **Original Music**: François de Roubaix; **Wr**: Pierre Drouot, Jean Ferry, Manfred R. Köhler, Harry Kümel; **Cinematography**: François de Roubaix; **Editing**: Denis Bonan, August Verschueren, Hans Zeiler.

The Day of the Beast (*El día de la bestia*)
Spain/Italy, 1995 – 103 mins
Álex de la Iglesia

Following up on his genre-blending sci-fi/action/comedy *Accion mutante* (1993), Spanish director Álex de la Iglesia impresses again with his equally irreverent second feature, *The Day of the Beast*. A pitch-black horror-comedy, *Beast* proves that Iglesia and the young and upcoming film-makers in the Spanish horror field are more than capable of crafting films of considerable technical skill and cinematic merit.

Father Ángel Beriartúa (Álex Angulo) has spent the last twenty-five years trying to decipher a hidden code in the Apocalypse of St John. Finally cracking it, he discovers that the Anti-Christ is due to be born on Christmas Eve in 1995. Determined to stop the return of Satan, Ángel begins committing as many sins as possible in order to become close to evil. Unfortunately for Ángel, the only person who believes his prophecy is José María (Santiago Segura), the frenzied proprietor of a heavy-metal music shop. Together the duo set out to determine the location of Satan's rebirth. Their plan involves kidnapping TV personality Professor Cavan (Armando De Razza) a psychic charlatan whose 'knowledge' Ángel believes will assist them. As the night progresses, the trio begin to see more and more evidence that Satan truly is returning. However, is it real or just a figment of their deranged imaginations?

The cinematic offspring of *The Exorcist* (1973) and *The Omen* (1976), *The Day of the Beast* adheres to their dark depictions of the devil. As with these earlier films, it is a serious man of the cloth who discovers and must confront the ultimate evil. At the same time, Iglesia bends the rules for comedic effect. Death-metal is used in incantations. LSD and store-bought bread are introduced as substitutes in sacrament. And the priest, usually the credible expert in Satan movies, is considered crazy except by two of society's fringe dwellers. However, Iglesia openly invites his audience to question the priest's quest. When the film ends, only the priest has truly seen the devil. Did our heroes prevent the return of Satan or simply confront evil in a human form? In addition to twisting accepted genre conventions, Iglesia takes the opportunity to comically malign many institutions of modern Spain. His presentation of Madrid is a virtual hell on earth, with police beatings, vigilantes, soulless TV execs and rampant Christmas commercialism.

Beast is also a significant film in terms of its critical reception in Spain and its international influence. The film won six out of fourteen nominations at the Goya Awards, Spain's highest film honour. It was the first full-fledged horror movie to be nominated since the Awards' inception in 1987. This helped to re-establish a critical base for genre efforts in Spain and garnered a mainstream acceptance for horror at levels previously unseen. *The Day of the Beast* also played at several international film festivals, launching a new foundation for Spanish horror and paving the way for film-makers such as Jaume Balagueró (*The Nameless*, 1999) and Alejandro Amenábar (*The Others*, 2001).   ww

Dir: Álex de la Iglesia; **Prod**: Claudio Gaeta, Fernando de Garcillán, Andrés Vicente Gómez, Antonio Saura; **Original Music**: Battista Lena; **Wr**: Jorge Guerricaechevarría, Álex de la Iglesia; **Cinematography**: Flavio Martínez Labiano; **Editing**: Teresa Font.

Deep Red (*Profondo rosso*, aka *The Hatchet Murders*)
Italy, 1975 – 130 mins
Dario Argento

Inspired by fellow Italian director Michelangelo Antonioni's *Blow-Up* (1966), *Deep Red* anticipates Dario Argento's later international reputation as a film-maker whose uniquely stylised approach to *giallo* thrillers transformed a genre noted for its relation to modern slasher horror into a meditation on the aesthetics of film-making itself. In Argento's hands, the *giallo*'s effects are also uncanny in that Argento's camerawork draws the viewer into a 'dense network of allusions' and 'bizarrely detailed *mise en scènes*' which are visually seductive and psychologically disorienting.[2]

If Argento's 1980 film *Inferno* suggests the director's affinity with the aesthetics of disorientation in Russian formalism,[3] *Deep Red* – a stylistically eerie exploration of murder, madness, paranoia and alienation – makes an early case for the director's development of an art-house sensibility. The eeriness achieved here recalls the paintings of American artist Edward Hopper, whose psychologically intense depictions of isolation in urban life inspired writers and film-makers such as Norman Mailer and Alfred Hitchcock. As if quoting from Hopper's paintings, scenes in *Deep Red* appear to insist on drawing attention to their own artifice and are marked by stark juxtapositions of colour and a hyperrealism that produce an uncanny disquiet. This disquieting effect continues throughout the film with Argento's camerawork and staging.

Thematically, *Deep Red* recalls its predecessor, *The Bird with the Crystal Plumage* (1970), in which the protagonist, who is witness to a brutal murder, comes to believe that a vital clue at the scene eludes him, leading him to conduct his own investigation into the crime. As in many Argento films, *Deep Red*'s motifs are consistent within his oeuvre:

The calm before the storm in Dario Argento's *Deep Red*

the traumatic primal scene of murder; the artistic outsider who feels compelled to play detective after witnessing a crime where something is not as it seems; the blurring and confusion of gender distinctions; and, of course, the fetishisation of murder, preferably by a black leather clad maniac.[4]

Deep Red features David Hemmings as Marcus Daly, a British pianist who witnesses the murder of his neighbour Helga Ulman (Macha Meril), a psychic who is killed after telepathically receiving 'perverted murderous thoughts' from 'a twisted mind' apparently located among members of the audience attending a parapsychology conference in Rome.

As the curtains close on this scene, the camera pulls back to give us the murderer's point of view and, like Ulman, the psychic, we are put into a state of hyper-vigilance in relation to this perspective as Ulman asserts that 'someone is watching'. Prior to the murder scene, the camera cuts to a world of uncanny objects made increasingly strange by lingering close-ups of items such as a small plastic doll, a doll resembling a red devil, cat's eye marbles and finally, knives that appear as harbingers of violence and death. As in other Argento films, the strange juxtaposition of objects functions to confuse the audience's point of view with the symbolic world of the psychopathic killer, while at the same time putting the audience in the dual position of being potential victim as well as detective.

As pianist-turned-detective, Marcus eventually solves the mystery of the killer's identity, but not before a number of other brutal deaths ensue, including that of a woman who meets her end by being scalded and strangled in an extended murder scene in a steam-filled bathroom. At its conclusion, the film's tension increases as Marcus returns to the scene of the first murder only to discover that the painting he thought contained a clue to the crime was actually a mirror in which the face of the killer had been reflected.

As in other films by Argento, stylistic camera techniques, detailed editing and a disturbing soundtrack combine to create an unsettling effect that assures *Deep Red* a significant place in the *giallo* genre and also makes it an extended contemplation on the aesthetics of horror cinema.   JC

Dir: Dario Argento; **Prod**: Claudio Argento, Salvatore Argento; **Original Music**: Goblins, Giorgio Gaslini; **Wr**: Dario Argento, Bernardino Zapponi; **Cinematography**: Luigi Kuveiller; **Editing**: Franco Fraticelli.

Déjà vu (Vec vidjeno)
Yugoslavia/UK, 1987 – 102 mins
Goran Markovic

Among the rare examples of horror in Serbian cinema, the terror is usually firmly rooted in reality. Such is the case with Goran Markovic's *Déjà vu*; disguised as a psycho-thriller, it offers a powerful condemnation of Tito's communist regime and its devastating effects on the people's psyche. *Déjà vu* concerns a troubled piano teacher, Mihailo (Mustafa Nadarevic, channelling the intensity of a young Jack Nicholson), and his attempt to preserve his sanity through a love affair with a poor but industrious girl, Olgica (the lovely Anica Dobra in her big-screen debut, before she became the star of numerous European productions). Mihailo is hampered by memories of the past, when his bourgeois family was destroyed by the Communists. In the present (actually, the early 1970s, as the bulk of the film is told in flashback), Olgica is anxious to join the Party, but Mihailo keeps witnessing the 'already seen' cycle of evil that will follow. When Olgica finally leaves him for a younger man, Mihailo snaps and goes on a killing spree.

Horror conventions are used in *Déjà vu* with greater skill and consistency than in *Variola vera* (1981), Markovic's earlier opus, in which the true story of a minor smallpox outbreak becomes a parable for the corrupted ex-Yugoslav society. *Déjà vu*'s complex form, clearly influenced by horror auteurs such as Dario Argento and Brian De Palma, is closely related to its content, and the director's main concern, obvious in his non-genre films, has never been more powerfully depicted: the way the past is reflected in the present, and the manner in which 'evi' is passed down from one generation to the next.

Markovic here deals metaphorically with an inheritance of evil typical in the Balkans, though certainly not uncommon in the rest of middle-Europe's ex-Communist countries. This is a region where the victims of yesteryear seem destined to grow into the tormentors of today, in turn guaranteeing the transformation of their own victims into the evildoers of tomorrow. The wrongs are never really balanced or corrected, only enriched with new injustices and new victims. Everything remains the same, as if 'already seen': only the protagonists are different. And that is the real horror, as evidenced in the civil wars that ensued after Yugoslavia's break-up, only four short years after *Déjà vu*'s release.

Subsequent Serbian efforts in the horror genre have either been unconvincing allegories, like *Full Moon over Belgrade* (1993), or solid homages to American slasher flicks, like *T. T. Syndrome* (2001), which sorely lack both the artistry and ambition of Markovic's psycho-thriller. What makes *Déjà vu* so special is that it manages to strongly indict a repressive political system while simultaneously functioning as a suspenseful and compelling genre movie.

Déjà vu's political allegory was sufficiently subdued for foreign audiences to respond to the universal aspects of its story about a man driven insane by demons both personal and collective. It was screened at the Fantasporto International Horror and Fantasy Film Festival in Spain, and is favourably reviewed by Kim Newman in Phil Hardy's oft-referenced *Overlook Film Encyclopedia: Horror* (1994). A successful picture that received critical as well as commercial acclaim, *Déjà vu* won several major Yugoslav film awards in 1987.   DO

Dir: Goran Markovic; **Prod**: Aleksandar Stojanovic; **Original Music**: Zoran Simjanovic; **Wr**: Goran Markovic; **Cinematography**: Zivko Zalar; **Editing**: Snezana Ivanovic.

Dellamorte Dellamore (aka *Cemetery Man*)
Italy/France/Germany, 1994 – 100 mins
Michele Soavi

With appropriate virtuosity, Michele Soavi's *Dellamorte Dellamore* (literally 'of death, of love') ended the Italian zombie cycle epitomised in the films of Lucio Fulci and marked the final chapter of the great era of Italian horror. Based on a novel by Tiziano Sclavi, the film became a minor cult phenomenon and in turn inspired Sclavi's wildly popular comic book, *Dylan Dog*. Cemetery settings, rotting zombies and operatic stylisation notwithstanding, the film's synergy is less Italian than international and postmodern. While channelling mentors Fulci, Dario Argento and Federico Fellini, Soavi quotes just as often from *Citizen Kane* (1941), *The Seventh Seal* (1957), *Vertigo* (1958), *The Evil Dead* (1981) and *Brazil* (1985). The film is a delirious fusion of zombie gorefest and European art film, blending splatter comedy with surreal fantasy and philosophical rumination.

   As a comedy alone, *Dellamorte Dellamore* is unique among Italian horror films, modulating between Romeroesque social satire, 'splatstick' (à la Sam Raimi and Peter Jackson) and the blackest of humour. Francesco Dellamorte (a deadpan Rupert Everett) is everyman: uneducated, unambitious, stuck in his literally dead-end job as cemetery caretaker – seeing to it that the deceased (who return as flesh-eating zombies after seven days) stay properly dead and buried. After a collision between bikers and a bus full of boy scouts and nuns, Dellamorte and his morbidly obese, mute, idiot-savant assistant Gnaghi (French musician François Hadji-Lazaro) are sorely tested. 'Returners' queue up at his office as, bleary eyed, smoking a cigarette or answering the phone, Dellamorte barely pauses to blow another head off. Election-obsessed city officials are hilariously oblivious to the problem (and, by implication, all social problems), and town-hall clerk Franco (Anton Alexander), buried in paperwork, is his double. Concluding that the (dying) living and the living dead are essentially alike, he becomes a serial killer – and no one notices.

Dellamorte Dellamore lives up to its titular second term as well, with the death-drive setting the parameters of romance. Although rumoured to be impotent, Dellamorte makes love to and loses the same woman (the ethereally voluptuous Anna Falchi, identified only as 'She') in increasingly necrophilic and then carnal incarnations. In a drooling, slapstick version of the theme, Gnaghi is infatuated with the irrepressible remains of the mayor's thirteen-year-old daughter Valentina (Fabiana Formica), installing her decapitated head inside the shell of his exploded TV set. Outside such variations on the monstrous-feminine, the zombies reflect a general state of entropy, their orality and aggression subsumed by melancholy and the compulsion simply to return.

Thus the film's third act shifts into a philosophical meditation, with a non-conclusion worthy of Samuel Beckett. 'Past this town is the rest of the world', Francesco speculates, as he and Gnaghi at last set out to find, at the end of a dark tunnel, the end of the road. Just before the closing credits, the camera dollies out to frame them as figures within a snow globe, an image that opened the film and now hints that the world of the movie may have been their own morose projection. The shot also wryly enshrines them with Laurel and Hardy, Quixote and Sancho Panza, or Estragon and Vladimir from *Waiting for Godot*. Pretentiously self-aware, endlessly interpretable, quoting and commenting on subjects from Italian politics to issues of identity, love, obsession and the nature of existence, *Dellamorte Dellamore* is *über* Eurotrash; it is equally, perhaps, an ancestor of *Shaun of the Dead* (2004) and the rom-zom-com. LB

Dir: Michele Soavi; **Prod**: Conchita Airoldi, Heinz Bibo, Tilde Corsi, Dino Di Dionisio, Gianni Romoli, Michele Soavi; **Original Music**: Riccardo Biseo, Manuel De Sica; **Wr**: Gianni Romoli, Tiziano Sclavi (novel); **Cinematography**: Mauro Marchetti; **Editing**: Franco Fraticelli.

Demons (*Dèmoni*)
Italy, 1985 – 93 mins
Lamberto Bava

If one film sums up what had become of Eurohorror in the 1980s, it's *Demons*. In 1985, producer Dario Argento and director Lamberto Bava had track records, but were not in a good career space – they needed a hit and *Demons* was it, establishing a franchise which ran to an official sequel (Bava's *Demons 2* [1986]) and at least three rival stabs at a third film: Bava's *Demons III: The Ogre* (1988), longtime hack Umberto Lenzi's opportunist *Black Demons* (1991) and Michele Soavi's *The Church* (1989). Bava and Argento have script credits, along with Franco Ferrini and genre mainstay Dardano Sacchetti; *Demons* is the sort of picture it takes at least four people (none of whose first language is that that the film is shot in, English) to write: it wasn't so much scripted as assembled, with scenes or ideas from different participants – including effects man Sergio Stivaletti – loosely strung together on a central premise (extra points for doing a mini-adaptation of Nabokov's *Laughter in the Dark* as a subplot). In the notion of a film erupting into reality, there's a parallel with Woody Allen's *The Purple Rose of Cairo* (1985), though a more likely precedent is Giuliano Montaldo's underrated *Closed Circuit*, a 1978 Italian TV movie in which the police investigate a mysterious, fatal shooting incident in a cinema where a spaghetti Western is screening and forensics establish that the bullet was made in America in the nineteenth century.

Time has not been kind to the 80s, and *Demons* has many of the problems of 80s' cinema: everyone wears a puffy jacket and has puffier hair, characters like the coke-snorting punks or the black pimp and his girlfriends come from a middle-aged imagination rather than the streets of Berlin (where the film was shot) and the use of contemporary artists on the soundtrack (Mötley Crüe, Saxon, Billy Idol, Rick Springfield) is opportunist rather than apt. The obvious model (even more obvious in *Demons 2*) is David Cronenberg's *Shivers* (1975), where we barely get time to register who characters are before orgiastic chaos engulfs them, but the specific inspiration for the demons themselves is Sam Raimi's *The Evil Dead* (1981, released as *La Casa* in Italy, prompting Lenzi to make several spurious *Casa* sequels exported as the *Ghosthouse* series).

Demons is a cynical picture, unconcerned with any of its characters: the mysterious usherette played by Nicoletta Elmi (formerly a child horror star in *Deep Red* [1975], *Flesh for Frankenstein* [1973] and *The Cursed Medallion* [1975]) *might* be part of the demonic plot, but this is forgotten when she gets killed like everyone else in the mêlée. The cinema setting, an enclosed but cavernous space, is the high concept of *Demons* – but, unlike Bigas Luna's *Anguish* (1987), the film doesn't take advantage of the multiple levels of reality on offer: the characters in the film on screen in the movie theatre are thin, hysterical clichés, but so are the ones in the audience; and the film-within-a-film sequences – which find kids unwisely poking around the tomb of Nostradamus – are stylistically exactly like the movie's supposed reality.   KN

Dir: Lamberto Bava; **Prod**: Dario Argento; **Wr**: Dario Argento, Lamberto Bava, Franco Ferrini, Dardano Sacchetti; **Cinematography**: Gianlorenzo Battaglia; **Editing**: Piero Bozza, Franco Fraticelli.

The Devil's Backbone (*El espinazo del diablo*)
Spain/Mexico, 2001 – 108 mins
Guillermo del Toro

> What is a ghost? A tragedy condemned to repeat itself time and again?
> An instant of pain, perhaps. Something dead which still seems to be alive.
> An emotion suspended in time. Like a blurred photograph. Like an insect
> trapped in amber.

These words form the literal and conceptual frame (the 'spine', if you
will) of Guillermo del Toro's *The Devil's Backbone*. We hear them spoken
in voiceover as the film opens and again as it concludes, but one of del
Toro's distinctive accomplishments is to keep these questions about
defining a ghost evolving throughout the film as a whole. Indeed, *The
Devil's Backbone* emerges as one of the horror genre's most ambitious
and sophisticated meditations on the ghost's many meanings –
emotional, psychological, historical, philosophical, spiritual, supernatural.

The Devil's Backbone takes place in Spain during the 1930s, as civil
war tears the nation apart. Young Carlos (Fernando Tielve), his father
killed by the Fascists, is deposited at a remote country orphanage that
houses the boys of Loyalists. The orphanage is haunted – by the war,
which has left behind a bomb that failed to explode in the main
courtyard; by a love too long deferred between its two overseers,
Carmen (Marisa Paredes) and Casares (Federico Luppi); by the seething
resentment of Jacinto (Eduardo Noriega), a young man who feels he has
given his best years to the orphanage and can only imagine stealing its
hidden stash of gold and burning it to the ground as a means of
balancing the scales; and by 'the one who sighs', the ghost of a child
who died in mysterious circumstances and refuses to rest until justice is
served.

This is the Mexican director del Toro's third full-length feature,
following the wonderfully imaginative *Cronos* (1993) and the technically

impressive but less compelling *Mimic* (1997). All of del Toro's films, including the subsequent *Blade II* (2002) and *Hellboy* (2004), reflect the director's passionate enthusiasm for the horror genre and its visual iconography, but it is *The Devil's Backbone* that stands thus far as his most personal and satisfying work. As a tale of ghosts understood in the broad but challenging terms of what del Toro calls 'unfinished business', the film recalls the mournful, intricately layered hauntings of Edgar Allan Poe and the long cinematic line indebted to Poe's touch, from Jean Epstein's *The Fall of the House of Usher* (1928) to M. Night Shyamalan's *The Sixth Sense* (1999). But perhaps the film's closest relative is Victor Erice's *The Spirit of the Beehive* (1973), a Spanish art film that also turns to Gothic conceits and the subjectivity of children in order to grapple with the traumatic impact of the Spanish Civil War.

The Devil's Backbone is that rare ghost film set substantially in bright, piercing daylight, where the wide open spaces outside the orphanage become more threatening than the labyrinthine passages within it. In fact, when the film ends with the benevolent spirit of Casares escorting the surviving children outside the decimated orphanage and into the war-torn world beyond, we can only hope that ghosts continue to need us as much as we need them. AL

Dir: Guillermo del Toro; **Prod**: Agustín Almodóvar, Pedro Almodóvar, Rosa Bosch, Bertha Navarro, Michel Ruben, Guillermo del Toro, Alfonso Cuarón (uncredited); **Original Music**: Javier Navarrete; **Wr**: Guillermo del Toro, Antonio Trashorras, David Muñoz; **Cinematography**: Guillermo Navarro; **Editing**: Guillermo Navarro.

Les Diaboliques (aka *Diabolique*, *The Devils*, *The Fiends*)
France, 1955 – 114 mins
Henri-Georges Clouzot

Directed by Henri-Georges Clouzot, and following his international hit *Wages of Fear* (1953), *Les Diaboliques* helped to usher in the 'modern' phase of the European horror-thriller.[5] Inspiring an envious Alfred Hitchcock to make *Psycho* (1960), and drawing on a novel by Pierre Boileau and Thomas Narcejac – as did Hitchcock's *Vertigo* (1958) – *Les Diaboliques* is a wholly remarkable study in sadism and suspense.[6]

The film's narrative focuses on the wife and mistress of a tyrannical schoolteacher, Delasalle (Paul Meurisse), who decide to plot together to murder him. However, Delasalle's supposedly dead body vanishes, and the two women (played by Simone Signoret and Vera Clouzot) are menaced by the re-appearance of their presumed victim's freshly laundered clothes. Is this a sign that Delasalle has survived, that his vengeful spirit is at work, or that an unknown blackmailer has witnessed the crime?

Les Diaboliques earns its place as a 'literally breathtaking' horror classic partly thanks to its stunning use of a final shock twist – a by now much-imitated device – but also partially thanks to its naturalistic focus on the everyday lives of perpetrators and victims of murder. Rather than being a detective-led crime tale, or indeed ultimately supernatural in tone, *Les Diaboliques* thematically explores the sadistic psychologies of its lead characters.[7]

Ernest Mandel, analysing the history of the crime story, quotes writers Boileau and Narcejac on the nature of their characters' exploits: 'One becomes a victim as soon as one is present at events whose definitive meaning one is unable to decipher, as soon as the real becomes a trap, as soon as everyday life is turned upside down'.[8] This is certainly what happens to *Les Diaboliques'* murderers, who are unable to decipher the true meaning of the disappearance of Delasalle's body. But, of course, it is also the psychological position of the film's viewers, who are subjected to a cinematic 'trap' and thereby become horrified victims in a related, visceral sense, being unable to fully decipher the filmic world and narrative until the final reveal.

Though French film critics of the 1960s tended to value Hitchcock's films over Clouzot's,[9] US auteurists and reviewers frequently favoured the French director.[10] These responses show that Clouzot and Hitchcock's critical reputations have been closely related, with the two directors engaging in a history-making power struggle to create the ultimate horror-thriller masterpiece. Here, European and Hollywood horror have powerfully informed and influenced one another.   MH

Dir: Henri-Georges Clouzot; Prod: Henri-Georges Clouzot; **Original Music**: Georges Van Parys; **Wr**: Pierre Boileau and Thomas Narcejac (novel), Jérôme Géronimi, Frédéric Grendel, René Masson; **Cinematography**: Armand Thirard; **Editing**: Madeleine Gug.

Don't Torture a Duckling (Non si sevizia un paperino)
Italy, 1972 – 110 mins
Lucio Fulci

Italy, 1972. In a small village in the deep South, a killer is strangling young boys. As none of the suspects arrested by the authorities proves to be the culprit, the townspeople's sorrow turns into superstitious fury, adding new atrocities to the ones committed by the serial killer. Only when a reporter from a northern city and a strikingly beautiful and shockingly liberated young woman (herself one of the main suspects) stumble upon a mutilated Donald Duck doll does the murderer's identity begin to take shape. And yet even the final, precipitating events re-establish little more than the impossibility for this closed, backward community to adapt to the changing times.

Considered by many – including the director himself – to be Lucio Fulci's masterpiece, this gem of a *giallo* contains two of the most striking sequences in all of Italian cinema. The four-minute seduction scene where 70s' sexpot Barbara Bouchet, in full frontal nudity, teasingly invites one of the young local boys (and a would-be victim!) to 'go to bed with her' caused a predictable scandal, complete with angry citizens' letters to the authorities and charges against Fulci, Bouchet and the film's producer for 'corruption of a minor'.

If this scene recalls Fulci's sex comedies (at least half of the fifty-four pictures he made are not horror films, thus making even more remarkable the titles of 'godfather of horror' and 'master of the macabre' that Fulci went on to earn) and can perhaps be seen as a sapient attempt to secure free publicity, the sequence of the murder of the *maciara* – the witch of the village wrongfully believed to be the killer – masterfully orchestrates all the themes and stylistic choices that make *Don't Torture a Duckling* such a highly original and extraordinarily powerful *giallo*.

In the opening shot, an empty highway dramatically placed atop high cement pillars snakes across the deserted countryside of Italy's impoverished South. Thus, Fulci immediately establishes the film's basic and unresolvable conflict: a modernity fuelled by economic development traversing an ancient, almost archaic, rural community, disrupting its age-old rhythms, attacking its religious values and ridiculing its deep residue of superstition, without at the same time being able to offer any positive alternative values.

Riz Ortolani's score, juxtaposing the 'typical' pulsating jazz chords of early 1970s' Italian *gialli* with plaintive popular chants throughout the film, continues to evoke this basic clash until, in the excruciatingly graphic lynching of the *maciara*, Fulci turns to diegetic music to achieve a shattering effect of profound poignancy. By an old cemetery, to the sound of a car radio playing a frantic rock song, a group of male villagers slowly surround the *maciara*, their slow, threatening approach choreographed with the fluidity of a Sergio Leone duel. When the lynching begins, with chains, fists and bats, the *maciara*'s open wounds project us into the full-fledged horror of Fulci's 1981 classic, *The Beyond*. But then, as the violence continues, the radio station suddenly switches to a melodic romantic song which Ortolani composed for the voice of Ornella Vanoni, then the Italian chanteuse of modern love and loneliness.

After the men leave the scene of the crime, the *maciara*, blood-covered and still accompanied by Vanoni's excruciatingly beautiful voice, drags herself to the edge of the highway. A few cars pass by. It must be Sunday, for they are all family cars heading to the beach. Fathers drive. Children wear colourful summer clothes. Mothers sport large sunglasses. One young girl holds a big green and blue ball. No one stops.　CU

Dir: Lucio Fulci; **Prod**: Renato Jaboni; **Original Music**: Riz Ortolani; **Wr**: Gianfranco Clerici, Lucio Fulci, Roberto Gianviti; **Cinematography**: Sergio D'Offizi; **Editing**: Ornella Micheli.

The Door with Seven Locks (*Die Tür mit den sieben Schlossern*)
Germany, 1962 – 95 mins
Alfred Vohrer

Although film adaptations of the blood-and-thunder novels of British writer Edgar Wallace (1875–1932) date back to 1916, his works achieved their greatest cinematic exposure when they became the basis for an inexpensive series of West German films – familiarly called *krimis*, from the term *Taschenkrimi* (pocket crime novel) – starting in 1959 with *The Fellowship of the Frog*. This first film caught on with the German public (not surprisingly since Wallace had always enjoyed a huge popularity in Germany) and a series was born. By 1962, when Alfred Vohrer made *The Door with Seven Locks*, an impressive eleven such pictures had been cranked out, including Vohrer's own *Dead Eyes of London*, made the previous year.

The formula for the *krimis* was straightforward and simple. Take a Wallace novel, update the story and violence content (it's hardly surprising that the black-and-white *Door with Seven Locks* boasts a bullet-riddled, blood-red main title), plug in either Joachim Fuchsberger or Heinz Drache as the detective hero, throw in the comic antics of house comedian Eddi Arent as the detective's sidekick, brazen out the fact that the supposedly English settings were inescapably German – *et voilà, a krimi*. The amazing thing is that it worked, though not quite perfectly. The attempts at creating England via stock shots, portraits of Queen Elizabeth II and the odd British sports car (especially, since they often didn't worry about finding a right-hand-drive model) fooled no one. Production values were sketchy, with old dark castles often looking like nothing so much as overlit sound stages. But the films were fun (in part due to their shortcomings) and exciting. They were also surprisingly faithful to the Wallace originals.

That's very much the case with *The Door with Seven Locks*. It certainly amps up the violence and the horror, but it follows the plot and incidents of Wallace's novel quite closely with its story of a Scotland Yard man (Drache) on the trail of a series of murders that are related to a set of keys. The manner of the investigation – his encounter with a grubby thief (Klaus Kinski) who's become convinced that success at a job he was hired to do would have meant his death, his dealings with a pretty librarian (Sabina Sesselmann) who turns out to be involved in the case, etc. – is straight out of the novel, as is the solution to the mystery. All of this makes the film a respectable version of the book, but its greater import in the realm of horror – indeed, that of the entire series – lies in the additional elements, in the increased horror content.

The earlier *krimis* had all taken the horror to much higher levels than anything previously seen on the screen – not horror in the traditional sense, but the horror of violence itself. By today's standards, these things seem fairly tame. At the time they were startling, over-the-top and even a bit tasteless. Vohrer's *Dead Eyes of London* was certainly far less genteel than the 1939 British version, *Dark Eyes of London*, though oddly the first film had been considered tasteless at the time. The addition of wrestler Adi Berber (best described as the German Tor Johnson) helped up the horror ante there, and his presence here does much the same. But Vohrer and screenwriter Harald Petersson-Giertz don't stop there. They've added poisonous snakes, machine guns, shock cuts to dead faces – and they've turned Wallace's deranged behavioural scientist into the stark-raving mad scientist, Staletti (Pinkas Braun). Staletti in the film comes complete with subterranean laboratory and loopy medical theories about grafting a man's head onto a monkey. In essence, the film has taken what was already a pulp thriller and increased its pulp quotient to a point where it topples over into something like a true horror film. That it also very nearly topples over into unintentional humour is another matter, but not necessarily an unfortunate one. The very absurdity of it is part of the charm.   KH

Dir: Alfred Vohrer; **Prod**: Horst Wendlandt; **Original Music**: Peter Thomas; **Wr**: Harald Petersson-Giertz, Johannes Kai, G. F. Hummel; **Cinematography**: Karl Lob; **Art**: Siegfried Mews, Helmut Nentwig.

The Ear (*Ucho*)
Czechoslovakia, 1970 – 94 mins
Karel Kachyna

Shot under the watchful eyes of the Soviet occupying forces as the post-1968 Warsaw Pact invasion period known as Normalisation began its repressive stranglehold on Czech film production, Karel Kachyna's daring political horror-noir *The Ear* was withheld from circulation immediately upon completion. Nothing short of the Velvet Revolution and a subsequent return to democratic principles in 1989 was necessary to get the two-decade ban removed and the picture screened to art-house audiences, and occasionally on Czech television.

Ludvík (Radoslav Brzobohaty) is a senior ministry official in the bureaucracy of Prague's ruling Communist Party. Anna (Jirina Bohdalová) is his alcoholic wife, daughter of a small-town pub-owner. The couple have a young son, and live in a comfortable home on a quiet street in a nice neighbourhood. Initially, the cruel insults, nasty looks and open hostility they direct towards one another seem like mere character development, at most a developing subplot. It is only later that we realise their complex and multifaceted marital relationship is at the very centre of *The Ear*'s concerns, at once allegorising, commenting on and distinguishing itself from the likewise complex relationship between a ruthless, oppressive political regime and its justifiably paranoid populace.

The events in *The Ear* take place over the course of one very long evening. Returning home from a seemingly casual Party function, Ludvík and Anna find their front gate open and the spare set of keys missing from its usual spot. At first dismissed by the couple as inconsequential, other strange findings – including a power outage and dead phone lines – make them wonder whether they aren't being observed by the suspicious and unethical Communist authorities.

In his mind's eye, Ludvík begins replaying scenes from the social function earlier that night. What seemed innocuous when first

Burning the evidence in Karel Kachyna's *The Ear*

experienced now takes on the surreal quality of a nightmare, as every sentence spoken to Ludvík – 'Sorry, the comrades are listening'; 'Didn't they speak to you?'; 'They're all trained spies' – becomes pregnant with meaning and signifies great personal danger in retrospect. Connecting the dots and focusing on the fact that his immediate superior (also a close friend) was recently taken away on trumped-up charges of anti-Communist activities, Ludvík comes to believe that he is the current target of Party suspicion, and that his own arrest is imminent.

Anguished by the thought that his comfortable if joyless home life may be over, desperate to get rid of any materials that could be cited as evidence of his untrustworthiness, Ludvík starts burning his papers and correspondence. Anna, loose-lipped from heavy drinking and convinced that her husband is being paranoid, needles him incessantly about the deteriorating state of their relationship and his utter lack of interest in her both sexually and emotionally.

Temporarily putting a halt to the couple's ongoing row is an apparently spontaneous late-night visit from a number of Ludvík's Party comrades. Fearful of their underlying motives, Ludvík plays the role of good host, and the already inebriated gang of bureaucrats proceeds to get stupefyingly drunk. When they finally leave, Anna and Ludvík start bickering again, only to find proof that their house is indeed bugged – that the 'Ear' has been listening to their private conversations and intimate confessions, many of which could be construed as rebellious or at least not in complete accord with strict Communist principles.

It is at this point, late in the film, when the precarious reality of their situation becomes manifest, that a previously submerged – though always present – dynamic in Ludvík and Anna's relationship rises to the surface. Expressing great tenderness, protectiveness and depth of feeling towards one another, the couple discuss how to proceed once the authorities come to take Ludvík away. Anna cries hysterically, Ludvík tries to comfort her and the *Who's Afraid of Virginia Woolf*-style psychological warfare comes to an end as Big Brother closes in. The analogies established earlier between marriage (the personal/private relations between individuals) and citizenship (the political/public relations between a country's government and its denizens) – both of which frequently involve suspicion, hypocrisy, resentments, tarnished ideals, secrets and lies – now diminish in import. Instead we become sensitive to the disanalogies: the limitless capacity of those in power to plot, to conspire, to utilise advanced technology or the threat thereof in order to terrorise, manipulate and control.

The Ear ends on an ironic and chilling note. The power in the house suddenly returns, and Ludvík receives a phone call telling him that he has in fact received a promotion. Instead of evincing joy at the 'good' news, the couple sits quietly in the living room, more mystified than ever by the Party's curious methods and motivations. Anna's final words ring in our ears as the closing credits run: 'I'm scared'. As well she should be.   SJS

Dir: Karel Kachyna; **Prod**: Karel Vejrík; **Original Music**: Svatopluk Havelka; **Wr**: Karel Kachyna, Jan Procházka, Ladislav Winkelhöfer; **Cinematography**: Josef Illík; **Editing**: Miroslav Hájek.

Eyes Without a Face (*Les Yeux sans visage*, aka *The Horror Chamber of Dr Faustus*)
France, 1960 – 88 mins
Georges Franju

Dr Génessier (Pierre Brasseur) – a surgeon obsessed with repairing his daughter's ravaged face, ruined in a car accident that he caused – kidnaps students in order to use their faces as donor tissue. Based on the novel by Jean Redon, the adaptation by Pierre Boileau and Thomas Narcejec bears similar themes to their novels *Les Diaboliques* and *Vertigo*, notably the concern with the everyday world going awry and the victim as central character. Though the police are present in the film, the investigative subplot is peripheral and they fail to find the missing girls. The story turns on Génessier's daughter Christiane (Edith Scob) and her increasing despair – Scob's performance here is key. About to undergo yet another transplant, it is she who frees the latest victim and turns on her father. The final iconic scenes depict her setting the dogs on Génessier and wandering into the woods alone with her doves. The film is equally memorable for Franju's ethereal imagery and Boileau–Narcejac's evocative dialogue.

Lauded by art-house patrons as well as horror connoisseurs, *Eyes Without a Face* is rooted in both the *fantastique* and modernist cinema, echoing the poetry of Cocteau and Resnais. It combines the elements of Frankensteinian scientific horror – the mad doctor, the gore, the tortured victims – with masks (a frequent trope of horror cinema from *The Phantom of the Opera* [1925] to *Onibaba* [1964] and plastic-surgery thrillers such as *The Stolen Face* [1930] and *Corruption* [1967]). The atmosphere plays heavily on shadow and eerie lighting. Faces are frequently hidden, only the eyes visible (the bandaged head of the victim Edna [Juliette Mayniel], Génessier's surgical attire and not least Christiane's mask). In the use of these masks and the frequent references to mirrors and reflections, identity and sanity become central concerns. Car drives and long, slow walks through the house punctuate the

narrative, suggesting a journey into madness. Christiane's impassive and flawless face – the transplant is as immobile as her porcelain mask – lends her a ghostlike presence as she haunts the corridors of the house. Her silent wanderings, as well as her seclusion in her attic room, suggest parallels to the Gothic novel and its attendant horrors.

The six-minute long surgery scene is the pivotal moment of horror in the film (the explicitness of the scalpel biting through the flesh and the lifting off of the amputated face remain agonising), but Franju creates the real horrors in the spectator's imagination by keeping Christiane's ruined face hidden – by mask, back of the head shots or unfocused camerawork. It is only in the medico-scientific detail (the analysis of Christiane's decaying face in particular) that Franju dwells on the visual. Here, obsession is a key theme: Génessier's obsession in particular. It is ironic that in the dubbed English-language version, the scene depicting Génessier's caring side was cut, emphasing his monstrosity at the cost of an added layer of reality and Franju's intent to make a film about the normal acting abnormally.

Despite being edited and retitled *The Horror Chamber of Dr. Faustus* in its dubbed English-language version, thus emphasising the horror, *Eyes Without a Face* has come to be recognised as a key example of cultural cinema and the *fantastique*. It has cultural resonances that spread from the novels of Clive Barker (in particular *The Damnation Game*) to new wave music (the title of the Billy Idol song). Franju's work includes documentary, realism and surrealism. *Eyes Without a Face* is all these things at once, and something more than just a horror movie.   BC

Dir: Georges Franju; **Prod**: Jules Borkon; **Original Music**: Maurice Jarre; **Wr**: Jean Redon (novel), Pierre Boileau and Thomas Narcejec, Pierre Gascar, Claude Sautet; **Cinematography**: Eugen Schüfftan; **Editing**: Gilbert Natot.

(Opposite page) Prisoner of the flesh: Edith Scob in *Eyes Without a Face*

Fascination
France, 1979 – 80 mins
Jean Rollin

Arguably the finest work of cinematic art ever made using porn stars,
Jean Rollin's psychological thriller *Fascination* is also an acquired taste.
This is the textbook definition of 'indulgent', but that is the essence of
Rollin's appeal: don't come calling if you're looking for the safe, the
familiar or the glossy. By sticking to his own personal aesthetics, without
regard to commercial imperatives or the opinion of the conventional film
industry, Rollin has earned legions of loyal fans around the world. Of
course, it doesn't hurt that his pictures feature lots of naked breasts.

Although some of the cast are laughably amateur, Rollin is blessed
with a true screen presence in Brigitte Lahaie. Still on the upswing of a
rise to fame in France's X-rated movie business as one of its top draws,
this is the third of her seven collaborations with Rollin. Casting a porn
star made sense: Lahaie was already comfortable with performing in the
nude, and evidently nonchalant about letting softcore slide into hardcore.
Fascination takes place in that same fantasy world depicted by
pornography, in which any interaction with a woman is likely to end in
sex. In fact, the initial set-up seems almost ideal porn territory.

Mark (Jean-Marie Lemair) is a thief on the run from his former
colleagues who ducks into a seemingly deserted chateau to hide out.
Inside he discovers a pair of sexy young things (Lahaie and Franca Mai),
alone, helpless and underclothed. Sure enough, bed-hopping ensues, but
these girls are neither helpless nor as alone as they seem, and they are
constantly remarking on his impending doom. Because these threats and
warnings issue from what he perceives as sexpots, Mark utterly fails to
take their dire comments seriously until his fate is sealed. He assumes he's
safe because he is a man with a gun, but in fact this film is placing him
in the role usually reserved for the girl: helpless victim, sexually exploited.

Euro-horror of the 1970s commonly relied on nudity and gore as
exploitation hooks, a way to snag audiences in a tight market.

Unsurprisingly, this tended towards misogyny more often than not. Nubile female victims sadistically abused by male villains or used as sexual fodder by male heroes were stock in trade. *Fascination* subverts this tradition with a refreshing depiction of female power.

The storytelling is simple and unaffected. Rollin took enormous inspiration from the classic silent-era thrillers of Louis Feuillade, and more so than most of Feuillade's followers he has adapted that silent-movie style for the modern age. The spare dialogue could easily have been reduced down to intertitles, or disposed of entirely. Once the situation is established, the narrative relies on visuals rather than dialogue to advance the plot. And what visuals they are, too: lush painterly images, surrealist in style and almost fattening to look at. Had René Magritte been hired by *Playboy* to make a vampire thriller, it would have looked a lot like this. The movie has a delirious dreamlike aura that is hard to shake off afterwards. Few film-makers could extract so much from such impoverished resources, but Rollin's confident imagination fuels his films in ways cash simply could not.   DK

Dir: Jean Rollin; **Prod**: Joe De Lara; **Original Music**: Philippe d'Aram; **Wr**: Jean Rollin; **Cinematography**: Georgie Fromentin; **Editing**: Dominique Saint-Cyr.

Four Flies on Grey Velvet (*4 mosche di velluto grigio*)
Italy/France, 1971 – 105 mins
Dario Argento

The *giallo Four Flies on Grey Velvet* completes Dario Argento's famed Italian 'Animal Trilogy' initiated by his directorial debut *The Bird with the Crystal Plumage* (1970) and second film *The Cat o' Nine Tails* (1971). The three films are linked not only through their cryptic animal titles but also in the way that they are formal deconstructions of murder mystery conventions. The trilogy, and the *giallo* in general, places greater emphasis on the staging of murder than on the hermeneutics of investigation, leading to the *giallo*'s associations with the horror genre rather than the thriller. These early *gialli* also reveal Argento's penchant for exploring the possibilities of form and music (*Four Flies* opens with an unusual point-of-view shot from inside a guitar, for example), paving the way for his more structurally complex and experimental later films.

At the heart of nearly all Argento's *gialli* lies the psychologically damaged individual who is the victim of repressive family structures. For Argento it is the family and its regulated organisation of gender and sexuality that gives birth to psychopaths. In *Four Flies on Grey Velvet*, the killer turns out to be Nina Tobias, played by a rather androgynous Mimsy Farmer, as the wife of the main protagonist Roberto (Michael Brandon). It turns out Nina was raised as a boy by her father, enforcing a gender not her own through physical beatings and cruelty. In turn she marries Roberto because he looks similar to her father and thus continues the cycle of torment. Roberto also has recurring dreams of decapitation, soliciting us to read the characters through a Freudian lens.

The clue in the film's title refers to the image of four flies, revealed through forensic retinal photography, imprinted on the back of the eye of one of the victims. It is Nina's pendant, a fly in resin, that finally catches Roberto's eye as it swings in front of him while trying to usher her out the door to safety.

Argento saves his *coup de grâce* until last with one of the most visually experimental and poetic deaths of any of his killers. Without CGI and predating by nearly three decades the now exhausted slow-motion camera effects of *The Matrix* trilogy (1999–2003), during her escape Nina crashes her getaway car into the back of a lorry. The film speed slows down from twenty-four frames per second to 30,000 frames per second in order to capture every twist of metal and exploding shard of glass. Captured this way by the scientific Pentazet camera, Nina's death is so stunning that it becomes transcendental in both aesthetic and effect. This truly spectacular death is also accompanied by Ennio Morricone's theme, 'Nina nana in blu', the music referring to a nursery rhyme and children's song. In other words, the music here reminds us of the origin of Nina's psychosis in a tragic childhood past, a device later used in Argento's *Deep Red* (1975), where a nursery rhyme is used to orchestrate the murders whose origin is, as always, organised around the theme of family.   GN

Dir: Dario Argento; **Prod**: Salvatore Argento; **Original Music**: Ennio Morricone; **Wr**: Dario Argento, Luigi Cozzi, Mario Foglietti, Bryan Edgar Wallace; **Cinematography**: Franco Di Giacomo; **Editing**: Franco Di Giacomo.

The Fourth Man (*De vierde man*)
Netherlands, 1983 – 102 mins
Paul Verhoeven

A beguiling portrait of a manipulative artist masquerading as an erotic horror film, Paul Verhoeven's *The Fourth Man* holds up numerous mirrors to its own perverse countenance so craftily that everyone from highbrow critics to casual gore hounds can walk away completely sated. The unlikely protagonist, Gerard Reve (whose 'dream'-like last name is derived from the author of the source novel), is first introduced as an alcohol-sodden, half-naked wreck (Jeroen Krabbé) fantasising about strangling his male violinist companion. When he travels to Flushing, he becomes entangled with Christine Halsslag (Renée Soutendijk), a beautician/literary enthusiast whose current out-of-town lover, Herman (Thom Hoffman), suffers from a lack of sexual endurance that leaves her unsatisfied. Gerard's machinations to claim Herman for himself reveal that Christine's past three lovers all died violent deaths and one of her current male bedmates may be next.

Beautifully adapted by Verhoeven's regular Dutch screenwriter, Gerard Soeteman, the film's text juggles a number of cultural references from fairytales (Gerard's 'witch' accusations to Christine) to Biblical stories (particularly 'Samson and Delilah', whose figurative emasculation scenario is echoed explicitly in the film's most notorious moment), all professed by Verhoeven to be tactics used to please stuffy European critics. However, its most beguiling aspect is its humourous adoption of surrealist themes and images, from cheeky wordplay (black widow Christine's short-circuiting salon sign transforms into 'spin', the Dutch term for 'spider') to startling *trompe-l'oeil* concoctions like an eyeball-styled doorknob, a revolver-shaped key hidden among a clutch of crimson roses and the Buñuel-worthy blasphemy of a sweaty, Speedo-clad Herman on a crucifix awaiting Gerard's services. Even the viewer is left unspared, particularly the gasp-inducing sequence in which Gerard pleasures himself at a keyhole while Christine and her boyfriend copulate on the other side;

Jeroen Krabbé kills his lover (or does he?) in *The Fourth Man*

when the entire theatrical audience peers in for a closer look as well, it's clear that no one is above Gerard's dubious but all-too-human behaviour. The denouement in which a nerve-wracked Gerard is hauled away by his dream-saviour 'Maria' (Geert de Jong) while a Cupid-lipped Christine targets her next man, is both open-ended, hilarious and unnerving, leaving the impression that all these mad characters were bound to collide in a bloody mess before zig-zagging away again on their own trajectories.

Never a director to shy away from sexual activity or violence on screen, Verhoeven caused a minor stir in English-speaking territories with his unflinching depiction of frontal nudity, genital mutilation, eyeball violence and simulated love-making (though it's genteel compared to his previous pan-sexual film, *Spetters* [1980]). Perhaps this aesthetic but shocking material was intended to distract conservative types from noticing that the film boasted not only a semi-sympathetic gay lead character but a completely unorthodox narrative in which very little actually happens; even the single 'real' moment of violence at the end can't be directly attributed to human malice, but rather the blackly comic hand of fate. This wry balancing act proved successful enough for Verhoeven to attempt it again with *Basic Instinct* (1992), a Hollywood variant with an even more disposable and ultimately open-ended plot which 'straightens' out the male lead character and gives its spider-woman villain a lesbian slant instead. However, that slick and sinister concoction – hampered by Joe Eszterhas's much ballyhooed but facile script – proves that, despite swapping scissors for ice picks, there's no substitute for the real thing.   NT

Dir: Paul Verhoeven; **Prod**: Rob Houwer; **Original Music**: Loek Dikker; **Wr**: Gerard Reve (novel), Gerard Soeteman; **Cinematography**: Jan de Bont; **Editing**: Ine Schenkkan.

Funny Games
Austria, 1997 – 109 mins
Michael Haneke

Michael Haneke's *Funny Games* is both an unnerving horror film and a critical interrogation of the pleasures we derive from such grisly fare. This is hardly a surprise coming from a director whose work has always appealed more to the art-house than the grind-house crowd. The film's story is simple. A family – mother, father and teenage son – are spending a weekend in a country house by the lake when two young men appear. The two strangers, clad in immaculate tennis whites and polite to a fault, first insinuate themselves into the house, then sadistically terrorise the family, finally murdering all three victims. Their first appearance, as they come strolling over from the house next door, suggests that they have

Playing for keeps: Michael Haneke's *Funny Games*

already killed another family, just as, by the end of the film, they are about to move on to another house by the lake.

Home invasion has been a staple of the thriller genre, starting with such noir-ish American gangster films as *Key Largo* (1948) and *Desperate Hours* (1955, remade 1990), and then moving squarely into the horror genre with 1970s' slasher films like *When a Stranger Calls* (1979) or the films in the *Nightmare on Elm Street* series (1984, *et al.*). Like its precursors, *Funny Games* exploits our unease about the invasion of private spaces and the transformation of the home as a space of safety and comfort into a deadly prison that isolates us from the larger community outside. The privacy of the home also stands for the integrity of the bourgeois patriarchal family, that other target of critical examination in the horror film: will the family stand up to the pressure? Can it be defended, or, more alarmingly, is it even worth defending?

Haneke's use of such a familiar theme raises audience expectations, which *Funny Games* then goes on to disappoint with grim determination. Genre audiences might expect the family to overcome their internal differences and fight back against the invaders; to see the invaders expelled from the home and the zone of safety re-established. The more sadistically the invaders behave, the more we anticipate the pleasures of retribution. *Funny Games* resolutely denies us these pleasures. Once the course of events is set, the final outcome is as grim as it is inevitable. Watching such helplessness in the face of sadistic violence is a game that, after all, turns out to be not so funny at all.

It is this strategic denial of pleasure that makes *Funny Games* a fascinating experiment in genre deconstruction. The film's violence is all the more shocking for being unspectacular, even banal. When the son is murdered with casual brutality, the camera lingers endlessly on the helpless agony of the survivors instead of dramatising the murder itself. Haneke grants his villains moments when they knowingly smirk and wink at the camera, and in one brief scene, when the mother manages to grab a shotgun and shoot one of the two intruders in a desperate attempt to fight back, the other one grabs a TV remote control and puts the film literally in reverse for a few seconds to alter the outcome of the scene. Disappointed viewers may realise how much they depend on being catered to and how 'safe' the pleasures of more conventional horror films really are. For fans of the horror film, the experience of *Funny Games* may be all the more harrowing.   SH

Dir: Michael Haneke; **Prod**: Veit Heiduschka; **Wr**: Michael Haneke; **Cinematography**: Jürgen Jürges; **Editing**: Andreas Prochaska.

The Girl Who Knew Too Much (*La ragazza che sapeva troppo*, aka *The Evil Eye*)
Italy, 1963 — 88 mins
Mario Bava

Directed by Mario Bava, *The Girl Who Knew Too Much* is the first Italian *giallo* and, together with Alfred Hitchcock's *Psycho* and Michael Powell's *Peeping Tom* (both 1960), is one of the early precursors of the American slasher movie. The *giallo* is perhaps best described as a hybrid of the horror and detective genres in that it offsets the viscerality of horror in the grotesque and baroque set pieces for which it is noted with the intellectualism of the detective thriller: the term itself originates from the yellow covers of pulp fictions published in Italy in the 1930s.

The *Girl Who Knew Too Much* narrates the story of Nora Draiston (Leticia Roman), a naive young woman, who, while visiting her sick aunt in Italy, witnesses a murder one dark and rainy night after fleeing from the house where her aunt has suddenly passed away. With the help of an Italian doctor, Marcello Bassi (John Saxon), with whom she becomes romantically involved, Nora seeks to solve the mystery of what she saw that night, as the next morning the body seems to have mysteriously disappeared. These initial sequences set up what will become one of the main conventions of the *giallo*: the foreign outsider who accidentally witnesses a crime and subsequently undertakes a private investigation into the mystery.

The multiplicity of its intertextual referencing is a distinguishing feature of Bava's film. Nora's experience in hospital, where she is accused of being a raving drunk, indicates a continuing dialogue with the work of Hitchcock (an innocent character's mistaken identity), as does the title (a clear reference to Hitch's *The Man Who Knew Too Much* [1956]). Newspaper clippings detailing the exploits of a so-called 'alphabet killer' self-reflexively refer back to the work of the queen of detective fiction, Agatha Christie. And it is no coincidence that the first shot of Nora on the plane shows her holding a lurid pulp fiction novel. Just as Nora's ravings about a murder are dismissed as paranoia, her insistence on seeing herself as the next/fourth victim are attributed to her appetite for detective fiction.

By focalising the narrative through Nora, Bava's *giallo* sets the trend for films such as *Halloween* (1978) and can be said to be the foundational text for the heroine character. At the same time, while Nora's naivety and sexual inexperience are similar to those of the 'final girl' in the American slasher film, she is neither a target of male psychosexual fury or of female revenge. Nora insists on solving the mystery of what she 'saw' that night, refusing to heed patriarchal warnings (the doctors) to leave the deductive process to the symbolic agents of the law (the police). And, by focalising the narrative purely through Nora's subjective and negotiated vision, the film works as a meta-commentary on the nature of seeing and its relationship to violence, which by association implicates the spectator within the cinematic frame.

Setting the trend for many subsequent *gialli*, the film subverts traditional gender representations in the horror genre. Just as Nora is no damsel-in-distress, the figure behind the murders is revealed to be a woman, Laura Terrani (Valentina Cortesa). While Laura descends into a recognisable psychosis, there is method in her madness, in clear opposition to the frenzy within which the male monster in the psychological horror film operates. Having killed her sister, Laura then murders two other victims in order to suggest a psychosexual motivation that would lead the police (as embedded viewers) off the right track. And Nora remains convinced that, because of the nature of the crimes, the murderer must be a man until the final denouement in which Laura reveals that it was her and not her husband who was responsible. In this way, while the *giallo* influences the slasher film, it also anticipates the postmodern contemporary horror films of directors such as Kevin Williamson and Wes Craven, and the new wave of French horror movies such as Alexandre Aja's recent *High Tension* (2003).   CB

Dir: Mario Bava; **Prod**: Massimo De Rita; **Original Music**: Roberto Nicolosi; **Wr**: Mario Bava, Enzo Corbucci, Ennio De Concini, Eliana De Sabata, Mino Guerrini, Franco Prosperi; **Cinematography**: Mario Bava; **Editing**: Mario Serandrei.

The Golem: How He Came into the World (*Der Golem, wie er in die Welt kam,* aka *The Golem*)
Germany, 1920 – 85 mins
Carl Boese, Paul Wegener

Based on Jewish folk tales from Eastern Europe, *The Golem* tells of a mystically animated man of clay brought to life to protect Prague's sixteenth-century ghetto from socially pervasive and state-sanctioned anti-Semitism. The final part of Wegener's 'golem trilogy', alongside *Monster of Fate* (1914) and *The Golem and the Dancer* (1916), it encapsulates – as did Wegener's *The Student of Prague* (1913) – a sentiment common to German Expressionist films of this period: that human arrogance had led to the horrors of World War I and the social and economic terrors of the post-war period. Hence the learned Rabbi Löw (Albert Steinrück) predicts disaster for the Jewish people by astronomical means. He magically animates a giant statue and takes it to the emperor's castle where, to great visual effect, he conjures a portal to the past that cinematically depicts significant moments in the history of the Jewish people.

Rescued by the golem (played by Wegener himself) from a curse hurled at the anti-Semitic court by Moses, the emperor rescinds an earlier proclamation that would have cleared the Jewish ghetto and fulfilled the rabbi's prophesy. But the golem remains an unstable entity – his susceptibility to control by the demon Astaroth leading him to run amok when revived by the servant Famulus (Ernst Deutsch), himself insanely angry that the rabbi's daughter Miriam (Lyda Salmonova) has fallen in love with the Gentile courtier Florian (Lothar Müthel). Throwing Florian from a tower, abducting Miriam and burning the rabbi's house to the ground, the golem is only stopped when a decidedly Aryan child removes the Star of David that has magically given him life, the film closing with the Star of David lying abandoned in the mud.

Beauty and the Beast: Paul Wegener's *The Golem*

Certainly the association of Jews with magical practices and the purposeful desecration of the Star of David has left the film open to charges of complicity with right-wing German anti-Semitism, but this would be to marginalise its engaging portrayal of the historic abuses of Jewish communities in Europe. The film avoids, moreover, the vulgar ethnic stereotyping of contemporary films such as F. W. Murnau's *Nosferatu* (1922), while repudiating the sentiments of the hate films of the 1940s such as *Jud Süss* (1940), which sought to justify the horrors of the holocaust by insistently equating Jews with dubious financial dealings.

And beyond such historically and culturally specific concerns, *The Golem* has been of enormous thematic and stylistic influence. Its depiction of the hubris entailed by Löw's monster-making activities would work its way into numerous films from *Metropolis* (1927) to *The Terminator* (1984), while its Expressionist stylisation would be disseminated by its cinematographer Karl Freund throughout Universal's classic monster movies, James Whale's *Frankenstein* (1931) drawing directly on the animation of the golem and its interaction with an innocent child. Although overshadowed by contemporary works such as *The Cabinet of Dr Caligari* (1919), *The Golem* remains a masterwork of German Expressionist cinema, being politically significant, stylistically influential and pioneering in its use of special visual effects. It most certainly deserves a far wider audience.   LB

Dir: Carl Boese, Paul Wegener; **Prod**: Paul Davidson; **Original Music**: Hans Landsberger; **Wr**: Henrik Galeen, Gustav Meyrink (novel), Paul Wegener; **Cinematography**: Karl Freund, Guido Seeber.

The Grapes of Death (*Les Raisons de la mort*, aka *Pesticide*)
France, 1978 – 90 mins
Jean Rollin

Jean Rollin's usual proclivity for the various perversions of decrepit bourgeoisie vampires is evident in this film, a rare example of lyricism in a zombie movie. Here Rollin retains the languid scenes of women exploring crumbling castles and cemeteries which emerge as the calcified wounds of wild landscapes. Hypnotic close-ups of females whose fear incarnates in their faces more as trance than horror punctuate the rotting, suppurating visages of those affected by the plague.

The plague in *The Grapes of Death* is not that of vampirism, but comes from a source no less sanguine or bourgeois – wine. In the little village near the vineyard of Roubles, something has happened to the wine. Elizabeth (Marie-George Pascal) returns to her village to find it the site of a pastoral apocalypse. Roubles is the interstitial space between a military base and a nuclear power plant (bingo!), and so Rollin hedges his bets with the possible sources of the infected wine which has turned the villagers, the winemakers and even the mayor into the living dead.

But Rollin's zombies are not like others. They have the contemplative calm of Lucio Fulci's zombies; indeed much of the film anticipates Fulci's *The Beyond* (1981) – most explicitly the delirious fetishism of the white eyes of the blind girl Lucy (Mirella Rancelot). But they also have a kind of confused sympathetic residue of childlike humanity. Technically these living dead have not died, simply developed wounds which signify their inevitable somnambulistic insanity. Their violence seems to quiver between a horror at harming their beloved and a non-specific urge to tear – though not eat – their victims. Love is an important part of the zombies' turpitude. The nameless farmer (Serge Marquand) has slit the throat of his wife and subsequently his daughter, but this was not a murderous compulsion; rather, it was a bizarre attempt at euthanasia. In the film's most enigmatic scenes, Lucy's lover Lucas (Paul Bisciglia) crucifies her on a rustic door and decapitates her, later to passionately kiss her head (which he refuses to relinquish).

Rollin's humorous cynicism of the bourgeois is poignantly evident when Elizabeth finds her saviours in Paul (Felix Marten) and his friend (Patrice Valota) who don't like wine, drinking only beer. But her saviours are far from redeemers, their militant culling of the zombies compelling Elizabeth to eradicate them when they attempt to execute her lover. Paul's final words 'This is crazy' reifies the poignancy of the situation.

The village is a polis of miasmic insanity in which the villagers are individual wounds from a double nosology born of modern science and warfare. The final scene emphasises this irresolvable insanity, as a slash of blood cuts a trajectory across Elizabeth's face: Rollin's sanguine signature. The film's rudimentary premise, neither logical nor illogical, allows it to gift to the viewer magical scenes framed and composed as visceral phantasmagoric *tableaux vivants*. Rollin's work is unique, and his ability to make plague both seductive and sympathetic shares more with social perceptions of disease than most zombie films. Beyond complex or trite metaphors of physical and mental epidemics, the film is visually stunning and ambiguously provocative thematically and aesthetically.   PMacC

Dir: Jean Rollin; **Prod**: Jean-Marie Ghanassia, Claude Guedj, Christian Ruh; **Original Music**: Philippe Sissman; **Wr**: Jean-Pierre Bouyxou, Christian Meunier, Jean Rollin; **Cinematography**: Claude Bécognée; **Editing**: Dominique Saint-Cyr, Christian Stoianovich.

Häxan: Witchcraft Through the Ages (Häxan, aka The Witches)
Denmark/Sweden, 1922 – 82 mins
Benjamin Christensen

Between 1919 and 1921, Danish film-maker Benjamin Christensen researched, wrote and directed one of the oddest of all horror movies. *Häxan* explores the history of European witchcraft, in particular the witch craze of 1450 to 1700. The film, which is divided into seven 'chapters', is a fascinating blend of scholarship, dramatic reconstruction and cultural criticism.

Chapter One is a lecture on the history of witchcraft. Belief in witchcraft, in Christensen's view, results from ignorance of the workings of the universe. But those accused of practising witchcraft were not thought merely to have magical powers. Christensen demonstrates that, by the Middle Ages, witches were thought to have renounced Christianity and made a pact with Satan. The association of witchcraft with apostasy and diabolism thus accounts for the murderous fury of the witch craze.

Chapters Two to Six illustrate common beliefs about witchcraft. The opening part of Chapter Two depicts a witch in her kitchen as she concocts potions out of loathsome ingredients. Chapters Three to Five depict a witch trial from beginning to end. An old woman is accused of bewitching a man. She proclaims her innocence, but under torture she tells of how she attended a sabbat where she saw members of the man's family. In this fashion, says Christensen, a witch trial could quickly consume more innocent victims. Chapter Six points out, however, that some who were accused of witchcraft sincerely confessed to being witches. Here we see, for example, a nun who considers herself possessed and asks that she be burned at the stake.

Chapter Seven argues that there is an important connection between belief in witches and hysteria. According to the classical theory of hysteria, hysterics exhibit symptoms, for example, sleep-walking and loss of bodily

A party from hell: Benjamin Christensen's *The Witches*

sensation, which have no discernible neurological or physiological cause. Instead, the cause is to be located in repressed beliefs and desires. Consequently, in an era disposed as a matter of theology to believe in witches, hysterical symptoms seem to untutored observers – including the hysterics themselves – to be the product of witchcraft and demonic possession. Christensen juxtaposes the kleptomania of a modern hysterical woman in Chapter Seven with the odd behaviour of the nun in Chapter Six who seizes a statue of the baby Jesus and then later spits on it. This comparison suggests that neurosis in general, and thus not merely hysteria, stands behind a belief in witchcraft.

Christensen relies on such famous witch-hunting manuals as Heinrich Kramer and James Sprenger's *Malleus Maleficarum* (*The Hammer against the Witches*) from 1486 and Francesco Guazzo's *Compendium Maleficarum* (*The Book of Witches*) from 1608. His views on the connection between belief in witchcraft and mental illness stem from the psychiatric work of Jean-Martin Charcot and his followers, including Sigmund Freud. (A full bibliography of Christensen's sources can be found among the extras on the DVD available from the Criterion Collection.)

Häxan is such an eccentric film that it does not have a clear place in cinema history. When it was released in 1922, it was well-received by many critics, but did poorly at the box office. And despite its obvious excellence, Häxan seems to have had little influence on subsequent films in the horror genre.   CB

Dir: Benjamin Christensen; **Original Music**: Launy Grøndahl, **Wr**: Benjamin Christensen; **Cinematography**: Johan Ankerstjerne; **Editing**: Edla Hansen.

High Tension (*Haute tension*, aka *Switchblade Romance*)
France, 2003 – 91 mins
Alexandre Aja

High Tension is a stylish French slasher movie that has provoked
controversy among horror fans for two reasons. One has to do with the
film's alleged relation to its source material, while the other concerns the
film's surprise twist ending (and reader beware, the twist is revealed
below).

On its release, *High Tension*, like many horror films, did not attract
much attention from mainstream critics. However, fans writing on the
internet detected resemblances between its plot – which involves a cat-
and-mouse contest between a serial killer and a resourceful heroine –
and the plot of the Dean Koontz novel *Intensity*. In both, the killer wipes
out the occupants of a house in which the heroine is staying as a guest,
in both she conceals herself in the killer's vehicle and in both there is a
scene of carnage at a service station ending with the heroine giving
chase in a stolen car. Whatever the merits of the case for Koontz, it has
to be acknowledged that there are important differences between the
two texts as well. While *Intensity* culminates in a classic showdown
between its heroine and the irredeemably evil villain, *High Tension*
follows an altogether more perverse trajectory by revealing that the killer
and the heroine are the same person, with the former a psychological
projection of the latter's murderousness. This is the twist that upset a
number of horror fans, one that spoiled the pleasure afforded by what
initially appeared to be a straightforward slasher in which Cécile de
France's close-cropped and androgynous heroine was the manly Final Girl
often featured in this kind of movie.

However, it is worth pointing out that this twist, far from being the
last-minute nonsensical imposition it is sometimes made out to be,
actually structures the film as a whole. The main narrative is very
explicitly set up as a flashback from the decidedly unreliable perspective

of the de France character, and the opening scene depicts her beginning to tell her story. Underlining her unreliability, the flashback itself commences with de France waking from a dream – which itself turns out to be taken from the climax of the film – in which she is being chased through a wood. When asked who is chasing her, she replies that she is chasing herself.

High Tension emerges from this as a kind of game, a knowledgeable appropriation of the American slasher format – the director Alexandre Aja has spoken in interviews of his love for American horror films – that at the same time playfully undermines slasher conventions. It is clearly not meant to be taken too seriously. The idea that the psychological double of the youthful de France is a fat, middle-aged man is particularly ludicrous, and while the lesbianism of her character – and the association of this with her violence – might well raise the hackles of a politically sensitive audience, one suspects that for the film-makers this too is just part of the game, a game that is by turns amusing, inventive and cheerfully irresponsible.

High Tension's slickness clearly appealed to Hollywood, and Alexandre Aja would go on (in 2006) to direct a successful remake of Wes Craven's 1977 horror classic, *The Hills Have Eyes*.   PH

Dir: Alexandre Aja; **Prod**: Alexandre Arcady, Andrei Boncea, Luc Besson (uncredited), Robert Benmussa; **Original Music**: François Eudes; **Wr**: Alexandre Aja, Gregory Levasseur; **Cinematography**: Maxime Alexandre; **Editing**: Baxter, Sophie Vermersch.

The Horrible Doctor Hichcock (*L'orribile segreto del Dottor Hichcock*, aka *Raptus*)
Italy, 1962 – 88 mins
Riccardo Freda

Am I the only one who first experienced Riccardo Freda's moody and
morose evocation of necrophilia, *The Horrible Dr Hichcock*, on late-night
television in the mid-1960s; surrendered to its insinuations of nasty
business in the laboratory and unnatural urges for dead flesh even as I
wondered just how such an obviously taboo-breaking narrative managed
to evade the censor's attention? What Hitchcock alluded to in *Vertigo*
(1958) or Edgar Ulmer inserted in the elaborate paraphernalia of *The
Black Cat* (1934), Freda brought out in the open: the spectacle of a man
intent on having sex with the dead. The fact that the plot itself often left
logic behind and replaced it with a vividly articulated atmosphere of
Gothic decay and social suffocation allowed the nightmarish material
temporarily to remain a matter of subtext. The director's visual acuity and
dedication to décor brought to mind the lavish wide-screen interiors of
Roger Corman's Poe adaptations, while the examination of lingering,
unappetising emotions alluded to Jack Clayton's rendering of Henry
James's *The Turn of the Screw* in *The Innocents* (1961).Yet something
more lurid was involved here, and wove a spell that these other films
barely seemed to touch upon.

   In London, 1885, Dr Bernard Hichcock (Robert Fleming) cements his
professional reputation with a superior anaesthetic, while at home he
engages in a disturbing amorous relationship with his wife, Margaretha
(Maria Teresa Vianello), which involves the use of his drug to render her
into a near-death state. Overwhelmed with intensity, Hichcock
accidentally overdoses his spouse, and is left alone with no outlet for his
affections. Twelve years pass, and he returns from the continent with a
new bride, Cynthia (Barbara Steele). She rapidly discovers that neither the
doctor nor his dour servant, Martha (Harriet White), wish her to become
settled in a new environment. Her nights become filled with

presentiments of some unseen presence, and the appearance of a skull under her pillow insinuates that a dire fate might await her. Her eventual discovery of her husband's compulsions brings her to breaking point.

As much as Freda enlivened the thematic repertoire of the European horror film, it was his deft visual design and elaboration of Steele's iconic status as a major actress in the genre that made *The Horrible Dr Hichcock* such a seminal film. Steele's wide, dark eyes could evoke anguish even when in repose. While Mario Bava inaugurated her career with the dual role as vampire and romantic lead in *The Mask of Satan* (1960), Freda here dwells upon the actress's status as victim, a role she took on again in their subsequent collaboration, *The Ghost* (1963). He smothered her in a wealth of Victorian bric-a-brac that made the art direction of the period's Hammer films seem almost anaemic by comparison, and let his camera record her dismay and emotional dissolution. Steele reports that Freda did little to direct her in either film, yet his masterful display of imperilled beauty sufficed to impart her haunting features upon the consciousnesses of enraptured moviegoers. Today, one yearns for a well-mastered DVD of the original European version of *The Horrible Dr Hichcock*, so that I, and others, need not depend upon our memories for the frisson that Freda let loose some forty years ago.   DS

Dir: Riccardo Freda; **Prod**: Ermanno Donati; **Original Music**: Roman Vlad; **Wr**: Ernesto Gastaldi; **Cinematography**: Raffaele Masciocchi; **Editing**: Ornella Micheli.

Hour of the Wolf (*Vargtimmen*)
Sweden, 1968 – 89 mins
Ingmar Bergman

Ingmar Bergman's one explicit horror film, *Hour of the Wolf*, centres on Johan (Max von Sydow), a famous painter who vacations on a remote island with his pregnant wife, Alma (Liv Ullman). The events are recounted as flashbacks, based on what the narrator has learned from Alma and from Johan's diary. Plagued by insomnia and agoraphobia, Johan fears the 'hour of the wolf', the hour before dawn, as he is persecuted by creatures he calls 'them', such as the 'Bird Man', an old woman whose face comes off with her hat, and a figure he labels 'ordinary', but is threatening all the same. Key characters from Johan's past also appear to torment him: a previous lover, Veronica Vogler (Ingrid Thulin), and a young boy. On the beach one day, Johan encounters a figure named Curator Heerbrand (Ulf Johansson) who enigmatically accuses the former of 'returning to the scene of the crime', which angers Johan. He finally meets Baron von Merkens (Erland Josephson), apparently the owner of the island, who admires Johan's paintings and claims to occupy a castle on the island. He issues a dinner invitation, which Johan is obliged to accept. At this castle of horrors Johan meets a Dracula figure, Archivist Lindhorst (Georg Rydeberg). Here, Johan confronts his past and also becomes a ritualistic victim (at least in his own mind) of the Archivist and the other dinner guests. From this experience Johan descends into madness and apparently also death – possibly by suicide.

The viewer is invited, at least initially, to be sympathetic towards Johan, and pity his tortured psychological states and fear of the dark, especially because his wife is an expectant mother. However, as the film progresses, and particularly at the climactic moment in the castle, Johan's past sins are re-enacted: his five-year illicit affair with Veronica (a married woman), and the apparent attempted molestation and murder of a young boy who had accompanied Johan on a fishing voyage. Johan is cast as a vampire who has cannibalised relationships for the sake of his

Haunted by the past and present: Max von Sydow in *Hour of the Wolf*

art; for this reason, apparently, he has been summoned to the castle to be held accountable – duped and ridiculed – by figures from his past. Still deeper in his past, though, is an account for Johan's disturbed personality, focusing on his traumatic childhood.

As a horror film with an emphasis on psychology, *Hour of the Wolf* can be seen as a more autobiographical version of Bergman's own, earlier *Through a Glass Darkly* (1961), which also contains a vampiric artist who keeps a diary, as well as the presence of a progressive madness, guilty secrets that haunt the characters, a setting on a remote

island and insects/supernatural predators. In part a Strindbergian
Kammerspiel, but also a work of confessional cinema, *Hour of the Wolf*'s
influence has been extensive and varied, clearly influencing films such as
Woody Allen's *Stardust Memories* (1980) and, in the horror genre,
pictures such as Oliver Stone's *Seizure* (1974) and David Cronenberg's
The Brood (1979).   RV and SV

Dir: Ingmar Bergman; **Prod**: Lars-Owe Carlberg; **Original Music**: Lars Johan Werle;
Wr: Ingmar Bergman; **Cinematography**: Sven Nykvist; **Editing**: Ulla Ryghe.

The House That Screamed (*La Residencia*)
Spain, 1969 – 104 mins
Narciso Ibáñez Serrador

Produced at the same time as Dario Argento's *The Bird with the Crystal Plumage* but a recipient of less acclaim, Narciso Ibáñez Serrador's Spanish horror film *The House That Screamed* shaped the horror genre by moving it away from the fantasy of ghosts, vampires and werewolves. While *The House That Screamed* doesn't belong to the burgeoning Italian *giallo* subgenre of the time, it helped to further establish a more realistic portrayal of horror that soon flourished in cinema worldwide.

Young Theresa (Cristina Galbo) finds herself enrolled in a girls' academy cloistered in a remote area of France. Immediately upon her arrival, two things are perfectly clear – headmistress Madame Fourneau (Lilli Palmer) regulates with strict authority, and Fourneau's student enforcer Irene (Mary Maude) is not afraid to impose these totalitarian ways. When Theresa proves too docile, she becomes the object of Irene's wrath. The one person Theresa does befriend is Fourneau's son Luis (John Moulder-Brown), a prying teenager kept away from the female population. But as Irene's intimidations intensify, Theresa decides to run away from the school, thus adding her name to a list of girls who have recently gone missing.

In terms of influence, the biggest model for *The House That Screamed* is obviously Alfred Hitchcock's *Psycho* (1960). Much like Norman Bates, young killer Luis is a product of an overprotective mother. However, Ibáñez Serrador ups the Oedipal factor by having Luis's mother witness her son's handiwork in the film's finale. The revelation that the son is killing to gain parts to create a woman in his mother's image is ample punishment and far more nihilistic than *Psycho*'s judicial conclusion. The director also provides a clever variation on Hitchcock's famous Janet Leigh elimination with the murder of Theresa twenty minutes before the film's end. The audience is then required to emotionally invest in Irene, a character previously vilified, as she begins to

unravel the mystery. Ibáñez Serrador actually performs this emotional
ploy a second time when Irene is killed and the heretofore villainous
Mme Fourneau becomes the final sympathetic character.

This is not to say that the picture lacks its own identity. Ibáñez
Serrador injects underlying themes of class status and conformity.
Theresa, the product of a broken family, is viciously mocked by Irene
when it is revealed that her mother works as a cabaret singer. Fourneau
represents the authoritarian leader who hands out the task of actual
abuse to others. Irene personifies the complicit follower as she enjoyably
metes out punishment to her classmates. Given the social and political
situation in Spain in the late 1960s (the country was still under Franco's
rule), it is not hard to imagine this being intentional. Regarding its own
legacy, *The House That Screamed* is one of the earliest examples of the
'child gone amuck' subgenre, showcased in films from *The Bad Seed*
(1956) to *Halloween* (1978). Ibáñez Serrador carried over his dismal
outlook on parent–child relations to his acclaimed *Who Can Kill a Child?*
(1976), where children as young as three become killers. This gloomy
strain is still seen in modern Spanish horror cinema, most notably in the
works of Jaume Balagueró.   ww

Dir: Narciso Ibáñez-Serrador; **Prod**: Arturo González, Jose M. Maldonado; **Original Music**:
Waldo de los Ríos; **Wr**: Narciso Ibáñez-Serrador, Juan Tébar; **Cinematography**: Manuel
Berenguer, Godofredo Pacheco (uncredited); **Editing** Mercedes Alonso, Reginald Mills.

House with the Laughing Windows (La casa dalle finestre che ridono)
Italy, 1976 – 110 mins
Pupi Avati

While Italian genre cinema often made use of trends and subgenres, *House with the Laughing Windows* does not clearly belong to any of these in particular, although it has sometimes been classified as a *giallo*. The film begins when the authorities of a small village commission an art expert, Stefano (Lino Capolicchio), to restore a fresco by a dead local painter named Buono Legnani (Tonino Corazzari). As his obsession for the painting that depicts the martyrdom of Saint Sebastian slowly grows, Stefano begins to understand how the mad artist managed to achieve such a vivid masterpiece and unwillingly puts his life and others' in jeopardy.

Shot in northern Italy, Pupi Avati's film makes great use of peaceful, sunny exterior locations that strongly contrast with dark and claustrophobic interiors more in the Gothic tradition. The village in which the action is set appears to be in a state of physical and moral decay, to the point where its inhabitants seem to deliberately cover up crimes in order to profit from the painter's celebrity – as Stefano will unfortunately discover in the end. An echo of the town's morbidity can be found in Legnani, who remains known as the Painter of Agony because he liked to portray dying people in order to try and capture the essence of death at work. However, as he wasn't content with what nature had to offer him, various 'models' were tortured and murdered – all in the name of art. This voyeuristic/artistic motif constitutes a kind of follow-up to Michael Powell's *Peeping Tom* (1960), and Avati would again tackle this subject matter and take it even further in *Zeder* (1983), where a movie camera is put inside a coffin as part of a weird scientific experiment.

Based on a script originally called *Blood Relations* and written by the director alone, *House with the Laughing Windows* brings to the fore a monstrous family since it was Legnani's two sisters, who, it turns out, actually committed the murders. Through their compulsive behaviour, and thanks to the use of a tape recorder that is put next to his burnt corpse and lets us hear his disturbingly ecstatic comments, the painter becomes a kind of living dead and continues to kill even after his death – something that a recurring image of the film (two shots of a mysterious and menacing hand) also hints at. But monstrosity is present as well through variations on the theme of androgyny, either from an auditory (the anonymous phone calls received by Stefano) or visual (the self-portrait of Legnani with a female body) source. The real identity of the priest whose church displays the painting combines both and thus enables Avati to take a poke at the clergy. This attack, like the setting of the film in Emilia-Romagna and the film's overall approach to the horror genre – a well-developed sense of atmosphere with a few very disturbing images – traces back to the director's own childhood, and contributes to *House with the Laughing Windows* particularly engrossing flavour.   FL

Dir: Pupi Avati; **Prod**: Antonio Avati, Gianni Minervini; **Original Music**: Amedeo Tommasi; **Wr**: Antonio Avati, Pupi Avati, Gianni Cavina, Maurizio Costanzo; **Cinematography**: Pasquale Rachini; **Editing**: Pasquale Rachini.

Hunchback of the Morgue (*El jorobado de la morgue*)
Spain, 1973 – 91 mins
Javier Aguirre

Made in 1972, when Paul Naschy's (aka Jacinto Molina) output was at its
most frenzied (he starred in eight films, scripting seven), *Hunchback of
the Morgue* channels the traditional hunchback story into a subtle
political commentary and provides an overt display of the crueller aspects
of Spanish horror, while adhering to actor/screenwriter Naschy's own
brand of Romantic-Gothic enchantments and his adoration of classic
monsters.

The Spanish horror film during the 1970s had a tendency to be
colder and more grim than its stylised '*la dolce vita*' counterpart in Italy.
The creators of Spanish horror had emerged from the country's bleak
landscape and childhood memories of a civil war, or else their parents'
reminiscences, in which atrocities by both sides had seared ugly images
into the national consciousness, hardening body and spirit alike. Attuned
to man's cruelties and the meaninglessness and disposability of life, these
film-makers vented their concerns and nightmares in what were
considered at the time simple exploitation programmers.

Hunchback's brutality and sickly baroque atmosphere stands out all
the more when juxtaposed with Naschy's sweet Romanticism, his
hunchback's adoration of the sympathetic female – a throwback to
Victor Hugo's seminal hunchback story, *Notre-Dame de Paris*. Yet a
hardened Spanish influence is clear; whereas Hugo placed his Quasimodo
in the breathtakingly beautiful, albeit mysterious, Notre Dame cathedral,
Naschy places his hunchback, Gotho, in a morgue and later in a
subterranean hell of vermin, body parts, screaming victims and a
primordial man-eating monster.

Budgetary restrictions limited the use of special effects or constructed
sets, mandating scenes of wincing realism. Madrid's morgue permitted
the use of a corpse for a head-severing scene, and though Naschy, as

Gotho, was unable to proceed after the initial cut, the scene still evokes queasiness and disgust. Real rats and the absolute stillness of actress Maria Elena Arpon were necessitated in another scene, in which Gotho has to chase away the rats nibbling and nestling on his love's dead body. Several of these rats were burned alive on screen, their panicked screeching echoing into legend among Euro-cult film aficionados.

Hunchback's political message made the film even more daring. Producer Manuel Leguineche, a noted journalist, and director Javier Aguirre, an experimental film-maker and film theorist, invested their own anti-Franquista commentary into the picture. They chanced a line that exposed the film's politics: 'You see, Gotho,' Dr Orla (Alberto Dalbés), the mad scientist, carefully says to Gotho, who has become a duped servant, 'how the most insignificant person can be of use to science and to humanity. All you have to do is let yourself be led by a real leader.' The censors were caught unawares and left the line alone.

Blatant political provocations were unheard of in Spanish cinema during General Franco's dictatorial rule. Many Spanish horror films, including this one, even had to change their fictional locales, usually to Portugal, France or Germany, so as not to tamper with the conceit that in Spain no monsters or evil could exist. But the film's evolving grotesquery and perversity, issuing as it did from the pit of Spain's monarchist and Inquisitorial past (literally so: the underground cellars that substituted for Dr Orla's lab of monstrosity and pain had once been used for Inquisitorial tortures), could not help but subliminally comment on the faith and tradition – and the iron-handed political stability – propping up contemporary Spanish society.

For his soulful performance as Gotho, Naschy won the Georges Méliès Award for best actor at the Second International Festival of Fantastic Cinema in Paris in 1973, advancing the cause of the Spanish *fantastique* in world cinema and further securing his position as Spain's premier horror man.   ML

Dir: Javier Aguirre; **Original Music**: Carmelo A. Bernaola; **Wr**: Javier Aguirre, Alberto S. Insúa, Jacinto Molina; **Cinematography**: Raúl Pérez Cubero; **Editing**: Raúl Pérez Cubero.

I Vampiri (aka *The Vampires*)
Italy, 1957 – 81 mins
Riccardo Freda, Mario Bava [uncredited]

Director Riccardo Freda made the leap from historical epics and peplums to Gothic horror with *I Vampiri*. Although the film was not a success at the box office, it predates the first wave of European horror – *The Curse of Frankenstein* (1957), *Horror of Dracula* (1958), *Eyes Without a Face* (France, 1960) – and rightly stakes its claim as the first post-World War II European horror film (and the first of the Italian sound era). *I Vampiri* is a modern reworking of the Countess Bathory tale, with the circa 100-year-old Duchess Margherita Du Grand (Gianna Maria Canale) kept young by Dr Julien Du Grand's (Antoine Balpêtré) experiments in cell reanimation and blood transfusions taken from young female victims. Du Grand procures the victims by blackmailing drug addict Joseph Seignoret (Paul Müller) into kidnapping women in exchange for a fix. A series of clues

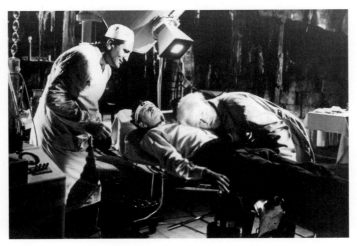

The doctor is in, unfortunately for the patient: Riccardo Freda's *I Vampiri*

lead reporter Pierre (Dario Michaëlis) and Inspector Chantal (Carlo D'Angelo) to the Du Grand castle, where they discover the dual identity of the Duchess (the young Giselle/the old Margherita) and bring an end to the serial murders.

It is a well-known fact that Mario Bava, the film's cinematographer, filled in for Freda on the last two days and had considerable input in reworking the script to complete the movie during the intense twelve-day shooting schedule. More importantly, *I Vampiri* establishes the strong visual style which would characterise the later Freda and Bava films, and would also mark an important aesthetic quality of European horror in general. This visual style includes a concentration on the 'plastics' of the image (pictorial beauty, a sculptural quality in the lighting and an architectural treatment of space through depth of field), the long take, sweeping tracking shots and assertive camera movements (camera shots that move independently of character or object movement).

A third important aspect of the picture is the way it transposes the accoutrements of the Gothic world (castles, labyrinthine structures, secret passageways, the theme of the double) into the modern world (contemporary Paris, the media, police investigation, medical science). Related to this, *I Vampiri* represents the inauguration of the 'medical horror' film, where a scientist/doctor sacrifices numerous young women in order to keep a loved one (usually a daughter or wife) eternally young and beautiful. The 'medical horror' film would become a mainstay of international horror, with such examples as: *Eyes Without a Face*, *Mill of the Stone Women* (1960), *The Awful Dr Orloff* (1962), *Atom Age Vampire* (1960), *The Horrible Dr Hichcock* (1962) and *Faceless* (1988).

Still another point of historical importance is the relationship of *I Vampiri* to the zombie movie. The character of Seignoret, who is killed by one of the doctor's assistants, is later brought back to life through Du Grand's experiments. Although a distant cry from his later flesh-eating and blood-drinking brethren, Seignoret represents Italian cinema's first 'zombie'.

As the above examples attest, *I Vampiri* is brimming with visual and conceptual ideas, many of which would shape the future of the European horror film. DT

Dir: Riccardo Freda, Mario Bava [uncredited, completed film]; **Prod**: Luigi Carpentieri, Ermanno Donati, Piero Donati; **Original Music**: Franco Mannino, Roman Vlad; **Wr**: Riccardo Freda, Piero Regnoli, J. V. Rhemo; **Cinematography**: Mario Bava; **Editing**: Roberto Cinquini.

In a Glass Cage (*Tras el cristal*)
Spain, 1986 – 112 mins
Agustí Villaronga

The first major production by Spanish writer–director Agustí Villaronga, *In a Glass Cage* explores the dialectic relationship between executioner and victim in an ambivalent tale of lust, death and transcendence. As in his later mystical thrillers *Moon Child* (1989) and *99.9* (1998), the film evokes a realm beyond social contracts and moral duties. It is inspired by Georges Bataille's account of the historical child murderer Gilles de Rais, along with the writings of the Marquis de Sade, blended with a totalitarian vision that links the film to Pier Paolo Pasolini's Fascism parable, *Salo, or The 120 Days of Sodom* (1975).

During World War II, Klaus (Günter Meisner) was a Nazi doctor who conducted fatal experiments on young boys. After the war he escapes to Spain, where he continues to perpetrate sex crimes against children until finally deciding to commit suicide by jumping off an old building, the scene of his latest offence. But his suicide attempt fails and he awakens in an iron lung in the home of his resentful wife Griselda (Marisa Paredes) and their daughter Rena (Gisèle Echevarría). One day, an adolescent boy named Angelo (David Sust) – 'Angel' in English – enters this strange family triangle and offers his services as a nurse. Although Griselda is offended, Klaus decides to give Angelo the desired post. A bizarre relationship unfolds between the two males, especially when Angelo informs Klaus that he has read his diaries and has been after him for a long time. But rather than slay the disabled murderer, Angelo starts to take after his patient and sacrifices boys to the old man. When Griselda becomes aware of these incidents, Angelo kills her. He begins transforming the house into a totalitarian microcosm, with walls of barbed wire. As a final destructive act, Angelo kills Klaus by forcing oral sex on him, letting him die outside the iron lung. In the end, Angelo himself lies in the medical machine (the 'glass cage' of the title) with young Rena as his nurse.

Villaronga is today known as an art-house director of stylistically similar dramas like *The Sea* (2002), another tale of violence, guilt and homosexual desire. Nearly all his films have connections with the horror and thriller genres, however, especially the Italian *giallo*, primarily in their use of artificial light, primary colours, minimal electronic scores and the open display of sexualised violence.

In a Glass Cage is particularly reminiscent of Stephen King's 1981 short story 'Apt Pupil', adapted for the screen by Bryan Singer in 1998. The horror arises through a mixture of texts concerning true wartime atrocities and staged acts of murder, culminating in the weird atmosphere of a blue-lit limbo. The film works like a nightmare, framed by the image of a snowglobe with a glockenspiel theme played throughout; this is visually restaged in the final scene where Angelo and Rena seem lost in a hermetic netherworld of death and desire. Thus, although Villaronga's films show a strong sense of style and aesthetics, it is no surprise that they are still widely considered 'underground' due to their extreme *vision du monde*.   MS

Dir: Agustí Villaronga; **Prod**: Teresa Enrich; **Original Music**: Javier Navarrete; **Wr**: Agustí Villaronga; **Cinematography**: Jaime Peracaula.

Inferno
Italy, 1980 – 107 mins
Dario Argento

Imagine combining *Psycho* (1960), *The Wizard of Oz* (1939) and Dante
Alighieri's early fourteenth-century poem, 'Inferno', which features a
descent into Hell. To this heady mix, add characters whose appearances
are so one-dimensionally strange and alienating they seem to have
stepped off a Brechtian stage. Include the almost-comic figure of Death
from an amateur stage production or a medieval morality play – and
don't forget evil and the supernatural. Set this hybrid construction to
selections from Verdi's 1842 opera *Nabucco* and discordant music from
Keith Emerson of Emerson, Lake and Palmer; illuminate the highly
stylised sets in surreal blues and reds, and have the characters speak
cryptically. The result is the profoundly haunting and disturbing dream-
logic of Dario Argento's *Inferno*, a film which appears to be self-
consciously masquerading as a *giallo*-style, Gothic opera – albeit
without singers. While *Inferno* has often been criticised for terrible
acting, dialogue and an incoherent plot, this compelling film – which
Argento calls his 'purest and most sincere' – seems less concerned with
traditional narrative trajectories than it does with the *art* of horror film-
making.

As the second instalment of a proposed trilogy featuring the 'Three
Mothers' – evil women who are also sisters intent on bringing death and
destruction into the world – *Inferno* follows Argento's *Suspiria* (1977).
Both films feature Mater Suspiriorum, the Mother of Sighs; Mater
Lacrimarum, the Mother of Tears; and Mater Tenebrarum, the Mother
of Darkness. The Mother of Sighs occupies a house in Freiburg, Germany
(which was destroyed in *Suspiria*); the house of Mater Lacrimarum is in
Rome; while Mater Tenebrarum, 'the youngest and cruellest', occupies
a house in New York. All of these houses were built for the 'mothers'
by the architect and alchemist E. Varelli, whose book, *The Three
Mothers*, ends up in the hands of Rose Elliot (Irene Miracle), a poet living

in New York who becomes obsessed with the suspicion that her apartment building is the dwelling place of some mysterious supernatural force.

Argento's colour schemes and imagery are bizarre. In *Inferno*, colour – morphing blues and red – is a language. Objects are surreal. A pipe without any ostensible purpose hangs suspended from the ceiling while a long, red wire protrudes from one end. Other pipes rise from floor to ceiling juxtaposed with Doric-style columns which, placed haphazardly, give the impression that one is backstage in an abandoned theatre. The camera follows a stream of water as it flows in a red and blue rivulet from a broken drainage pipe into a hole in the concrete floor of the cellar, which turns out to be the ceiling of a flooded room. When her keys fall into the hole, Rose casually removes her shoes, climbs into the overly blue water and swims in search of them. In one of the film's eeriest scenes, Rose swims languidly underwater in what we dimly perceive in the gloom is a flooded ballroom in which a poster bearing the name and image of 'Mater Tenebrarum' still hangs.

Some critics have found fault with Inferno at this point, claiming that

> it begins to fall apart, becoming less coherent with each turn in the flimsy plot. Its artful set-pieces and dreamlike mood and images come to naught without a solid structure in which to frame them. Characters say and do stupid things.[11]

It could be said, however, that 'the dreamlike mood and images' actually serve to enhance Argento's attempts at meditating on the conventions of horror cinema. As Maitland McDonagh asserts, the

> complex internal logic [of Argento's films] is connotative rather than denotative, metaphoric rather than metonymic . . .; images proceed from one to another not in the service of advancement of linear narrative, but by way of poetic connections, a kind of alchemical reasoning.[12]

Argento's reflections on horror conventions arguably rely on a series of 'correspondences' which 'move by a relation of counterparts and doubles, and [are] subject to dangerous distortions and interferences'.[13] Rather than being incoherent, therefore, *Inferno* demonstrates Argento's affinity for analogies and parallelisms by way of 'poetic connections' that give rise to the film's dream-logic.   JC

Dir: Dario Argento; **Prod**: Claudio Argento, Salvatore Argento, William Garroni; **Original Music**: Keith Emerson; **Wr**: Dario Argento, Daria Nicolodi (uncredited), Thomas De Quincey (novel 'Suspiria de Profundis', uncredited); **Cinematography**: Romano Albani; **Editing**: Romano Albani.

Kill, Baby . . . Kill! (aka *Operazione paura* [*Operation Fear*], aka *Don't Walk in the Park*, aka *Curse of the Dead*)
Italy, 1966 – 85 mins
Mario Bava

Made on a shoestring budget and released under the slightly less inept title *Operation Fear* in its native country – where its premiere was greeted with a standing ovation from none other than Luchino Visconti – this atmospheric chiller is arguably Mario Bava's crowning achievement in the vein of supernatural Gothic horror. While *Black Sunday* (1960) may be viewed as the last horror classic shot in black-and-white, *Kill, Baby . . . Kill!* provides a distillation of the fantastic in its purest form and in vibrant colour schemes, downplaying the display of gore and libido in favour of the mechanics of dread and oppression.

Trust no one: Mario Bava's *Kill, Baby ... Kill!*

Dr Paul Eswai (Giacomo Rossi-Stuart), a young coroner, comes to a remote mountain village overcome with fear and superstition, to perform an autopsy on a young maid who leapt to her death from the top of a tower. A silver coin embedded in the victim's heart is but the first of a long string of ancestral customs and shameful secrets which revolve around the figure of a blonde-haired little girl (actually played by a boy, which subliminally enhances the eeriness of the ghost-child's demeanour) clad in virginal white. Some two decades earlier she was trampled to death during a drunken festival, and her spectral apparition is now enough to compel guilt-ridden townsfolk to suicide. It soon transpires that her mother, the reclusive Baroness Graps (Giana Vivaldi), has been using her abilities as a medium to conjure up the vengeful spirit of Melissa (Valeria Valeri) while surrounding herself with howling ghostly presences she is unable to fully control. It will take the protagonist's dogged investigative efforts and a final showdown between the Baroness and the local sorceress to break the chain of bloodshed.

As usual with Bava, a hackneyed plot, stilted acting and subpar dialogue are all brilliantly transcended here by the sheer artistry of iconic sequences whose pictorial perfection and oneiric aura are simply indelible: the various visual synecdoches of Melissa (her ball bouncing down a hallway, her hand and/or face suddenly appearing behind a window, her swing); Dr Eswai chasing a fleeing figure through a succession of identical rooms, only to be confronted with his own mirror image; the vertigo-inducing shot of a spiral staircase; Melissa's sister's 'psychedelic' nightmare. So much so, in fact, that they will be rearticulated by other famous directors: the innocent-looking demon-child using the head of a decapitated actor as a replacement ball in Fellini's contribution to the 1967 horror anthology *Spirits of the Dead* ('Toby Dammit'), or the Devil in the deceptive guise of an angelic-looking girl in Martin Scorsese's *The Last Temptation of Christ* (1988); a man chasing his double through a time warp in the finale of David Lynch's *Twin Peaks* (1990–1).

Bava himself quotes liberally from his favourite masters, both literary (Poe and Mérimée, in particular) and filmic (for example, Murnau and

Dreyer, for the arrival of the protagonist in a carriage driven by a frightened coachman, as pallbearers are silhouetted against the horizon). But the miraculous alchemy of the film lies in the transfiguration of conventional Gothic paraphernalia (fog-shrouded labyrinthine streets; a haunted villa; cobwebbed hidden passageways; portraits; a family curse; the doppelgänger; science vs witchcraft) into Bava's own idiosyncrasies and haunting motifs (images as powerful simulacra; the return of the repressed; dislocation of the space–time continuum; non-Euclidian logic; hallucinatory confusion of illusion and reality).   PM

Dir: Mario Bava; **Prod**: Luciano Catenacci, Nando Pisani; **Original Music**: Carlo Rustichelli; **Wr**: Mario Bava, Romano Migliorini, Roberto Natale; **Cinematography**: Antonio Rinaldi, Mario Bava (uncredited); **Editing**: Romana Fortini.

The Kingdom (*Riget*)
Denmark/France/Germany/Sweden, 1994 – 279 mins
Morten Arnfred, Lars von Trier

Released as both a five-hour film at the 1994 Venice International Film
Festival and as a four-episode mini-series on Danish television, Lars von
Trier's *The Kingdom* soon found an enthusiastic international audience.
Its overwhelming critical and commercial success all but guaranteed a
second season, which aired in 1997, and provided the foundation for a
less-than-spectacular US adaptation helmed by bestselling horror writer
Stephen King (2004).

Set in Copenhagen's Rigshospital (or, 'The Hospital of the Danish
Kingdom'), a large, modern medical facility specialising in teaching and
steeped in urban legend, *The Kingdom* borrows heavily from two key
sources. The first of these is a French television programme, *Belphégor*
(1965), directed by Claude Barmas. Featuring eerie sequences in a
subterranean labyrinth hidden beneath the Louvre's Department of
Egyptology, *Belphégor*'s influence on *The Kingdom* is palpable, especially
in those sequences where von Trier capitalises upon Rigshospital's dimly
lit tunnels and elevator shafts to accent the ghost story at the mini-series'
core. Haunted by the restless spirit of a young girl who was murdered by
one of the hospital's doctors in 1919, Rigshospital becomes a site of
supernatural occurrences, psychic phenomena and unnerving – if not
always coherent – relationships between patients and staff.

Perhaps the most profound influence upon *The Kingdom*, however,
is David Lynch's *Twin Peaks*. Like Lynch's groundbreaking TV series,
The Kingdom features a plethora of grotesque characters, overlapping
storylines, darkly humorous sequences and tantalising narratological
diversions designed not so much to provide exposition as to sustain the
series' surreal, almost other-worldly tone. Over the course of *The
Kingdom*'s multiple storylines, drugs (mainly cocaine) routinely disappear
from the hospital's dispensary; nefarious hospital administrators form a
shadowy, enigmatic cult; the kitchen staff, composed of men and

women with Down's syndrome, articulate vital, almost preternatural insights; and mendacious characters regularly confound audience attempts at structuring meaning through an understanding of motive or action.

The Kingdom was largely financed by the Danish Broadcasting Company, and like 1988's Medea (based on an un-filmed screenplay by Carl Theodor Dreyer), von Trier's previous foray into television, it is a daring and technically ambitious work. Inspired by the hand-held, cinéma vérité aesthetic that invests Barry Levinson's US television series, Homicide: Life on the Street (1993–9), with an unsettling immediacy, von Trier's creative direction and Eric Kress's frenetic cinematography heighten The Kingdom's uncanny tone, as well as the audience's unease. Shooting primarily with available light and experimenting with radical jump-cuts during the editing process, von Trier purposefully disrupts conventional spectatorial pleasures. Violating conventional allocations of filmic space through the use of double exposures and a ferocious disregard for the 180-degree rule that dominated cinematic grammar for much of the medium's first century, von Trier's film-making style in The Kingdom would prove a valuable testing ground for cinematographic strategies further advanced in subsequent, similarly acclaimed works like Breaking the Waves (1996), Dancer in the Dark (2000), Dogville (2002) and Manderlay (2004). The primarily hand-held camerawork and reliance upon natural lighting that lends The Kingdom its disorienting perspective seems ideal for a ghost story set in an institution mired in sickness, rumour and myth. Likewise, von Trier's stylistic devices anticipate the Dogme 95 movement's famous 'Vow of Chastity', especially those prohibitions intended to eradicate static photography, overly fluid tracking shots and the manipulation of the filmed image through the use of special lighting, gels and filters.

This is not to suggest that such technological distortions do not occur in The Kingdom; Henrik Harpelund's skills as a Steadicam operator greatly enhance several crucial sequences, and the depiction of the ghost's spectral form inevitably necessitates the artful manipulation of the filmed image. That said, *The Kingdom* reveals Lars von Trier as one of the most original directors in contemporary European cinema, and should he ever deem that a third return to Rigshospital is in order, he will have little difficulty convincing audiences to place themselves under his care.   JMCR

Dir: Morten Arnfred, Lars von Trier; **Prod**: Sven Abrahamsen, Philippe Bober, Peter Aalbæk Jensen, Ole Reim, Ib Tardini; **Original Music**: Joachim Holbek; **Wr**: Tómas Gislason, Lars von Trier, Niels Vørsel; **Cinematography**: Eric Kress; **Editing**: Molly Marlene Stensgård, Jacob Thuesen.

Laurin
West Germany/Hungary, 1989 – 84 mins
Robert Sigl

Robert Sigl's *Laurin* tells the story of a little girl, Laurin (Dóra Szinetár), who lives in a small town in an unspecified European village around the turn of the century. Staying with her grandmother after her mother's tragic death, she becomes the centre of a plot that involves the disappearance of two little boys. The schoolmaster, a retired officer, is revealed as the killer, but dies himself as he attempts to murder Laurin.

If this plot synopsis amounts to little more than a rough sketch, it is for good reason. Like many first films, *Laurin* is somewhat ragged around the edges, falling short of its creator's ambitions. Shooting on a shoestring budget on location in Hungary, Sigl had to work with a cast (some of them amateurs) and crew able to communicate neither in German nor in English. Because of these challenges, the film is, by Sigl's own admission, flawed – there are occasional continuity problems, the plot is riddled with inconsistencies and coincidences, and some of the dialogue is painfully stilted, both in the English and the German dubbed version.

And yet, *Laurin* is an oddly compelling piece of auteurist film-making since Sigl is not really interested in the mechanics of realist storytelling. Instead, *Laurin* delves with great seriousness into a Freudian psychosexual landscape of childhood trauma, from which its child protagonist eventually emerges, despite her young age, with a sense of mature sexuality. Scenes of sexual voyeurism abound; Freudian primal scenes repeat themselves, linking disparate characters and points in time. Sigl conjures up a universe of fetishised objects – a music box, a pair of spectacles, a black kite, a spyglass, the nail on which the murderer is finally to impale himself – from which the events seem to emerge with an uncanny life of their own.

With its period setting and its dream logic, the film is an experiment in Gothic horror. Most of the key scenes do indeed take place during 'a dark and stormy night' at cemeteries and in underground caverns. Ominous portents are everywhere; dreams and nightmares are often prophetic. Despite the claptrap of the Gothic, however, *Laurin* succeeds as much as some of its more obvious cinematic predecessors: Carl Theodor Dreyer's *Vampyr* (1932), F. W. Murnau's *Nosferatu* (1922), Neil Jordan's *The Company of Wolves* (1984) or Werner Herzog's early films. Unapologetic about his film's stylised artificiality, Sigl himself cites literary works from German Romanticism, like E. T. A. Hoffman's or Theodor Storm's stories, as sources of inspiration. The Grimms' fairytales also come to mind, especially in a scene in which the little girl, wearing a red coat, encounters a mysterious black dog who appears at crucial moments in the story.

Though Sigl has kept a number of projects related to the fantastic or the horror genre under development, he has, since *Laurin*, gone on to work mostly in television (two slasher films he made for German TV have gone straight to video in the US: *School's Out* [1999] and *Dead Island: School's Out 2* [2001]). Given Sigl's unique vision in his debut film, horror fans should pay attention whenever he gets another chance to make a feature. SH

Dir: Robert Sigl; **Prod**: Andreas Bareiß, György Onódi, Róbert Prokopp, Bernhard Stampfer; **Original Music**: Hans Jansen, Jacques Zwart; **Wr**: Ádám Rozgonyi, Robert Sigl; **Cinematography**: Nyika Jancsó; **Editing**: Teri Losonci.

Let Sleeping Corpses Lie (Non si deve profanare il sonno dei morti, aka The Living Dead at Manchester Morgue)
Spain/Italy, 1974 – 93 mins
Jorge Grau

As antiques dealer George (Ray Lovelock) heads out of London for the weekend, he leaves a city in an active state of decay. From the very opening frames of Jorge Grau's 1974 shocker, modern society is on the edge of collapse. This is a world so depraved that a woman can strip nude and run through traffic without meriting even a batted eye from the jaded commuters. When the zombie apocalypse comes the following afternoon, we cannot help but see the walking dead not as the cause of civilisation's collapse, but as one of its many symptoms.

In the wake of George Romero's bold reinvention of the genre in 1968, zombie movies became a popular genre for European horror makers. Too popular, perhaps, because while movies about undead corpses eating human flesh were a dime a dozen, good ones were much scarcer. *Let Sleeping Corpses Lie* was not a commercial hit on its original run, but has lingered in the imaginations of fans for decades hence. Along with those elements obviously copied from *Night of the Living Dead* (and, for that matter, *Dirty Harry* [1971]), Grau infuses his film with carefully established atmosphere and suspense. Where most Eurozombie outings jump right into post-apocalyptic survival plots, Grau holds off on the central menace until the movie is more than half over. Of course, the audience knows what's coming, between familiarity with the genre and the title itself. Nevertheless, Grau confidently defers the big zombie reveal until late – and when it comes, it's a doozy. The gore effects, largely attributed to Gianetto de Rossi, stunned theatregoers and appalled censors.

To maintain suspense while waiting for the sleeping corpses to stop lying, Grau and screenwriters Sandro Continenza and Marcello Coscia toss Lovelock's character in with a young lady (Christine Galbo) on her way to an unhappy family reunion. They accidentally become prime suspects in a grisly murder, investigated by a hard-boiled cop played by Arthur Kennedy. He finds it much easier to believe these rebellious youngsters, with their unkempt hair, are Satanist mass killers than, say, that the dead have come back to life. The dramatic tension leading up to – and continuing during – the zombie plague is all about the era's culture clashes. Lovelock not only looks a bit like a hippy, he shares their anti-establishment views on the evils of scientific progress. Once he starts to realise that an experimental pest-control procedure may be at fault for the resurrection of the dead, he loses himself in angrily denouncing the machine instead of, you know, turning the thing off. Meanwhile, the authorities can offer no protection from the zombies because they are too preoccupied with their own prejudices against the younger generation.

One could easily substitute discussion of Vietnam protesters and Agent Orange and maintain the basic plot dynamics; odd, since this isn't an American film at all. The cast features an Italian, a Spaniard and a Massachusetts boy playing the Englishman, with bits of the actual UK countryside joining Italian and Spanish sound stages as the supposedly British locales. The director is Spanish, the production was co-financed by Spaniards and Italians and was greeted with hostility by the authorities (censors, reviewers) of every European country. The culture clashes now seem dated, the once gut-wrenching effects tame, but the overall dramatic punch has not dimmed in power one jot.   DK

Dir: Jorge Grau; **Prod**: Edmondo Amati, Manuel Pérez; **Original Music**: Giuliano Sorgini; **Wr**: Juan Cobos, Sandro Continenza, Marcello Coscia, Miguel Rubio; **Cinematography**: Francisco Sempere; **Editing**: Domingo García, Vincenzo Tomassi.

The Lift (*De Lift*, aka *Goin' Up*)
Netherlands, 1983 – 99 mins
Dick Maas

A country as neat and tidy as the Netherlands, and a society as open as the Dutch, does not seem to have the culture of fear that is the ideal breeding ground for horror narratives. There are no serial killers, no vast woods or high fortresses and no monsters to speak of. So it comes as hardly a surprise that until a few years ago there was no *polder horror* film culture.

Dick Maas's *The Lift* was the first Dutch film to fill that gap. The film tells the straightforward story of a lift gone bonkers, and the efforts of one man – technician Felix Adelaar (Huub Stapel) – and a female journalist (Willeke Van Ammelrooy) to both stop the device in its

Death by elevator in Dick Maas's *The Lift*

murderous antics and unravel the covert experiments of the manufacturing company: Rising Sun Electronics. Although critics reacted with vitriol and denounced it, *The Lift* became a huge box-office success and was one of the first Dutch films ever to do well internationally. A jury presided over by John Carpenter awarded it first prize at the Avoriaz genre festival.

It is not difficult to see Carpenter's influence on *The Lift*. It shares with *The Thing* (1982) and *Assault on Precinct 13* (1976) an emphasis on one claustrophobic location, and it has the focus on an object of heavy-duty technology in common with *Christine* (1983) – an added problem is that this particular object (a big box in a dark shaft, going up and down) is practically impossible to capture on camera. *The Lift* ingeniously uses back lighting to create an atmosphere of danger. Like many of Carpenter's movies, *The Lift* relies on dry wit as a relief from tension; one can only zoom in on opening and closing doors so often. It also has a protagonist who is both naively bewildered by what happens and obsessed with conquering the obstacle put in front of him (why doesn't he just take the stairs?). It is to Stapel's credit that he manages to make the most of this ambiguity simply through looking alternately determined or overwhelmed, like a combination of Kurt Russell and James Woods. It also helps him overcome some seriously crippled dialogue (most hilariously: 'Shall I get some green soap?'). Next to Stapel, Van Ammelrooy's role is reduced to that of nosy sidekick but her appeal to audiences at the time as one of the sexiest Dutch actresses should not be overlooked.

Thematically, *The Lift* shares the implicit concerns of much modern horror that technology harbours evil, and that its manipulation by nebulous corporations and corrupt authorities is detrimental to the physical well-being of humans. Maas doesn't really make much of this premise, but its presence nevertheless gives the film some depth. Interestingly enough, this is a concern also at the heart of the work of compatriot Paul Verhoeven, with whom Maas shared both box-office success and local critical hostility. The unease of Dutch film culture with genre cinema eventually drove Verhoeven to Hollywood. Maas never really made that move, although he did find himself directing a US remake of *The Lift*, entitled *Down* (aka *The Shaft*, 2001), featuring Naomi Watts.

Since *The Lift*, Dutch horror has included the complex *The Vanishing* (George Sluizer, 1988), the outrageous *Intensive Care* (Dorna Van Rouveroy, 1991) and the unpretentious *Wednesday* (Jean-Paul Arends and Bob Embregts, 2005). Next to that there are numerous *Nether-horror* shorts. It is still a long way from a horror tradition comparable to other European countries such as Italy, Spain or France, but for a tolerant nation that, until the early twenty-first-century assassinations of politician Pim Fortuyn and film-maker Theo Van Gogh, prided itself on its ability to resolve any conflict peacefully, it is nevertheless fascinating to see an increase in films in which the means of conflict resolution involve the violent use of hooks, wires and guillotine-sharp lifts.   EM

Dir: Dick Maas; **Prod**: Matthijs van Heijningen; **Original Music**: Dick Maas; **Wr**: Dick Maas; **Cinematography**: Marc Felperlaan; **Editing**: Hans van Dongen.

Lips of Blood (*Lèvres de sang*)
France, 1975 – 90 mins
Jean Rollin

The films of Jean Rollin have always tended to sacrifice a coherent narrative in favour of a surrealist style, filled with images that reflect the film-maker's childhood influences and artistic affinities; *Lips of Blood* is in many ways the epitome of all these concerns. It is certainly Rollin's most romantic film.

The story follows a young man named Frederic (Jean-Loup Philippe) who is still very much attached to his mother and has yet to sever that umbilical cord. When he sees the photo of a castle at a party, Frederick has a flashback: a touching childhood encounter with a young woman at that very castle. This sparks an obsession to find her. But those who can help him with his quest are determined to stop him. Foremost is his mother, who had entombed the woman – a vampire – for eternity in the castle, determined to save future victims. Frederic's quest unleashes a bevy of semi-nude vampire beauties who resume their murderous ways, but also help rejoin the separated lovers. In the end, Frederic makes the ultimate sacrifice by joining the ranks of the undead so that he may spend eternity with his true love.

The problem most have with appreciating *Lips of Blood* is that it's a horror film without scares, an erotic film without sex and a showcase of scenes more concerned with satisfying the film-maker's personal obsessions than the audience. Despite its low-budget production values, clumsy acting and slow pacing, however, it is still a film deserving of affection for it represents the triumph of a film-maker realising his most personal artistic ambitions.

Lips of Blood was produced by Jean-Marie Ghanassia, a young man with a small budget who had admired Rollin's previous efforts and gave him complete creative control. Rollin embraced this opportunity and devised a script that could not only be commercial but also encompass elements that enchanted him, such as the finale on the beaches of

Dieppe. As a young boy, Rollin had once visited this beach while on vacation with his family and found it fascinating, sad and stimulating. Hence, the Dieppe beach is a setting that appears often in Rollin's films, though arguably nowhere as romantically as in *Lips of Blood*, with the two lovers floating out to sea in a coffin, seeking a new life elsewhere.

The production became a troubled one when one of the backers suddenly withdrew, forcing Rollin to frantically cut out and rewrite scenes to reduce a four-week shooting schedule to three. Most of what was lost, by Rollin's own admission, was the film's structure and rhythm. Yet he fought hard to maintain his desired ending at Dieppe, for that was clearly a bigger concern than narrative lucidity. After all, this was a story of a man trying to recapture a memory from his youth and give it eternal life and, if art truly imitates life, *Lips of Blood* is one of Rollin's greatest successes.   DW

Dir: Jean Rollin; **Prod**: Jean-Marie Ghanassia, Lionel Wallmann; **Original Music**: Didier William Lepauw; **Wr**: Jean-Loup Philippe, Jean Rollin; **Cinematography**: Jean-François Robin.

Lisa and the Devil (*Lisa e il diavolo*)
Italy, 1972 – 95 mins
Mario Bava, Alfredo Leone

Lisa and the Devil centres on the eponymous Lisa Reiner (Elke Sommer) who is holidaying with friends in Spain when she becomes lost in a maze of village streets, finally chancing upon a car that will take her away from these surroundings. Unfortunately, the vehicle breaks down by a villa inhabited by a blind countess, her deranged son Maximilian (Alessio Orano) and their mysterious servant Leandro (Telly Savalas). Believing Lisa to be the reincarnation of his lost love, Elena, Maximilian kills off most of the members in Lisa's party, including his own mother, so that Lisa can remain with him forever. By the end of the film, it is discovered that Leandro has been orchestrating the entire sequence of events with his satanic powers. Leandro-as-Devil eliminates Maximilian, then forces Lisa to transform herself back into the corpse of Elena. Disguised as an aeroplane pilot, Leandro transports all the dead humans into an afterlife where they will be forced to relive the same scenario over and over again for all eternity.

While *Lisa and the Devil* is not as popular as some of Mario Bava's earlier works, including *Black Sunday* (1960) and *Baron Blood* (1972), it remains a psychologically disturbing film reminiscent of such ghostly horror classics as *The Innocents* (1961) and *Carnival of Souls* (1962). In both of these films, a female protagonist (like Bava's Lisa) is preyed upon by demonic forces that either leave her alone and abandoned for the remainder of her human existence or compel her to accept the fate that she is trying so hard to resist (i.e., her own death). What elevates *Lisa and the Devil* above the standard ghost tale is the inclusion of the ultimate trickster character, the Devil himself (played with such fiendish delight by Savalas), in the storyline. As the credits roll, we see Leandro-as-Devil playing cards, setting the destinies of those humans who intersect his path with each hand that he draws. In a later scene, Leandro creates mannequins that bear an astonishing resemblance to the key players, suggesting he is the 'grand puppet-master' over them. And the pilot role he assumes at the end effectively illustrates his control over the 'plane' of human existence as well as what lies beyond. While contemporary cinematic tricksters such as Freddy Krueger (Robert Englund) in the *Nightmare on Elm Street* series (1984–present) and Chucky of the *Child's Play* franchise (1988–2005) contain more comical features, Savalas's Leandro manages to evoke a sinister and more dangerous dimension to the Devil's nature. For instance, the extended stares that Leandro gives Lisa are so all-consuming that no recent horror trickster comes close to portraying the same level of menace.

Lisa and the Devil was re-edited and re-released as *The House of Exorcism* in 1975 to cash in on the success of *The Exorcist* (1973). One should avoid this later version as it barely retains the essential core of the original production.   JI

Dir: Mario Bava, Alfredo Leone; **Prod**: José Gutiérrez Maesso, Alfredo Leone; **Original Music**: Joaquín Rodrigo, Carlo Savina; **Wr**: Mario Bava, Alberto Cittini, Alfredo Leone, Giorgio Maulini, Romano Migliorini, Roberto Natale; **Cinematography**: Cecilio Paniagua; **Editing**: Carlo Reali.

Maléfique
France, 2002 – 90 mins
Eric Valette

Eric Valette's début feature is both visually and narratively a prime example of an unexpected mini-surge of Gallic horror films in the last decade or so, partly initiated by 'Bee Movies', a subsidiary of Fidélité Productions that, prior to *Maléfique*, had released three low-budgeters with varying degrees of success and quality. After creating a buzz at the San Sebastian and Sitges festivals, the film was awarded the Jury Prize at the 2003 Gérardmer International Festival of Fantastic Film in France.

With the exception of a couple of scenes (at the start and close of the film), the story is entirely set in a claustrophobic penitentiary cell shared by four prisoners: Carrère (Gérald Laroche), the latest arrival, is a middle-aged white-collar embezzler whose hopes of being bailed out and reunited with his family are quickly dashed; Lassalle (Philippe Laudenbach), older and taciturn, is a scholar who murdered his wife in a sudden bout of near dementia; Pâquerette (Dimitri Rataud) is a mentally retarded twenty-year-old with a literal fixation in the oral stage (when but a child, he ate his baby sister and now swallows every object he can snatch up); and finally Marcus (Clovis Cornillac) is a pre-op transsexual body-builder who acts as a substitute, occasionally breast-feeding, mother for his protégé, Pâquerette, while bullying Carrère in the daytime and sodomising Lassalle at night. The fortuitous discovery of an occult grimoire vaguely reminiscent of Lovecraft's *Necronomicon* (in actuality, a journal full of cabalistic signs and incantations, once kept by an inmate obsessed with self-rejuvenation) does not take long to affect the group's dynamics as it may hold the key to an unconventional escape route by granting wishes . . .

Contrary to what this partial synopsis might suggest, the film is much more inventive than derivative or reductive. It skilfully eschews known tropes (courtesy of a literate script) and stock figures of the horror repertoire. Thanks to uniformly inspired performances, the cast resembles less some gallery of monsters or over-the-top crazies than a colourful *family* of offbeat, yet multidimensional characters. Not the least of the film's merits is that it astutely walks a tightrope, managing to blend supposedly immiscible ingredients without lapsing into ridicule or caricature. Gory or supernatural moments thus co-exist or alternate with more realistic elements from daily prison life enlivened by quirky, although not overwritten, dialogue. Wisely averting an over-use of CGI and animatronics, the film still packs a punch with some impressive special effects sequences, as when every joint in the levitating body of the unfortunate Pâquerette is violently twisted and dislocated by invisible forces, or fantastical Freudian imagery (most notably the eye in the vagina).

As an old-style B-movie played unabashedly straight, *Maléfique* stands as one of the most original efforts in recent French horror fare, and is surprisingly rife with philosophical implications: *libido sciendi* or the quest for total knowledge; desire for immortality and *regressus ad uterum*; and the respective statuses of word – both written and spoken – and image – both video and film.   PM

Dir: Eric Valette; **Prod**: Olivier Delbosc, Marc Missonnier, Franck Ribière; **Original Music**: Eric Sampieri; **Wr**: Alexandre Charlot, Franck Magnier, François Cognard; **Cinematography**: Jean-Marc Bouzou; **Editing**: Luc Golfin.

Malpertuis (aka *Malpertuis: The Legend of Doom House*)
France/Belgium/West Germany, 1971 – 124 mins
Harry Kümel

*Malpertui*s must be one of the most ambitious horror films ever made. It is horror of the most exploitative kind, featuring gushes of blood, ghosts lurking in alleys, flame-spitting blasphemists and psychotic scientists. It is also a feverishly hellish nightmare, a surreal fantasy, a mystery story and a philosophical tract. Borrowing imagery from Rubens' voluptuous biblical evocations, Bosch's phantasmagorical carnivals of cruelty and Magritte's casually shocking paradoxes, it is filled with saints, patriarchs, whores, misfits, bowler hats and strange lantern posts.

The storyline of *Malpertuis*, based on a novel by Jean Ray, is convoluted and complex. Jan (Mathieu Carrière) is a sailor who, after a night on the town, falls in love with a mysterious girl, Alice (Susan Hampshire). He loses sight of her, and in his subsequent quest for her is abducted, assaulted and almost cut to pieces. While visiting his uncle, Cassavius (Orson Welles), Jan discovers that the girl also has another identity. As Gorgon, the goddess of darkness and death, she tells him Cassavius has found the last of the ancient gods on an island, kidnapped them and has bound them to him by a testament, shackling them inside his giant Gothic house, Malpertuis ('tuis' is old Flemish for 'house').

While the themes of terror, torture and betrayal give the story of the gods' captivity a sense of pressing relevance, *Malpertuis* is first and foremost a visual *tour de force*. At times it all seems a bit overwhelming in its grandiloquence. The set design, costumes and make-up, and arrays of dazzling angles, mesmerising depths, stupendous wide-angle shots and quick, almost crashing zooms, create a continuously fantastic atmosphere in which it is easy to doubt the reliability of one's senses. The lighting in the film is simply magnificent. Seldom do films have such deep scarlet tones (Francis Ford Coppola's *Bram Stoker's Dracula* [1992],

The gods must be crazy: Harry Kümel's *Malpertuis*

a film with which *Malpertuis* shares a passion for style and blasphemy, is one exception). And in the middle of all this lies a bedridden, red-nosed Orson Welles, one of cinema's most prolific icons, lording over the story like a curious hybrid of Jabba the Hut and Zeus.

At the time of production, director Harry Kümel was viewed as one of the most prodigious directors working in Europe. His debut feature *Monsieur Hawarden* (1969) had earned him critical acclaim, and *Daughters of Darkness* (1971) was one of the most successful films ever to come from Belgium. It allowed Kümel (then still only thirty-two) to demand almost total control and enabled him to enlist any cast and crew, including veteran screenwriter Jean Ferry (who had also worked on *Daughters of Darkness*), cinematographer Gerry Fisher and French chanteuse Sylvia Vartan (and her beau of the time, Johnny Halliday, who has an uncredited cameo role). Casting Welles was undoubtedly Kümel's most significant coup. He claims to have had John Huston and Peter

Ustinov in mind as well, but no one could have played the part of Cassavius better than Welles. His reputation adds so much weight to the film that it almost seems to become his project.

In the end, though, *Malpertuis* is definitely Kümel's movie. It manages a quasi-perfect balance between art and trash, what *The Times* called a 'surreal league of its own'. In what is a striking similarity with Welles' experiences on *The Magnificent Ambersons* (1942), Kümel was ultimately not given final cut, and the version premiered at the Cannes Film Festival in 1972 was twenty minutes shorter than what he had in mind (the DVD usually includes both versions). With such a bad start to its release trajectory, *Malpertuis* did not do well commercially. These days, *Malpertuis* has started receiving the attention it deserves, but at the time Kümel's ambitions were denounced as megalomaniac, as if he were a fevered madman who had, Icarus-like, tried to fly too close to the sun.   EM

Dir: Harry Kümel; **Prod**: Paul Laffargue, Ritta Laffargue, Pierre Levie; **Original Music**: Georges Delerue; **Wr**: Jean Ferry, Jean Ray (novel); **Cinematography**: Gerry Fisher; **Editing**: Richard Marden.

Man Bites Dog (aka *C'est arrivé près de chez vous* [*It Happened in Your Neighbourhood*])
Belgium, 1992 – 96 mins
Rémy Belvaux, André Bonzel, Benoît Poelvoorde

A low-budget Belgian horror movie with strong cult status, *Man Bites Dog* revolves around a film crew shooting a documentary about Benoît the serial killer (Benoît Poelvoorde). The crew follows Ben when he visits his parents, attends a bar and recites his poetry. They also follow him when he rapes and murders people: men, women, young and old. Despite its comic aspects, *Man Bites Dog* is truly disturbing, not only because Ben commits his violent acts so cold-bloodedly, but also because the film crew witnessing the brutality seems far from bothered by it. In fact, as the narrative unfolds, the crew becomes more and more involved in the various murders. Not only do they finance the documentary with the money Ben has stolen from his victims, they also help him dispose of the bodies – and they finally participate in the rape of a female victim in front of her husband. The picture ends when both Ben and the crew are gunned down by another serial killer – one with his own documentary crew, no less.

   Man Bites Dog can be considered a mockumentary, a film made to look like a documentary despite its fictional status. The documentary look is achieved through the use of hand-held cameras and in-camera editing that gives the impression that the entire production is being shot with hardly any intrusion from the film-makers. This heightens the illusion of immediacy and creates a false sense of authenticity, even though the spectator may be aware of the film's fictional content. *Man Bites Dog* was also shot using grainy black-and-white 16mm stock, like many cinéma vérité documentaries. This grainy quality is heightened by the reliance on natural lighting, understood to be part of the 'authentic' look of the vérité style. Most of the picture is shot in long takes, implying an exact temporal correspondence between the duration of the event and the duration of the image. Furthermore, the film was shot on location with non-professional actors, the sound was recorded live and the film makes almost no use of non-diegetic sound, all of which creates a stronger illusion of reality. All the actors – especially Ben – gaze directly into the camera. This form of direct address is a convention of documentary realism and places the viewer into the position of direct witness.

What ultimately shocks the viewer in *Man Bites Dog* is not so much Ben's casualness and emotional detachment towards his murderous activities. It is shocking primarily because it questions the boundary between the observant and the participant in violence and, in so doing, invites viewers to redefine their own relationship with violence in the media. Like Michael Haneke's *Funny Games* (1997) and Oliver Stone's *Natural Born Killers* (1994), *Man Bites Dog* raises the issue of public fascination with serial killers. Rémy (Rémy Belvaux), the director of the documentary within the film, keeps on shooting even though two of his soundmen have died in the process. The filming does not end as long as there is an audience willing to keep watching.

The gang rape is by any standard the film's most disturbing sequence, because it takes away the 'entertainment value' of violence, reminding viewers of their relation to on-screen horrors they find disgusting and repulsive off screen. This scene, witnessed in viciously graphic detail, forces us to abandon our position of safe voyeurism, the violence becoming painful and disturbing precisely because we are confronted with it – so to speak – against our will. This scene changes the whole movie, as *Man Bites Dog* can no longer be seen merely as a 'snuff satire'.

While the crew gets increasingly involved in Ben's monstrous acts, Ben himself gains increasing control in the shooting of the documentary. Late in the film, Ben attacks a postman who manages to escape, an event that is stretched out several times in slow- and reverse-motion. In the next shot, Ben appears to be sitting behind the editing table, accusing the film-makers of not coming to his aid but instead continuing to shoot. This suggests a collision between the representation and what is being represented – the core of the film's 'ethical pursuit'. The violence here is representation, representation is violence, and it is from this in-between space that the terror in *Man Bites Dog* emerges.   TL

Dir: Rémy Belvaux; **Prod**: Rémy Belvaux, André Bonzel, Benoît Poelvoorde; **Original Music**: Jean-Marc Chenut, Laurence Dufrene; **Wr**: Rémy Belvaux, André Bonzel, Benoît Poelvoorde, Vincent Tavier; **Cinematography**: André Bonzel; **Editing**: Rémy Belvaux, Eric Dardill.

Mark of the Devil (*Hexen bis aufs Blut gequält*, aka *Burn, Witch, Burn*, aka *Austria 1700*, aka *Hexen*, aka *Satan*)
West Germany, 1970 – 95 mins
Michael Armstrong, Adrian Hoven [uncredited]

Mark of the Devil was conceived in the spirit of exploitation, merely intended to capitalise on the success of Michael Reeves' *Witchfinder General* (aka *Conqueror Worm*, 1968). But its determination to salivate over the gruesome details of torture, wrapped in a story where only sadness and injustice survive, make a painful impression few ever forget.

The action begins in a small seventeenth-century Austrian village where Albino (Reggie Nalder), the local witch-hunter, terrorises the population. The post-credit sequence sets the tone with Albino orchestrating a public execution in which a man's hands are amputated before he is tarred and feathered. The scene then lingers on two women who are slowly lowered into a bonfire. Hope eventually rides into town in the form of Count Cumberland (Herbert Lom), a well-respected witchfinder and apparently morally upright official. His devoted assistant Christian (Udo Kier) is confident justice and order will now be restored. But when Christian becomes smitten with an accused witch who he knows to be innocent – a buxom bar wench named Vanessa (Olivera Vuco) – it sets in motion a sequence of events that ultimately leads to his own tragic and gruesome end.

Mark of the Devil has its weaknesses. The acting lacks the realism the story demands, the camera is sometimes zoom-happy and the gaudy score, rather than enhancing the action, more often deflates it. The torture scenes, however, deliver a rich measure of sadistic glee. Henchmen habitually seek the 'mark of the devil' by poking victims with long needles. Later, in the torture chamber, there is ample footage of villagers being whipped, stretched on a rack and stuck with hot pokers. Then, in the film's most infamous scene, a young innocent named Jeni (Gaby Fuchs) has her tongue ripped out by pliers.

Little is explained about Jeni's character, even though her torment is the most prominently featured. But it hardly matters, for her main function in the story is to be nude, bound, female and writhing. This is foremost why *Mark of the Devil* is often seen as an early entry in the 'sex and sadism' genre popular in the 1970s (eg, *Ilsa: She Wolf of the SS* [1975]). But it's the film's ending – reeking in cynicism, injustice and nihilism – that packs the biggest punch. Few films before or since have dared a climax where the innocent suffer, the villain gets away and the hero is slaughtered by an angry mob. Films such as *The Parallax View* and *Chinatown* (both 1974) are a better comparison in this context.

But the lasting memory of *Mark of the Devil* is still its exploitative qualities, epitomised by much of its marketing. When released in the US in 1972, patrons were given stomach distress bags that screamed, 'This VOMIT BAG and the PRICE of one ADMISSION will enable YOU to SEE . . . the first film rated V for violence'. These have since become a popular collectible among film fans, and secured *Mark of the Devil* its place as one of the most memorable horror films of all time.   DG

Dir: Michael Armstrong, Adrian Hoven (uncredited); **Prod**: Adrian Hoven; **Original Music**: Michael Holm; **Wr**: Michael Armstrong, Adrian Hoven; **Cinematography**: Ernst W. Kalinke; **Editing**: Siegrun Jäger.

The Mark of the Wolfman (*La marca del hombre-lobo, The Werewolf's Mark,* aka *Frankenstein's Bloody Terror,* aka *The Vampire of Dr Dracula*)
Spain, 1968 – 78 mins
Enrique López Eguiluz

Important as the film that introduced Spanish horror icon Paul Naschy and his werewolf creation, Waldemar Daninsky, *The Mark of the Wolfman* was also significant in being the first Spanish movie that dared to employ the mythology of Universal's classic monsters popular worldwide since the 1930s and 40s. The film's success, domestically and internationally, further validated horror as a suitable and lucrative genre for Spanish film-makers.

Born in Madrid as Jacinto Molina Alvarez in 1934, the future Paul Naschy struggled to find his niche, studying for a career in architecture while competing with considerable success in weightlifting contests that couldn't support his livelihood. On occasion, Molina worked in cinema as an extra or assistant. At thirty-three, he began his horror career by scripting *The Mark of the Wolfman*. When no suitable actor could be found to play the role of the werewolf (Lon Chaney Jr had to decline because of poor health and physical condition), Molina took on the role himself at the suggestion of the German co-production company, Alpha Films. Because the Germans felt his Spanish name would negatively effect the sale of the film internationally, Molina changed it to Paul Naschy, getting the forename from the current pope at the time, Paul VI, and the surname from a Hungarian weightlifter he knew, Imre Nagy.

The Mark of the Wolfman was an ornate production using real castles and locations for its sets, and filmed in colour, 70mm, stereo sound and, amazingly, 3D. Part fairytale, part Gothic chiller, it harvested the traditions that went before and stimulated new ones. Rather than inhabiting the more distant Victorian world of Hammer's interpretation of Universal's classic monsters, Naschy's supernatural entities were placed in the modern world, though secured to a Gothic and romantic past. The werewolf character, Waldemar Daninsky, is first seen speeding down a road in a red sports car, dressed as Mephistopheles, a scene that clearly joins up the distant world of macabre superstition and Satanism with the contemporary world of speed and sleek machinery. As one of the two vampires in the film, Julian Ugarte gave a unique homoerotic cast to his character, while the typical sexual underpinnings of the vampire were made more manifest than in Universal's day, though still within the bounds of decency suitable for Spanish cinema of that time. As a product of modern society, Waldemar Daninsky was far more raging and brutal a werewolf than his Universal inspiration, Lawrence Talbot.

The Mark of the Wolfman anchored Naschy's career as a major horror figure in Spanish cinema. He would go on to star in eleven more Waldemar Daninsky films, and become his own horror factory, scripting and starring in many horror movies, and later adding directing and producing to the mix. His most mature and impressive works came in the late 1970s and the 1980s. Ironically, changes in the international film business began to devastate world horror and exploitation cinema, and Naschy's best pictures were little seen, financially unsuccessful and personally ruinous.

In 2001, Naschy stepped out of the shadows of horror and cult cinema to receive Spain's highest honour, the Gold Medal for Fine Arts, from the hands of the King of Spain himself, Juan Carlos.   ML

Dir: Enrique López Eguiluz; **Prod**: Maximiliano Pérez-Flores; **Original Music**: Ángel Arteaga; **Wr**: Jacinto Molina; **Cinematography**: Emilio Foriscot; **Editing**: Francisco Jaumandreu.

The Mask of Satan (*La maschera del demonio*, aka *Mask of the Demon*, aka *Black Sunday*)
Italy, 1960 – 85 mins
Mario Bava

The Mask of Satan is a film of many faces. It first gained international prominence in a significantly censored version entitled *Black Sunday*, distributed by American International Pictures and given a new score by Lex Baxter. But the original version of Mario Bava's feature directorial début is actually a brilliant exercise in creating the bleak mood and atmosphere of a Gothic fairytale. Shot almost entirely on an Italian sound stage and never hiding its artificial settings, this black-and-white horror classic successfully evokes a constantly dreamlike ambience.

The Mask of Satan begins with a shock: in the seventeenth century, the young woman Asa (Barbara Steele) of the Vajda family and her brother/lover Javutich (Arturo Dominici) are sentenced to death by the Inquisition for practising witchcraft. After Asa curses her persecutors' heritage, an iron mask with long nails inside is hammered onto her face. Then she is bound to the stake to be burned by the 'purifying fire'; only a sudden rain puts an unexpected end to the event. Two centuries later, in 1830, the travelling doctors Gorobec (John Richardson) and Kruvajan (Andrea Checchi) have a carriage accident and are forced to rest by Asa's decaying tomb. There the handsome young Gorobec meets Katia (Steele again), a descendant of the Vajda clan, and promptly falls in love with her. Trouble begins when Kruvajan accidentally revives Asa's corpse by spilling some blood over her body during an attack by a bat. Along with her lover Javutich, also reincarnated, Asa seeks to fulfil her oath of revenge and begins terrorising Katia and her father. Gorobec stands by Katia's side and fights for her life, while others are killed in horrible ways. In the end, Asa is finally burned at the stake, her spirit exorcised forever.

In the double role of Asa/Katia, the dark and strangely beautiful British actress Barbara Steele established herself as a famous 'scream queen' who would subsequently appear in genre films by Michael

The mask must go on: Barbara Steele in *Mask of the Demon*

Reeves, David Cronenberg, Jonathan Demme, Joe Dante and others. Her cult status will always be connected with Bava's early masterpiece and two scenes in particular: when Katia first appears in the old ruins with two dogs on a leash, and in the scene where she speaks to her double in a single shot.

Bava sought to capture the essence of the classic literary Gothic fiction by recreating all the essential elements – dark tombs, a haunted castle, bats, rainstorms, a *belle dame sans merci*, a *femme fragile*, the family curse, etc. – and combining them with the horrific images of early 60s' genre cinema inspired by Britain's Hammer films. His expressive camera is always in motion, and some clever editing manages to produce astonishing subjective effects. All of the above, along with Bava's will to stretch the boundaries of the staging of sexual and gruesome acts (torture, executions, burning faces, mutilated corpses), give *The Mask of Satan* the impressive power to affect viewers today. Moreover, the film's fairytale cruelties obviously inspired later film-makers, such as Tim Burton, to follow a similar path. MS

Dir: Mario Bava; **Prod**: Massimo De Rita; **Original Music**: Roberto Nicolosi; **Wr**: Nikolai Gogol (story), Ennio De Concini, Mario Serandrei, Mario Bava; **Cinematography**: Mario Bava; **Editing**: Mario Serandrei.

Mill of the Stone Women (Il mulino delle donne di pietra, aka *Drops of Blood*, aka *Horror of the Stone Women*, aka *The Horrible Mill Women)*
Italy/France, 1960 – 95 mins
Georgio Ferroni

Released in August 1960, just a few weeks after Mario Bava's groundbreaking *Black Sunday* (aka *The Mask of Satan*), *Mill of the Stone Women* is set in nineteenth-century Holland and adapted from a novel by the Flemish author Pieter Van Veigen. It tells the story of Hans von Arnam (Pierre Brice), a young art student who visits Professor Gregorius Wahl's (Robert Boehme) windmill in order to collect information about his famous carousel of wax figures. His brief affair with Wahl's mysteriously attractive daughter, Elfi (Scilla Gabel), leads to tragic consequences for everyone involved.

While Ferroni's film misleadingly begins with a watered-down landscape of misty canals and makes consistent use of local colour, it soon turns out to be a skilful exercise in Technicolor Gothic narrative, a subgenre that Italian horror directors would largely tackle during the 1960s. Wahl's windmill is in fact nothing more than a medieval castle whose sinister corridors conceal several dark secrets. Among them, the theme of human bodies covered with wax and carefully displayed for public exhibition in the carousel traces back to Michael Curtiz's *Mystery of the Wax Museum* (1933) and its remake – André De Toth's *House of Wax* (1953) – although the movie equally draws its inspiration from German Expressionist cinema. Like Paul Leni's *Waxworks* (1924), in which a statue of Jack the Ripper features prominently, the subject matter of the figures is not simply famous people but well-known female characters who committed murders or died in a gruesome way. They are all shown caught in the act (pouring poison, tied to a stake, etc.) and this particularity enables *Mill of the Stone Women* to address a murder as art/art as murder problematic that remains popular today. The splitting in two of the antagonist further establishes a distinction between Dr Loren

Bolem (Wolfgang Preiss), a Frankenstein-like scientist, and the mad artist, Professor Wahl, although both of them are monstrous in their own way.

Dedicated to Terence Fisher, this colour horror film – the first of the kind made in Italy – apparently recalls the Hammer tradition. However, for most contemporary viewers, its complex light and colour patterns, circular camera movements and use of strongly romantic music seem more akin to *The Whip and the Body* (1963), one of Bava's subsequent masterpieces. It also hints at various deviant sexual behaviours that are repressed under a firmly established patriarchal order. Apart from Elfi's nymphomania, which needs to be controlled and appears to be more central to the story than the blood sickness she has inherited from her ancestors, necrophilia is hinted at when Hans is aroused by the young girl's very still body – in fact, she keeps dying and coming back to life thanks to repeated transfusions. Wahl's strong attachment to his daughter, as well as his killing of Bolem – her would-be suitor – suggest the possibility of incest and the ending itself emphasises this disturbing idea. Interestingly, this same year saw the release of another film with similar concerns but whose aesthetic bias differs radically: Georges Franju's French horror classic, *Eyes Without a Face*.   FL

Dir: Giorgio Ferroni; **Prod**: Giorgio Stegani; **Original Music**: Carlo Innocenzi; **Wr**: Remigio Del Grosso, Giorgio Ferroni, Ugo Liberatore, Giorgio Stegani; Pieter Van Veigen (novel); **Cinematography**: Pier Ludovico Pavoni; **Editing**: Antonietta Zita.

Nekromantik
West Germany, 1987 – 75 mins
Jörg Buttgereit

Prefaced by an epigraph that warns of the 'grossly offensive' nature of the film that follows, Jörg Buttgereit's *Nekromantik* addresses the last great erotic taboo: that of sexual congress with the dead. It does so to address a significant political taboo within its country of origin, the evils perpetrated by the Nazi regime with the compliance of the majority of the German people. It focuses on the frequently surreal misadventures of a couple of Berlin-based necrophiliacs, intercut with the pontifications of a television psychologist, documentary footage of animal slaughter, scenes from a decidedly misogynistic slasher movie and soft-focus slow-motion pastoral dream sequences. Thus, it depicts not only the psychological degeneration of the ultimately suicidal protagonist Rob (Daktari Lorenz), whose girlfriend leaves him and takes their latest corpse-lover with her, but the socio-cultural ramifications of *Die unbewaltigte Vergangenheit*: the past that has not been adequately addressed by German culture and society.

In this respect, *Nekromantik* shows itself to be rather more thematically complex and technically sophisticated than its low budget and shocking subject matter might imply, sharing a range of artistic and ideological concerns with the canonic auteurs of German cinema: specifically Volker Schlondörff, Hans Jürgen Syberberg, Werner Herzog and Rainer Werner Fassbinder. In keeping with the concerns of such directors, *Nekromantik* is thus predicated on a belief in a quintessentially irrational German unconscious as historically evinced in Goethe's rendering of the Faust legend, E. T. A. Hoffman's tales of the *unheimlich* in prose and the horror tales of Weimar cinema such as Robert Wiene's *The Cabinet of Dr Caligari* (1919), Paul Wegener's *The Golem* (1920) and F. W. Murnau's *Nosferatu* (1922).

Appropriated by the Nazis and subsequently repressed, along with the cultural memory of the dreadful deeds perpetrated by ordinary

German people, this irrational tradition erupts in each of Buttgereit's films: from the early back-projections he created for the experimental noise band *Einsturzende Neubauten* to the feature films *The Death King* (1990), *Nekromantik II* (1991) and *Schramm* (1993). It manifests itself in a wilful disruption of linear temporality, the insertion of dream sequences and the inclusion of absurdist parodies of art-house films. Early in Buttgereit's career, in films such as *Bloody Excesses in the Leader's Bunker* (1982), moreover, it entailed the insertion of real-life concentration-camp footage. But its most distinctive manifestation appears in the *Nekromantik* films in the form of disgusting erotic encounters with the deliquescing dead.

Avoiding the censorship to which the post-reunification *Nekromantik II* was subject, *Nekromantik* remains a highly contentious movie. Although shocking in subject matter and unremittingly visceral in its portrayal of sex and death, it is not gratuitously distasteful. Instead it sets out to expose the complicity of the film medium in the ideological manipulation of the individual that may culminate in acts of bloody violence. It points, moreover, to the ways in which film itself can bring about a re-sensitisation to the horrors of the past.   LB

Dir: Jörg Buttgereit; **Prod**: Manfred O. Jelinski; **Original Music**: Hermann Kopp, Daktari Lorenz, John Boy Walton; **Wr**: Jörg Buttgereit, Franz Rodenkirchen; **Cinematography**: Uwe Bohrer; **Editing**: Jörg Buttgereit, Manfred O. Jelinski.

Night Watch (*Nochnoi dozor*)
Russia, 2004 – 115 mins
Timur Bekmambetov

Set in contemporary Moscow, *Night Watch* tells the story of an ancient and eternal impasse between the supernatural forces of Light and Dark. The eponymous Night Watch are the Light Others who issue permits to and police the Dark Others. Anton Gorodetsky (Konstantin Khabensky), an Other who is recruited to the Night Watch after seeking to win back his wife by killing her unborn child, becomes a key player in a struggle over the destiny of a prophesied child. Though learning the boy is his son, he becomes distracted by the case of a cursed woman who seems to be inviting the destruction of Moscow. In a final epic showdown, Anton saves Moscow, but the boy chooses the side of the Dark Others.

Night Watch is an epic fantasy with dystopic overtones and a dark subtext, borrowing heavily from such franchises as *The Lord of the Rings* and *Star Wars*. Scenes in which characters grasp fluorescent lights are a clear homage to the lightsabre, and characters move in and out of the Gloom – a twilight realm – just as Frodo does with the One Ring. Moreover, with its literary roots (the film is an adaptation of the first third of an epic novel) and political subtext, it also alludes to Mikhail Bulgakov's *The Master and Margarita*.

The effects used to recreate a gritty urban environment peopled by Mafia-styled warlocks, shapeshifters and other supernatural creatures are as noteworthy as those in many Hollywood films. The amalgam of computer and in-camera effects are arguably as technically significant as those in *The Matrix* series. *Night Watch*, however, seems anything but derivative. Notable features include animated and computer-game-style sequences, jump-cuts and disjointed editing which gives an impressionistic feel, and extremes of both shallow focus and close-up.

Hard to categorise generically, the film can be read as fairytale or epic quest, with its central narrative opposition between Night and Day, or as a refreshing take on the vampire genre in which the vampire hunter tracks his prey by drinking blood and the vampires can be seen only in mirrors. *Night Watch* does more than simply hybridise genres, though, treading a fine line in ambiguity by making the Light Others more ethically conflicted than their Dark counterparts – who are straightforwardly and unambiguously evil.

As the title suggests, much of the action is set at night: shadows, twilight and obscurity being key themes which underscore the moral uncertainty of the Night Watch itself. The film derives a sense of the uncanny and the grotesque from the repeated motifs of birds, spiders, blood and strange, contorted, mutant toys. Birds especially are used as signifiers of doom; great flocks of crows silhouetted darkly against a grey sky are a frequent sight. Blood as a signifier of both life and death is given added import through the use of effects shots depicting vessels and spaces inside the body. The sound design, too, is a key dimension of the horror, with the use of heightened sound during quiet moments and ethereal choral music played over slow-motion sequences.

Night Watch was a huge hit in Russia, becoming the most successful film of the post-Soviet era. In overseas territories, the picture also broke the conventions of subtitling with its innovative and imaginative subtitles, frequently animated and integrated into the visual surface of the film itself.   BC

Dir: Timur Bekmambetov; **Prod**: Varvara Avdyushko, Igor Bondarenko, Konstantin Ernst, Arthur Gorson, Aleksei Kublitsky, Aleksei Kulibin, Anatoli Maksimov; **Original Music**: Yuri Poteyenko; **Wr**: Timur Bekmambetov, Laeta Kalogridis, Sergei Lukyanenko (novel): **Cinematography**: Sergei Trofimov; **Editing**: Dmitri Kiselev.

Nightwatch (Nattevagten)
Denmark, 1994 – 105 mins
Ole Bornedal

The Danish film *Nightwatch* was considered a surprise success when it hit the film festival circuit in 1994, a scene more accustomed to art-house dramas than thrill-a-minute genre films. But Denmark, and Scandinavian cinema in general, has always had a tradition of making genre movies, particularly crime stories. The strong craftsmanship of this unabashed thriller – rooted in a story where the characters learn to appreciate the lives they have by facing death and mutilation – was too rich a combination to escape notice.

The lead character in *Nightwatch* is Martin (Nikolaj Coster-Waldau), a young law student who accepts a job as a night watchman at a mortuary. His best friend, Jens (Kim Bodnia), is a boozing, reckless soul

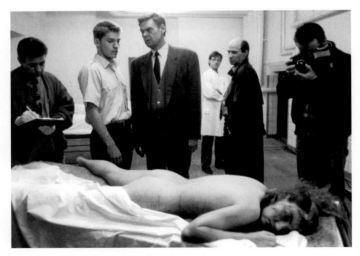

Of morgues and murder: Ole Bornedal's *Nightwatch*

who is bored with life. What binds them – besides their respective girlfriends – is their unwillingness to follow the road to adulthood. To wit, Jens makes a bet with Martin; that for two weeks they will play a game of chicken. They will challenge each other to commit acts that could have dire consequences. 'The stakes? Freedom', says Jens. Whoever backs down first must marry his girlfriend.

It is when Jens challenges Martin to have sex with Joyce (Rikke Louise Andersson), a seventeen-year-old prostitute, that Martin's life goes on a collision course with a serial killer, and the thriller portion of the film kicks in. This terror aspect is little else than a subplot at first, alluded to most prominently when we observe Martin spending his evenings, isolated, watching over the mortuary that houses the murder victims. This eerie setting is exploited for all its creepiness in the first half of the movie, mostly by contrasting darkness with bright lights, and extreme noise with deathly silence.

Throughout, *Nightwatch* drops clues that turn out to be pivotal to the serial killer story, climaxing in a sequence of events that is milked for maximum suspense and thrills. But, more crucially, it gives the characters a taste of death that drives them to embrace life more than ever before. This overriding theme is stated when Inspector Wörmer (Ulf Pilgaard), the chief investigator of the killings, urges Martin to examine a vat filled with body parts, and says 'It makes you appreciate life, doesn't it?' Later on, the sight of dead bodies unleashes the only moment of eroticism between Martin and his girlfriend. The ample references to necrophilia also enhance this thematic thread.

It is this life-versus-death theme that was unfortunately de-emphasised in the 1997 Hollywood remake of *Nightwatch* (also directed by Bornedal). The remake follows the original quite closely – often shot by shot – but by truncating many of the more personal scenes, the serial killer story becomes the film's focus. The box-office failure of this remake has since prevented the original from being distributed in North America. Still, *Nightwatch* stands as an ideal case study for horror in cinema: that to make a great terror film, it is not enough to have characters in jeopardy, but characters that are worth knowing and caring about.   DW

Dir: Ole Bornedal; **Prod**: Michael Obel; **Original Music**: Joachim Holbek, Knud Odde, The Sandmen, Sort Sol; **Wr**: Ole Bornedal; **Cinematography**: Dan Laustsen; **Editing**: Camilla Skousen.

Nosferatu: A Symphony of Horror (*Nosferatu: Eine Symphonie des Grauens*, aka *Nosferatu the Vampire*, aka *Nosferatu*, aka *Terror of Dracula*)
Germany, 1922 – 94 mins
F. W. Murnau

Released in 1922, F. W. Murnau's *Nosferatu: A Symphony of Horrors* is the earliest remaining cinematic adaptation of Bram Stoker's *Dracula*. The adaptation was made without permission, and Stoker's widow later brought a successful lawsuit against the film. The names of the characters and several key plot elements were altered in the adaptation, but the basic premise remains intact: Hutter (Gustav von Wangenheim), a clerk in an estate agent's office, takes leave of his young wife Ellen (Greta Schroeder), and, on instructions from his employer, travels across Europe to a remote mountainous region where the local people live in fear and superstition. A ghostly coachman escorts him to a dark castle where he is met by his host, the cadaverous Count Orlok (Max Schreck).

In the course of their transactions, the Count sees a picture of Hutter's wife, and a destructive process of obsession and pursuit is set in motion. Hutter soon discovers that his host is a vampire and manages to flee. While Hutter races home to Ellen, the vampire makes a parallel voyage, his coffin stowed in the hull of a ship. Accompanied by scores of rats, he terrorises and kills the crew and the ship's captain en route to Bremen. His arrival marks the beginning of a 'plague' that mysteriously sweeps through the town. He is ultimately destroyed when Ellen martyrs herself by keeping the vampire with her until dawn, when the sun's rays shoot through the monster, reducing him to dust.

The film employs the poetic language of dreams, using spatial terms and relationships to evoke interior states of being. *Nosferatu* traces each character's journey into an uncharted territory of longing, desire and terror, creating an entirely uncomfortable and haunting experience for the viewer. As the vampire, Schreck is skeletal and rodent-like – and relentlessly grotesque. Under Murnau's direction he created a series of

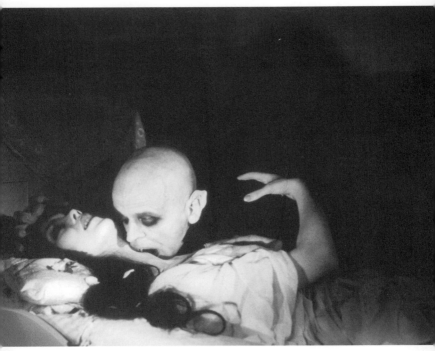

Eros and Thanatos intermingle in F. W. Murnau's *Nosferatu*

indelible images, such as the vampire carrying his own coffin through the streets of Bremen, and the shadow of his outstretched claws.

Murnau's expressive camerawork, notably his use of angular shots and spatial relationships to create atmosphere and emotional effects, has been widely discussed. Beyond analysing the technical achievements of the film, each new generation of critics and scholars has looked anew at *Nosferatu*, pondering every possible angle of interpretation. Some of these readings have included speculation as to whether the film metaphorically reflected the prevalent anti-Semitic attitudes of Weimar

Germany, or whether perhaps the vampire's abject and terrifying qualities mirrored Murnau's sense of ostracism as a gay man in that place and time.

A milestone achievement in creating the language and vocabulary of cinematic horror, *Nosferatu* enjoyed critical success from the time of its initial release. Artists and fans continue to draw inspiration from this early masterwork, and *Nosferatu* references, imitations and spoofs continue to appear in popular culture. In 1979, director Werner Herzog made his own version of the picture, and E. Elias Merhige's *Shadow of the Vampire* (2000) offers a colourful account of the film's genesis.   RG

Dir: F. W. Murnau; **Prod**: Enrico Dieckmann, Albin Grau; **Original Music**: Hans Erdmann; **Wr**: Henrik Galeen, Bram Stoker (novel): **Cinematography**: Fritz Arno Wagner, Günther Krampf (uncredited).

Nosferatu the Vampire (*Nosferatu – Phantom der Nacht*)
Germany, 1979 – 107 mins
Werner Herzog

Whether or not one accepts Werner Herzog as a great director, few would question the fact that he is one of the most idiosyncratic of all film-makers – and one who goes where lesser mortals fear to tread. Nowhere is this more evident than in his decision to remake F. W. Murnau's *Nosferatu* (1922), one of the cornerstone works of German cinema by perhaps the greatest of all German film-makers. It takes a brave soul – or a seriously deluded one – to even consider such an undertaking, let alone actually do it. It takes something at least verging on genius to do it right.

Calling Herzog's film a remake, while technically correct, does it a grave disservice. Yes, it follows the outline of Murnau's film with reasonable fidelity, even to the point of duplicating some shots. There are also traces of other films within its confines, most notably Tod Browning's *Dracula* and Rouben Mamoulian's *Dr Jekyll and Mr Hyde* (both 1931), though both these films owe much to Murnau in the first place. But the overall sense of Herzog's version is more a combination of a reimagining and a meditation. Points that are suggested in Murnau's film – the equation of the vampire and the plague, the tide of rats that accompany both – are here taken to their logical extensions, creating a work of unusually unsettling power.

Murnau's picture is often lumped together with other German fantasy films of its era, seen as being part and parcel of the same creative impetus that fuelled Robert Wiene's *The Cabinet of Dr Caligari* (1919). As an example of Expressionist film-making there is some truth in that, but Murnau's film – his entire approach – is markedly different from the hermetic, studio-bound world of *Caligari*. His film takes place in something like the real world in real locations, creating its Expressionist tone through lighting and camerawork. Murnau found the unreal that lay beneath the real, crafting a work that was considerably more viscerally affecting than anything in *Caligari*. This too is the approach Herzog takes, but to even greater extremes. His Castle Dracula, for example, is merely a ruined outline against the sky when observed from a distance. That is the reality. The clean, whitewashed castle Jonathan Harker (Bruno Ganz) visits seems completely unconnected to this image, suggesting that perhaps it is an illusion held together by the strength of Count Dracula's (Klaus Kinski) will. Yet that sets up a dichotomy in the film's portrayal of the Count – one that is never fully reconciled.

There is little, if anything, magical about the Herzog–Kinski vision of Dracula. He never jerks upright magically from his coffin, doesn't *appear* to be both coach driver and host to Harker, doesn't load a wagonful of coffins at high speed or have a tarpaulin magically cover them, doesn't disappear in a puff of smoke when struck by sunlight, etc. Everything he does is laborious. He is presented as a tired, sick creature, eternally lonely, wanting to be a part of the world of life that is denied him. Even at his most repellent, there is an innate sadness to the creature and a disturbing sympathy for his plight. (It is far more this version of Dracula than Murnau's that's at the core of E. Elias Merhige's 2000 film, *Shadow of the Vampire*.) Yet this Dracula is even more an implacable force than Murnau's. His forward, evil momentum – the opening music used to evoke the feel of a flowing river is from Richard Wagner's *Das Rheingold* – comes on like a wave that cannot be stopped.

At the same time, Herzog has decidedly *not* tried to make a realistic film – note the deliberate sacrifice of realism for the sake of atmosphere in the lighting of the scene where Dracula's coach meets Harker on the road. The film he made is very much in the fantastic mode and exists in a world that feels very much a part of the silent film world of the original. If Murnau found the unreal beneath the real, Herzog took it one level deeper, resulting in a movie that is, if anything, even more chilling than its model.   KH

Dir: Werner Herzog; **Prod**: Michael Gruskoff, Werner Herzog, Daniel Toscan du Plantier; Score: Popol Vu; **Cinematography**: Jörg Schmidt-Reitwein; **Wr**: Werner Herzog; **Editing**: Beate Mainka-Jellinghaus.

Opera (aka *Terror at the Opera*)
Italy, 1987 – 95 mins
Dario Argento

Dario Argento's *Opera* centres on a production of Verdi's *Macbeth*, which traditionally carries a curse. People are murdered by an unknown assailant who forces a young diva named Betty (Cristina Marsillach) to watch, placing pins under her eyes to keep them open. Eventually it is disclosed that the killer is the police inspector assigned to solve the brutal crimes.

The literary tradition of the *giallo* (which literally translates as 'yellow' in Italian) began in 1929 when the Milanese Publishing house Mondadori launched a series of murder mysteries in yellow covers. These *gialli*, less a genre than a conceptual category, included horror stories, *policiers* and crime melodramas. Mario Bava's *The Girl Who Knew Too Much* (1963) is credited as the first cinematic *giallo*. But Argento has downplayed the influence of Bava, who tends to be more baroque and 'obvious', attributing his inspiration instead to such diverse film-makers as Lang, Hitchcock, Lewton, Tourneur, Fellini, Godard, Disney and Warhol.

Opera's aesthetic converges on several of Argento's stylistic trademarks. His plots contain explicit violence linked to the antagonist's past sexual history. To emphasise psychosexual transferrals between physical desire and its unattainability, lethal phallic instruments of penetration are ubiquitously placed in oneiric settings. Moreover, Argento often creates two narrative endings. In *Opera*, the first conclusion occurs with the presumptive death of the police inspector at Betty's hands. The second occurs with the inspector's capture after his murder of the stage director. As the film's coda attests, however, the entire experience has pushed Betty over the edge. Another device, the killer's synecdochic image consisting of gloved hands and black mask, becomes a correlative for his fractured and recurrent sadomasochistic fantasies enacted years earlier with Betty's mother. These fantasies so disrupt the movie's spatio-temporal flow that they appear to be displaced rather than subjective inserts from the murderer's point of view.

Also characteristic of Argento is *Opera*'s ambiguous viewpoint through the Steadicam's restless exploration of space, shattering the illusory perspective Hollywood films seek to establish: a logical and credible visual reference point obtained via shot and countershot. As the camera tracks the opera house or Betty's apartment, the focaliser is either not revealed or his face is obscured. The result is an incessant shifting between an objective, external, impersonal narrator outside the diegesis, and an agent through whom the audience observes the scene. Other camera manoeuvres foreground stylistic techniques with minimal narrative function, for example, intricate Louma crane and Sky-cam shots approximating the movement of ravens as they circle the opera house, or the camera performing an apparent free fall into space, detached from its mount.

Close-ups, which in conventional films reveal something significant, here disclose nothing. Hands stab Betty's lover through the throat, shoot a bullet through her agent's eye, but provide no clues to the slayer's identity. With traditional elucidating devices such as the shot-countershot and close-up rendered impotent, the audience is forced to use other senses that are likewise subverted. The killer's voice, for instance, is distorted so that the privileged position accorded human discourse loses its pre-eminent status as a means of character identification. All this makes *Opera* a mesmerising Argento thriller and a quintessential *giallo*.   MS

Dir: Dario Argento; **Prod**: Dario Argento, Ferdinando Caputo; **Original Music**: Brian Eno, Roger Eno, Daniel Lanois, Claudio Simonetti, Bill Wyman; **Wr**: Dario Argento, Franco Ferrini; **Cinematography**: Ronnie Taylor; **Editing**: Franco Fraticelli.

The Ordeal (*Calvaire*)
Belgium/France/Luxembourg, 2004 – 90 mins
Fabrice Du Welz

Belgium has garnered a reputation among connoisseurs as the originator of some of the darkest, bleakest and rawest realistic horror in Europe. Films such as *The Lonely Killers* (Boris Szulzinger, 1972), *Man Bites Dog* (Rémy Belvaux, André Bonzel, Benoît Poelvoorde, 1992) and *S.* (Guido Henderickx, 1998) testify to an acute awareness of the subconsciousness of the culture they are bred in.

The Ordeal fits that lineage perfectly, and in fact ups the ante considerably. The story is deviously simple. A few days before Christmas, Marc Stevens (Laurent Lucas) is a young *chanteur* travelling in the Fagnes area, a region akin to the Deep South of *Deliverance* (1972), or the Cornwall of *Straw Dogs* (1971). When his car breaks down, Marc finds refuge in a small hotel – as in *Psycho* (1960), ominously announced through mists of pouring rain. Owner Paul Bartel (Jackie Berroyer) first pretends to help him, but then betrays Marc's trust and keeps him in captivity. Dressed up as Bartel's former wife Gloria, Marc is tortured, paraded around and later nailed to a crucifix. Marc escapes when his captor's lodge is besieged by local farmers who first liberate the livestock and then proceed to rape Marc. In the snowed-under swamps he finally rids himself of his pursuers.

One does not need to be a devout Catholic to see the Biblical metaphors oozing out of this story like blood from Christ's wounds. Du Welz may have switched Easter for Christmas (Bartel jokes that fixing Marc's broken car might take until Easter), but the directness with which he shows suffering is only a little less literal than *The Passion of the Christ* (2004), and at least as gut-wrenching to watch. But there is more than just gore here. While stylistically dominated by harsh realism – the beginning of the film could be plucked from the Dardenne Brothers' oeuvre – the colours, camerawork and pace reference most of the modern horror canon, from *Psycho* through *Night of the Living Dead* (1968),

The Texas Chainsaw Massacre (1974) to *The Blair Witch Project* (1999). Veteran scream queen Brigitte Lahaie makes a cameo, and there is even a reference to *Snow White* in the form of seven eerie dwarves in red jumpsuits. As the story unfolds, the style gradually changes: realism makes way for dark, expressionist lighting (sometimes even complete darkness) and cinematographer Benoît Debie (who also shot Gaspar Noé's brilliant, disturbing *Irréversible* [2002]) increasingly alternates hand-held shots with smooth, elaborate tracking shots. *The Ordeal* is completely void of music save three diegetic punctures, the third of which is a wild piano sarabande in the local bar with rural zombies performing a tribal dance. If you consider this comedic, think again: Du Welz makes it as uncanny as the 'one of us' mantra in *Freaks* (1932), a battle cry more than a celebration.

In the end, *The Ordeal* is more than a stew of golden horror moments and Christian iconography. Like most recent Belgian horror films, it is saturated with the rural abductions and rape scandals that rocked Belgian society in the mid- to late 1990s. It is impossible to see the film outside that framework, the same way any inferences to topical issues of torture (for example, Guantanamo Bay, Abu Ghraib) cannot be ignored.

With such weighty themes, *The Ordeal*'s successful reception – which began at the *L'Âge d'Or*, the annual festival of subversive cinema held by the Belgian Film Archive, followed by notable appearances at the festivals of Cannes, Edinburgh and Gérardmer – is all the more remarkable. It demonstrates how horror can hold up an ice-cold mirror to the society it reflects: decaying, stuck on absurd and violent rituals; incomprehensibly surreal, but also oh-so-recognisably real.   EM

Dir: Fabrice Du Welz; **Prod**: Michael Gentile, Eddy Géradon-Luyckx, Vincent Tavier; **Original Music**: Vincent Cahay; **Wr**: Fabrice Du Welz, Romain Protat; **Cinematography**: Benoît Debie; **Editing**: Sabine Hubeaux.

Orgy of the Vampires (La orgia nocturna de los vampiros, aka The Vampires' Night Orgy)
Spain, 1972 – 84 mins
León Klimovsky

Orgy of the Vampires is an excellent example of the type of horror film produced in Spain during the early 1970s. It has energy, invention and abounds with generic clichés. It might best be described as 'cheap and cheerful'.

The film begins with a coffin being lowered into a grave. The rope holding it snaps and the coffin cracks open. Inside, the body has totally decomposed and worms and maggots abound. The credits roll as they squirm around a smouldering skull, all to the beat of a manic jazz pop score. The story that then unfolds involves a group of workers on their way to an isolated manor in the Spanish countryside. Tired, they decide to spend the night at an inn in an isolated village. When they arrive they meet another traveller (played by Jack Taylor), but can find no residents. As night falls, one of the occupants of the coach is attacked by a group of zombie-like vampire villagers. Back at the inn, other residents have begun to appear and mention a mysterious countess. In the morning the coach won't start, leaving the workers trapped. In a memorable, almost claustrophobic scene, two of the travellers are attacked on the coach by a horde of zombie villagers. In the end only two manage to escape, but when they attempt to report the horror they have encountered to the authorities, they are told it never happened. However, the final shot of the film is of the coach, the windows drenched in mud, leaving the audience wondering what might be within.

The film is directed with his usual efficiency by León Klimovsky. Klimovsky was an Argentine director who, after beginning his career in his homeland directing works that aspired to art, worked extensively in the Spanish commercial cinema of the 1960s and 70s. As a journeyman professional film-maker he was responsible for Westerns, comedies and war films, gaining a reputation for shooting quickly and to budget.

Such attributes made him a favourite with producers. Occasionally his movies would feature well-known names such as Jack Palance, but usually they would headline lesser-known actors.

Jack Taylor, the top-liner of this film, is one such actor. He starred in a number of horror films across Europe, working with the likes of Jesús Franco in *Succubus* (1968). Taylor was an American who found himself in demand initially in Mexico, where he starred in a number of movies for director Federico Curiel, and then in Europe. There he appeared in films such as *Billy the Kid* (1964), also for Klimovsky, and other Westerns for the likes of Amando de Ossorio. Adaptable, he found regular work on the European exploitation circuit without ever becoming a household name. Luis Ciges, who here takes the role of the gardener, played supporting roles in many Spanish genre films of this period. He found a sort of stardom later in life through his appearance in Javier Fesser's manic comedy, *The Miracle of P. Tinto* (1998).

It might not be the most distinctive example of Spanish horror cinema, but *Orgy of the Vampires* is certainly entertaining. As with a number of Klimovsky's films, what it lacks in originality it more than makes up for in atmosphere. AW

Dir: León Klimovsky; **Prod**: José Frade; **Wr**: Gabriel Burgos, Antonio Fos; **Cinematography**: Antonio L. Ballesteros; **Editing**: Antonio Ramírez de Loaysa.

The Perfume of the Lady in Black (Il profuoa della signora in nero)
Italy, 1974 – 101 mins
Francesco Barilli

Francisco Barilli's feature directorial début, *The Perfume of the Lady in Black*, is a subtle, unsettling work and one of the most accomplished psychological horror films to have emerged from Italy. While it shows some indebtedness to the *giallo*, it is too eclectic in its sources and inspirations to be truly representative of that subgenre.

Silvia Hacherman (superbly played by American-born actress Mimsy Farmer) is an unwed industrial scientist absorbed in her work. The routine of her life is disrupted when she attends a party at the home of an African couple knowledgeable in the practices of black magic. The discussion of voodoo rituals and human sacrifices – subsequently followed by a game of tennis, during which she pricks herself on a sharp nail protruding from her racket – seems to awaken traumatic memories from her childhood past. She may or may not have been sexually abused by her mother's lover, but is nonetheless tormented by a particularly vivid image of her mother, who died mysteriously and is the enigmatic figure alluded to in the film's title. A link is thus established between Silvia and her mother, the assumption being that if they do not share an identical fate, they are both victims of some sort of occult violence, a connection strengthened when, in the film's final moments, she dons her mother's black dress.

The conspiratorial elements of the plot – a young woman becoming entangled in a web of deceit and manipulation – were derived from English-language films such as Roman Polanski's *Rosemary's Baby* (1968), but the film also exhibits an affinity to Polanski's earlier *Repulsion* (1965), particularly in the rather subtle way it hints at Silvia's frigidity and inability to enjoy sex with her boyfriend. Moreover, the way in which Silvia's past (and future) becomes intermingled with her subjective fantasies and paranoid delusions reveals an indebtedness to films such as

Nicolas Roeg's *Don't Look Now* (1973) and, more distantly, *Hush . . . Hush, Sweet Charlotte* (1964), although it shares *Don't Look Now*'s catastrophic, unexpected and shocking finale. It even borrows the latter's figure of an evil imp, in this case an 'Alice in Wonderland' figure in a white dress who at first seems to be Silvia's inner child but later becomes a tormenting Fury, the subtle evocation of a similar figure in Mario Bava's *Kill, Baby . . . Kill!* (1966).

It was probably the film's fragmented, delirious style, with its strangely contradictory plot elements, that prevented it from securing a release in countries like the United States. Although little seen outside Europe, its reputation was solid among the cognoscenti of Italian horror and eventually, when its singularity was recognised, it became acknowledged as the classic work of horror cinema it is. As a result, its influence is difficult to measure. Unlike other masters of Italian horror, such as Dario Argento, Barilli, a painter, made few other films, and while *Perfume* exhibits an explicit link with the cannibalism subsequently depicted in other Italian horror movies of the period, his style is not nearly as florid or insistently graphic.   RU and SU

Dir: Francisco Barilli; **Prod**: Giovanni Bertolucci, Aldo U. Passalacqua; **Original Music**: Nicola Piovani; **Wr**: Francisco Barilli, Massimo D'Avak; **Cinematography**: Mario Masini; **Editing**: Enzo Micarelli.

Possession
France/West Germany, 1981 – 127 mins
Andrej Zulawski

A relentlessly bizarre cinematic nightmare, Andrej Zulawski's *Possession* is surely one of the most original, intense and unpredictable horror films to date. The plot is chaotic: Marc (Sam Neill) arrives home to Berlin earlier than expected to find that his wife Anna (Isabelle Adjani) has taken a lover, Heinrich (Heinz Bennet), and that their marriage is falling apart. He soon finds that Anna harbours other dark secrets as well – a slime-covered tentacled monster-lover she keeps hidden away in a rented flat, chief among them. Meanwhile, Marc develops a relationship with his son's schoolteacher (also played by Adjani), who bears an uncanny resemblance to his estranged wife. The narrative then gets even more complicated, with snooping private detectives, chase scenes, successive murders and monstrous births all developed against the backdrop of a divided Berlin. If these plot elements weren't sufficient to set *Possession* apart from the norm, the tenor of the piece is so hysterically overwrought and surreal that it cannot fail to agitate and disturb. Zulawski employs a constantly moving camera to highlight the sense of emotional turmoil and the effect is dizzying.

   Possession is intentionally melodramatic and unabashedly esoteric – using the surrealist tendencies of irrational exchange and anarchic disjuncture as its modus operandi – and it is Zulawski's simultaneously cerebral and bloody use of these techniques that gives the film its considerable impact. *Possession* explores the horror of a crumbling marriage, a horror located in a family in which secrets and lies have taken monstrous form. The plot hinges on the dreamlike conceit of stumbling on a terrible discovery as a result of arriving 'too early': your whole life is a lie; your spouse is cheating, everyone knows about it except you and, if not for a simple error in timing, you would have remained totally oblivious. The film employs the uncanny language of nightmare and, in so doing, bears some notable resemblance and a relationship to the work of other directors who deal in irrational cruelties, doubled characters and emotional pandemonium: Luis Buñuel, Ken Russell and David Lynch chief among them.

The film can also potentially be read as Zulawski's anguished farewell to Poland and a meditation on betrayal and deception on levels beyond the individual. Born in Ukraine, Zulawski was apprenticed to Andrej Wajda before making his first films. His work was controversial, being both stylistically excessive and implicitly critical of the political climate in the bloc, attributes which soon brought Zulawski into conflict with Polish authorities. His film *The Devil* (1972) was banned, and the Polish Ministry of Culture shut down production of his science-fiction film *On the Silver Globe* in 1978 when shooting was nearly complete. These and other traumas led to Zulawski leaving Poland; he has since primarily lived and worked in France. *Possession* was Zulawski's first picture after his expatriation and it garnered several notable awards, in particular for Adjani. Despite limited success at the box office upon its initial release, *Possession* is beloved among horror enthusiasts, and continues to mark an important achievement in the history of the genre.   RG

Dir: Andrej Zulawski; **Prod**: Marie-Laure Reyre; **Original Music**: Andrzej Korzynski; **Wr**: Andrej Zulawski, Frederic Tuten; **Cinematography**: Bruno Nuytten; **Editing**: Marie-Sophie Dubus, Suzanne Lang-Willar.

Schramm
Germany, 1993 – 75 mins
Jörg Buttgereit

Through a series of fragmented vignettes, we learn that Lothar
Schramm (Florian Koerner von Gustorf) is the 'Lipstick Killer', withdrawn,
fantasy-prone, psychotic and fixated upon Marianne (Monika M), a
prostitute who occupies the same seedy apartment block. Unable to
express his attraction either emotionally or physically, Lothar instead
agrees to accompany Marianne to the house of a group of wealthy
clients, constantly nurturing both his self-loathing and his hateful,
murderous resentment.

Having established himself as one of the most idiosyncratic figures
on the European horror scene with *Nekromantik* (1987), *The Death
King* (1990) and *Nekromantik II* (1991), director Jörg Buttgereit
embarked on this characteristically perverse entry in the serial killer
subgenre. Sadly, he has not directed a feature since. As in those earlier
efforts, *Schramm* obsessively and solemnly details the interrelationship of
sex and death, with an economical but textured insight into physical and
psychological decay. Much underrated, this is Buttgereit's most
accomplished film, belonging not only within the pantheon of
contemporary serial killer films but in a small German tradition that
includes Fritz Lang's *M* (1931) and Ulli Lommel's *The Tenderness of
Wolves* (1973).

Narratively spare, *Schramm*'s non-linear construction is guided by
the dying thoughts of Lothar, who is introduced sprawled semi-naked
on a floor splattered in blood and paint. A key element distinguishing
the film from its counterparts in the genre is its lack of interest in the
'seriality' of Lothar's murderous activity – he is only shown committing
one double murder in the early section of the movie. Even then,
Buttgereit seems more interested in the opportunity this affords for
Lothar to display his victims (two door-to-door Christians) in artful
sexual poses. Lothar's own death (revealed at the outset) is itself

depicted visually as a bizarre hybrid of human still-form and abstract Expressionism.

The departure from a narrative of victim accumulation allows the film to focus upon the subjectivity of its central figure. This imbues *Schramm* with a high degree of ambiguity in its depiction of 'reality', as Lothar indulges in fantasies of both emotional and physical potency (a romantic dance with Marianne, running a marathon) and extreme physical violation of himself (an eyeball extraction, a leg amputation and penis mutilation, all graphically portrayed). Underlying this fantasy life is the lethargy and squalor of his daily existence, redeemable only through a fantasy vision of impossibly idealised romance. Sexual expression is achieved not through actual pursuit of this ideal, but through grotesque liaisons with inflatable sex toys while the human object of longing is heard servicing clients in an adjacent apartment. This is a rare serial killer film whose chief concern is the level of detachment and pain of its human monster.

This imagined relationship merely serves to fuel the fatal misogyny that has informed Lothar's crimes. Given the film's degree of subjectivity, it is some achievement that it is able to distance itself from Lothar's hatred for women. The extent of this fear and mistrust of the opposite sex is exemplified by an imagined physical embodiment of the *vagina dentata*, a repulsive, Cronenbergian apparition that appears in a variety of fantasy scenarios. However, instead of attempting to explain Lothar's pathology, *Schramm* merely hints at psychoanalytic tropes, such as a traumatic childhood (depicted highly effectively through 8mm footage) and a dominant matriarch (embodied by a portrait of a woman who may or may not be Lothar's mother).

For a film so steeped in despair and nihilism, there is an undercurrent of the blackest humour. In a neat encapsulation of *Schramm*'s recurrent paralleling of the mundane with the monstrous, Lothar's own death is the result of a DIY accident, brought about by his attempt to cover up the evidence of his latest gruesome crime. The absurdity of this demise is given extra force by the events climaxing the film, which hint at both Lothar's spiritual damnation and Marianne's terrifying fate.   NJ

Dir: Jörg Buttgereit; **Prod**: Manfred O. Jelinski; **Original Music**: Max Müller, Gundula Schmitz; **Wr**: Jörg Buttgereit, Franz Rodenkirchen; **Cinematography**: Manfred O. Jelinski; **Editing**: Jörg Buttgereit, Manfred O. Jelinski, Franz Rodenkirchen.

Seven Blood-Stained Orchids (*Sette orchidee macchiate di rosso*, aka *Edgar Wallace – The Mystery of the Silver Half Moons*)
Italy, 1972 – 88 mins
Umberto Lenzi

Umberto Lenzi was one of the most prolific Italian film-makers of the 1960s and 70s. Some consider him an unsung maestro of lowbrow trash; others view him as an immoral, misogynistic, self-aggrandising hack. In either case, his body of work remains historically significant because of how closely it followed popular trends in Italian genre cinema: spy films and spaghetti Westerns in the late 60s; *giallo* thrillers, *poliziotteschi* crime films and cannibal epics throughout the 70s. *Seven Blood-Stained Orchids* arrived at the peak of the *giallo* craze, and was one of eight that Lenzi directed between 1969 and 1975. An obscure title for many years – it received no US release until the advent of DVDs – *Orchids* now stands out as one of the most archetypal of all *gialli*, a textbook illustration of the genre's filmic conventions and literary influences.

Exuding an atmosphere of sleazy decadence, the plotline reads like a checklist of *giallo* trademarks. A mysterious, black-gloved killer is brutally murdering a string of women, always leaving a silver half-moon pendant as a calling card. When one of the women (Uschi Glas) survives, she sets out with her fashion designer husband (Antonio Sabata) to unmask the killer, discovering that all the victims were guests at the same hotel two years earlier. Clues are unearthed at a satisfyingly brisk pace, and Lenzi punctuates the narrative with the kind of violent murder set pieces that had by then become a stock-in-trade of *giallo* cinema – the showstopper being a spectacular death by power drill.

The film's lurid, pulpy vibe perfectly captures the spirit of the yellow-jacketed crime paperbacks from which *giallo* cinema derived its name, and *Orchids* remains a fascinating example of how these literary antecedents were adapted for 1970s' film audiences. Two of the most significant crime and mystery writers can, in fact, be cited as key influences on Lenzi's picture: Cornell Woolrich and Edgar Wallace.

The primary source material for *Orchids* was a 1948 Woolrich novel, *Rendezvous in Black*. In Woolrich's version of the story, a man's fiancée is killed on the eve of their wedding when she is struck by a bottle thrown from a charter plane full of drunken men. The groom vows revenge by killing, on the anniversary of his fiancée's death, the person most precious to each passenger. By turning one of the slated victims into the protagonist, and by concealing the motives and identity of the avenger until the end, we can see how Lenzi molded the Woolrich tale to more closely fit the conventions and expectations of early 70s' *giallo* cinema.

The connection to Edgar Wallace is more convoluted and controversial. *Orchids* was an Italian–German co-production, with the German backing provided by Rialto. Throughout the 1960s, Rialto produced a successful run of over thirty Wallace-inspired *krimi* films that were very influential on the development of Italian *giallo* cinema, often using similar mystery structures and devices. The *krimi* influence on *Orchids* is most apparent in the clue of the silver half-moons and in the casting of Uschi Glas, a veteran of numerous *krimis*.

In Germany, Rialto released *Orchids* under the title *Edgar Wallace – The Mystery of the Silver Half Moons*, but the film was not actually based on any specific Wallace writings — a fraudulent advertising gambit that can only be interpreted as Rialto's attempt to capitalise on the Wallace name. However, by 1972, the Italian *giallo* had all but usurped the German *krimi*, and, alongside another Wallace-inspired *giallo*, *What Have You Done to Solange?* (1972), *Orchids* was the final release of Rialto's Wallace series.   AS

Dir: Umberto Lenzi; **Prod**: Lamberto Palmieri; **Original Music**: Riz Ortolani; **Wr**: Roberto Gianviti, Paul Hengge (credited on German prints), Umberto Lenzi, Edgar Wallace (uncredited in Italian version), Cornell Woolrich (novel, uncredited); **Cinematography**: Angelo Lotti; **Editing**: Eugenio Alabiso, Clarissa Ambach (German version).

Short Night of the Glass Dolls (*La corta notte delle bambole di vetro*, aka *Malastrana*)
Italy/West Germany/Yugoslavia, 1972 – 92 mins
Aldo Lado

The directorial début of Aldo Lado, *Short Night of the Glass Dolls* stands at the crossroads of two distinct schools of film-making in Italy: the *giallo* mystery-thriller and the political art-house film. A quick scan of the principal cast and crew reveals the coming together of talents from both traditions: actors Jean Sorel, Barbara Bach and Mario Adorf were all familiar faces from other notable *gialli*, whereas cinematographer Giuseppe Ruzzolini was a longtime collaborator of Pier Paolo Pasolini and actress Ingrid Thulin was a veteran of nine Ingmar Bergman films. Lado had himself already straddled both traditions – earning a story credit on a Hitchcockian thriller, *The Designated Victim* (1970), and an assistant director credit on Bernardo Bertolucci's *The Conformist* (1970) – and this melding of styles would soon become a defining characteristic of his oeuvre.

Much like Lado's *Who Saw Her Die?* (1972) and *Night Train Murders* (1975), *Short Night of the Glass Dolls* uses horror and *giallo* conventions as political metaphors for class oppression and the moral corruption of the social elite. The result is an unconventional *giallo* that eschews the more sensationalist aspects of the genre – black-gloved killers, straight razors, bisexual fashion models, etc. – to focus on a mystery narrative with heavy leanings towards Hitchcock, Polanski, Kafka and Marx.

The central premise is itself lifted from the 'Breakdown' episode of *Alfred Hitchcock Presents* (1955), in which a paralysed man is mistaken for dead and has no way of communicating to the people around him. In Hitchcock's version, the paralysis is the result of a car crash; in Lado's hands, it is something altogether more ominous and politically charged. He structures the film as a series of memories that the man has while lying in a Prague morgue. We learn that he was an American journalist named Gregory Moore (Sorel), and that his girlfriend mysteriously vanished after a high-society party. When his investigation uncovers the truth of her disappearance, the film comes full circle and we finally learn the sinister reasons for his catalepsy.

The first clue to his political aspirations is Lado's choice of Prague as the setting for the story. Not only is it the birthplace of Kafka, but the Prague Spring of 1968 had occurred less than three years earlier, and Czechoslovakia was still struggling under Soviet occupation. Lado uses this social context to give familiar horror and *giallo* devices a highly allegorical, Kafkaesque set of meanings. The horror convention of being buried alive, for example, is used as a metaphor for the silencing of political dissidents; Moore begins the film as an apolitical, womanising journalist, and the disappearance of his girlfriend prompts a political awakening that is met with a response from the social elite that both literally and figuratively puts him back to sleep.

The main thrust of the film's social critique is that the ruling classes expend the bodies of the young as a fuel to maintain power. To explore this theme, Lado borrows elements of the occultist conspiracy from *Rosemary's Baby* (1968), depicting the elderly elite as a secret society that engages in orgies where they literally feast on the blood of the young. Lado also redeploys the use of insect symbolism that was widespread in *giallo* films, employing a recurring motif of flightless butterflies as a symbol of the oppression of vibrant, freedom-seeking youth. Moore's girlfriend – a free spirit whose name, Mira Svodoba (Bach), connotes peace and freedom in Slavic – is herself closely aligned with the butterfly motif and functions as an embodiment of the youth movement. As a result, her mysterious disappearance and Moore's subsequent limbo between life and death serve as potent metaphors for life in a post-1968 Prague. AS

Dir: Aldo Lado; **Prod**: Enzo Doria, Luciano Volpato, Dieter Geissler; **Original Music**: Ennio Morricone; **Wr**: Aldo Lado, Ruediger von Spiess (additional dialogue); **Cinematography**: Giuseppe Ruzzolini; **Editing**: Jutta Brandstaedter, Mario Morra.

Spirits of the Dead (aka *Histoires extraordinaires*)

France/Italy, 1967 –120 mins

Federico Fellini, Louis Malle, Roger Vadim

Spirits of the Dead comprises three films based on stories by Edgar Allan Poe. The first of the three, 'Metzengerstein', directed by Roger Vadim, is set in a vague medieval past and focuses on the rivalry between two ancient families, the Metzengersteins and the Berlifitzings. The sadistic, licentious Contessa Fréderique von Metzengerstein (Jane Fonda) develops an incestuous passion for her rival, the animal-loving Wilhelm von Berlifitzing, aptly played by Peter Fonda. When Wilhelm refuses her advances, the Contessa exacts a cruel revenge, which only returns, supernaturally, to bring about her own destruction. 'William Wilson', the second film, directed by Louis Malle, connects with the first in its sadistic protagonist and in its use of the *doppelgänger* motif. Set in the nineteenth century, the titular character (Alain Delon) wins a game of cards against a bold woman, Giuseppina (Brigitte Bardot); he cheats to win, but is exposed by his double, who has dogged him incessantly, and whom he subsequently battles to the death. The spectacular final episode, 'Toby Dammit', directed by Federico Fellini, is based on Poe's story, 'Never Bet the Devil Your Head', but its setting is contemporary. The title character, played by Terence Stamp, is a celebrated British actor on assignment in Italy to make a film. He is a compulsive gambler and heavy drinker who makes the ultimate wager with the Devil – depicted as a blonde-haired little girl with a red bouncing ball, an idea derived from Mario Bava's *Kill, Baby . . . Kill!* (1966) – that he can drive his Ferrari across the divide of a collapsed bridge.

When eventually released in the United States by American International Pictures in 1969, the film enjoyed the distinction of being that country's first R-rated horror movie. American International, famously, had been the distributor of Roger Corman's series of films based on Poe's works, none of which had been rated 'R'. Unlike Corman's films,

Spirits of the Dead has a distinctly European sensibility; *Histoires extraordinaires* was the title Charles Baudelaire gave to his first volume of Poe translations (1856) and had also been used as the title of a 1949 film that contained adaptations of Poe stories, directed by Jean Faurez.

Spirits of the Dead forever altered the way the cinema adapted Edgar Allan Poe. With this film, Poe's work suddenly became dark and dangerous, featuring self-destructive and death-obsessed characters, riddles to themselves and others. Although Vadim's episode, for example, was set in the historical past, its stars were modern if not avant-garde. Its style was modern, experimental and innovative hence its influence cannot be under-estimated. The most celebrated of the three adaptations is 'Toby Dammit', which, in order to capture his protagonist's disorientation and self-loathing, employs a delirious, hallucinatory style that Fellini himself seldom matched in his subsequent films.   RU and SU

Dir: Federico Fellini, Louis Malle, Roger Vadim; **Prod**: Raymond Eger, Alberto Grimaldi; **Original Music**: Diego Masson (Segment 'William Wilson'), Jean Prodromidès (Segment 'Metzengerstein'), Nino Rota (Segment 'Toby Dammit'); **Wr**: (Segment 'Metzengerstein') Edgar Allan Poe (story), Roger Vadim, Pascal Cousin, Daniel Boulanger (Segment 'William Wilson') Edgar Allan Poe, Louis Malle, Clement Biddle Wood, Daniel Boulanger (Segment 'Toby Dammit') Edgar Allan Poe, Federico Fellini, Bernardino Zapponi; **Cinematography**: Tonino Delli Colli (Segment 'William Wilson'), Claude Renoir (Segment 'Metzengerstein'), Giuseppe Rotunno (Segment 'Toby Dammit'); **Editing**: Franco Arcalli (Segment 'William Wilson'), Suzanne Baron (Segment 'William Wilson'), Ruggero Mastroianni (Segment 'Toby Dammit'), Hélène Plemiannikov (Segment 'Metzengerstein').

The Stendhal Syndrome (La sindrome di Stendhal)
Italy, 1996 – 119 mins
Dario Argento

Dario Argento's *The Stendhal Syndrome* is named for a psychosomatic condition first described by the writer Stendhal (pseudonym of Marie-Henri Beyle), who, while visiting Florence in 1817, became dazed and emotional at the sight of Giotto's ceiling frescoes. Argento's daughter Asia plays Anna Manni, a police detective who has been assigned to track down a serial rapist-murderer in Florence. Afflicted with the syndrome at the Uffizi Gallery, where she hallucinates that paintings come to life, Anna is assisted by a seemingly helpful bystander who turns out to be the rapist; he soon turns her into his victim instead, stalking, kidnapping and raping her. Although she eventually frees herself and kills her assailant, Anna internalises the violence directed against her. In a state of psychosis, she alters her appearance and 'becomes' the rapist, murdering men as he had murdered women.

The Stendhal Syndrome departs from the Italian cinematic tradition of the *giallo* (after the yellow jackets of thriller novels) that Argento as Italy's premier horror auteur perfected in the 1970s and 80s (following forerunners like Mario Bava, Riccardo Freda and Lucio Fulci). The film is a hybrid: a psycho-thriller concerned with sexual violence against women but also, and most literally, an art film that weaves a vast range of canonical paintings into its sets and story. It shifts the *giallo*'s focus on *who* done it to the *effects* of violence, revealing its maniac's identity from the start and dispensing with the trademark black gloves and trench coat the *giallo* uses to keep us guessing. While *giallo* murders are extravagantly amoral set pieces aimed more at aesthetic pleasure than empathy, here the film invites us to identify with a psychologically developed protagonist experiencing chilling sexual violence.

Incompatible though *The Stendhal Syndrome*'s genres may seem, they become inextricably connected in the film. Not only does Anna first

Identity crisis: Asia Argento in *The Stendhal Syndrome*

encounter her assailant in the Uffizi Gallery (where Argento was the first director ever permitted to film), but the world of art represented there already mirrors the gendered and violent world of the story. After passing by masculine images of warfare (like Paolo Uccelli's *Battle of San Romano*) and Botticellian femininity, Anna is riveted by Caravaggio's painting of the decapitated Medusa, whose look of shock and rage anticipates Anna's own violation.

Her hallucinatory immersion into the sea depicted in Breughel's *Landscape with the Fall of Icarus* prefigures Anna's incremental loss of self throughout the film. *The Stendhal Syndrome* consistently connects Anna's assault by, and eventual fusion with, her pursuer to her erotic, symbiotic experience of art; the rapist is at once *art* lover and art *lover* who will catalyse a radical transference between the two characters. Hence, the film's two genres are really one that takes to an extreme the dialectic pervading Argento's work, in which violence has always been about beauty and beauty about violence.

The Stendhal Syndrome is unique in the radicality with which it relates aesthetics, culture and violence, but also in its having a feminist dimension that critiques patriarchy. While Argento, breaking with a tradition of Italian horror often maligned for its misogyny, has consistently challenged gender categories, his films normally eschew explicit social commentary. Far from a 'social action' film, however, *The Stendhal Syndrome* shows patriarchy as an all-consuming structure whose unequal power distribution can be eluded by no one. In responding to it with her own gendered aggression, the protagonist remains entrapped in its logic, repeating rather than escaping violence.   LSS

Dir: Dario Argento; **Prod:** Dario Argento, Giuseppe Colombo, Walter Massi; **Original Music:** Ennio Morricone; **Wr:** Dario Argento, Franco Ferrini, Graziella Magherini (novel); **Cinematography:** Giuseppe Rotunno; **Editing:** Angelo Nicolini.

Succubus (aka *Necronomicon – Geträumte Sünden* [*Necronomicon – Dreamt Sin*])
West Germany, 1968 – 82 mins
Jesús Franco

The Spaniard Jesús Franco, usually billed as 'Jess Franco', may be the most prolific film-maker since the silent era. Devotees claim that only by watching his entire output can his vision be appreciated. This is perhaps an impossible task: it may be that even the director hasn't seen *all* his films. The genres he most often returns to are horror and pornography, and much of his most distinctive work fits into an overlap between the two, frequently with Sadean or fetish themes – which makes him (along with Jean Rollin) one of the most oft-censored of major genre directors.

Succubus, shot in Lisbon and Berlin (presented as one composite European city), is one of a clutch of films Franco made with the mannish,

'Would you care for some whipping with your chains?': Jesus Franco's *Succubus*

inexpressive nudie star Janine Reynaud. It is hard to position in any particular genre: its macabre elements are too slight for horror, its sexuality too peculiar for porno (even as a limited-market 'kink' film it doesn't deliver) and its artiness is couched in exploitation terms (one trailer tries to sell the film with 'First, *La dolce vita* . . . now, *Succubus*!').

The film opens with redhead Lorna Green (Reynaud) as a dominatrix/torturer, tormenting, fondling and stabbing a chained-up man (Americo Coimbra) and a blonde woman, then reveals that this is artifice, a nightclub act analogous to striptease. Lorna's sense of reality is crumbling anyway: she's having an affair with Bill (Jack Taylor), her manager, but is apparently being mind-controlled by a sinister stranger (Michel Lemoine). It's a matter of debate as to how 'real' various scenes and incidents in the film are. There's a double reveal towards the end when it seems Bill and the Stranger are in league to kill Lorna, maybe as part of a spy plot from one of the other Franco-Reynaud films, but it turns out Bill is the intended victim, executed by Lorna. Even that's provisional.

What Franco is mostly interested in is staging more surreal, perverse sequences that just barely count as stripteases (a party where Reynaud strips while on the floor, only to be attacked by guests in animal masks, actually is an imitation of a scene in Fellini's *La dolce vita* [1960]) or horror. Lorna takes a female lover (Nathalie Lord) to her castle, but embraces turn to menace and mannequins seem to come to life (an effect at once disturbing and comical) and attack the other woman. Slathered between 'exploitable' elements are word games (Lorna has to give instant reactions to dropped names from Hitchcock and Henry Miller through Charlie Mingus and de Sade to Kafka and Godard) and references to popular culture (a pan across a row of Aurora monster hobby kits, with Lemoine – posing like Boris Karloff – added as a supposedly worthy new addition to the pantheon of Dracula, Godzilla, the Phantom and company). Franco works too fast to think about his films too much, which at best gives them an oneiric, hypnotic feel –

augmented here by an excellent mix of jazz and classical musical
arrangements on the soundtrack.   KN

Dir: Jesús Franco; **Prod**: Pier A. Caminnecci, Adrian Hoven; **Original Music**: Friedrich Gulda,
Jerry van Rooyen; **Wr**: Pier A. Caminnecci; **Cinematography**: Jorge Herrero, Franz Xaver
Lederle; **Editing**: Frizzi Schmidt.

Suspiria
Italy, 1977 – 97 mins
Dario Argento

Perhaps Dario Argento's most satisfying work both in the conventional terms of the horror genre and in terms of his own extraordinary vision, *Suspiria* was the director's first supernatural Gothic tale after four stylish *giallo* slasher movies. Like them, *Suspiria* was calculated for international, especially US distribution, released through 20th Century-Fox, starring newcomer Jessica Harper alongside Fritz Lang's favourite Hollywood actress, the venerable Joan Bennett, late of TV's Gothic soap opera *Dark Shadows* (1966). The script, co-written by Argento's frequent collaborator and former lover, actress Daria Nicolodi, was conceived as part of a trilogy, as yet uncompleted, whose second chapter was 1980's *Inferno*.

American dancer Suzy Banyon (Harper) arrives at a German academy where bizarre events lead to grisly murders. Her investigation reveals that the school's weird staff comprises a coven of witches headed by an ancient sorceress named Helena Marcos. Venturing into the school's hidden recesses, Suzy manages to kill 'The Black Queen' and flee as the structure erupts in flames, the classic Gothic finale. The plot is traditional, the form spectacular. *Suspiria* was shot on Eastman colour stock but printed on an old three-strip Technicolor printer and further manipulated in the laboratory – pushing Argento's characteristic *mise en scène* of bright, saturated colours to Expressionistic extremes.

Witches aside, *Suspiria*'s two most astonishing murder scenes suggest the work of a driven psychopath, particularly the massacre of two female students in their upper-floor apartment. The pounding electronic score (performed by Argento's group, Goblin) drives a spectacle of sadistic overkill in which the repeated slashing and stabbing of the first victim includes views inside her body of the knife piercing her quivering heart. In a later scene, another woman is trapped in an attic room as the killer – seen only as a probing straight-razor manipulating the latch – tries to break in. (A black-caped figure glimpsed striding down a dark hallway is likely Argento himself, varying his pattern of substituting his own hands in close-ups for those of his killers.) She escapes by piling up trunks to reach a high window, but jumps down to land in a surreal, blue-tinted room inexplicably filled floor to ceiling with coils of barbed wire that entangle her before a knife held in gloved hands slits her throat. The murder itself seems anti-climactic in comparison to the brilliant setting, sound and montage editing.

Because of *Suspiria*, Argento's films have all been successfully distributed in the US, but remain unacknowledged influences on the American slasher cycle that seemingly emerged full-grown with John Carpenter's *Halloween* (1978). The Italian maestro was years ahead of Carpenter in unsettling the audience through sustained identification with a prowling camera assumed to be the killer's vision. Yet Argento manipulates moving camera and point-of-view shots that are often only ambiguously attached to any particular character. The jarring technique matches the convoluted plots, which become no less disorienting for their wildly illogical 'explanations'. Helena Marcos's academy was originally 'a sort of school of dance and occult sciences', we are told – surely one attracting a very precise student profile! No matter, *Suspiria*'s attraction is its visual splendour and perversely inventive violence.   RW

Dir: Dario Argento; **Prod**: Claudio Argento, Salvatore Argento; **Original Music**: Dario Argento, Goblins; **Wr**: Thomas De Quincey (novel, uncredited), Dario Argento, Daria Nicolodi; **Cinematography**: Luciano Tovoli; **Editing**: Franco Fraticelli.

The Tenant (*Le Locataire*)
France, 1976 – 126 mins
Roman Polanski

The Tenant was the last thing anyone expected Roman Polanski would choose to follow up the success of *Chinatown* (1974). A relatively low-budget claustrophobic Kafkaesque horror film about a man who loses his identity and his sanity when he becomes convinced that there is a conspiracy to 'turn him into' the previous occupant of his apartment and drive him to duplicate her suicide? Hardly the stuff of blockbusters. But Polanski always evinced a tendency to balance his commercial works with distinctly personal ones – and no film in his *oeuvre* qualifies as more personal than *The Tenant*.

Not surprisingly, it met with a good deal of critical hostitlity upon its original release. Viewers expecting another *Chinatown* were disappointed (to put it mildly). Paramount, who probably only agreed to handle the project on the strength of *Rosemary's Baby* (1968) and *Chinatown*, had no idea what to do with the picture. It was a horror film, but it wasn't like any horror film they had dealt with before, and it had no stars. All it had was the Polanski name, so they settled on a vague ad campaign and the ludicrous tagline, 'Nobody does it to you like Roman Polanski' (a phrase that would take on new significance about a year later when Polanski was charged with having sex with a minor).

Even hardcore Polanski fans tended to shy away from *The Tenant*, finding it something of an unsatisfactory rehash of his first English-language film *Repulsion* (1965), with Polanski's Trelkovsky character a most unsatisfactory replacement for Catherine Deneuve's Carole Ledoux. The irony in this view lies in the fact that *Repulsion* had been a commercial undertaking to allow Polanski the wherewithal to make the more personal *Cul-de-sac* (1966). There is an undeniable similarity between the two films – both deal with the descent of the main character into madness – but taken as part of Polanski's overall body of work, *Repulsion* seems more like a rough sketch for the more accomplished later film.

Polanski and his usual writing partner Gerard Brach adapted a moderately effective novel by Roland Topor for the screenplay, transforming it into something extraordinary – a film that works on so many layers and levels that there never has been, and probably never can be, a definitive reading of it. As a result, it remains a strangely impenetrable work that refuses to give up all its mysteries no matter how closely one studies it. Perhaps the only horror film comparable to it in this regard is Stanley Kubrick's *The Shining* (1980), which, according to cinema legend, was born of Kubrick's desire to make a film like *The Tenant*.

Polanski's decision to play the lead gives the film part of its resonance, referring back to his own position as an outsider in France. It is impossible not to see something of Polanski's comment that one is always reminded of being a foreigner in Paris ('If you park your car wrong, it is not the fact that it's on the sidewalk that matters, but the fact that you speak with an accent') at every turn in the film. Little digs at his not being French are peppered throughout the movie, despite his every effort to blend in or be inconspicuous. In many ways, it's the image of a man driven to insanity simply because he's different from those around him. The over-the-top, almost operatic climax is as much the act of breaking out of his self-effacing persona as it is the final spiral into madness. Yet that is a simplification of a very complex narrative that, at bottom, questions the very essence of identity in the most chilling terms imaginable.

In some ways – most notably the abysmal dubbing of the non-English-speaking cast members – *The Tenant* is an awkward work, but it makes up for it in so many other ways that this hardly matters. The theatricality of its apartment-house setting (especially the courtyard), the

(Next page) Polanski directs himself in *The Tenant*

myriad cross-references to Polanski's other films, the rich, dark images of Sven Nykvist's camerawork, Philippe Sarde's haunting score and Polanski's incredibly brave performance all make it the director's finest and most complex horror film.   KH

Dir: Roman Polanski; **Prod**: Andrew Braunsberg; **Original Music**: Philippe Sarde; **Cinematography**: Sven Nykvist; **Wr**: Gerard Brach, Roman Polanski, Roland Topor (novel); **Art**: Pierre Guffroy; **Editing**: Françoise Bonnot.

Tenebre (Tenebrae, aka Unsane, aka Sotto gli occhi dell'assassino [Under the Eyes of the Assassin])
Italy, 1982 – 101 mins
Dario Argento

After two successive forays into supernatural horror territory (*Suspiria* [1977]; *Inferno* [1980]) that left fans begging for a closing chapter to the Three Mothers trilogy, Dario Argento surprisingly opted instead to return to the *giallo* which, by all accounts, had found its defining masterpiece with his own *Deep Red* (1975) and largely exhausted itself by the late 1970s. The result was a highly recursive and self-reflexive thriller, not to mention an over-the-top gory exercise, that radically revisited the genre by stretching its very limits.

The plot revolves around American crime writer Peter Neal (Anthony Franciosa) flying to Italy to promote his latest bestseller. It soon transpires that a criminal psychopath is using the eponymous book as a blueprint to eradicate what he perceives as human perversion. The body count baffles the police and Neal starts to investigate on his own. The last third of a particularly convoluted narrative, whose innumerable red herrings and identity instability far exceed the conventions of a typical *giallo*, provides a double whammy. Neal turns out to be an opportunistic maniac who stepped into the initial murderer's shoes (after eliminating him) in order to get rid of his ex-wife and her lover (a literal exemplification of the generic premise that a killer can hide another). After a fake suicide with the help of a movie prop razor, he suddenly resurrects into full view from behind a police inspector as the latter stoops down – a visual conflation of perpetrator and victim.

Argento further draws attention to the film-making process with other bravura moments and visual pyrotechnics, including an extended Louma crane sequence scored to the pounding music of regular collaborator Claudio Simonetti (from Italian prog-rock band, Goblins): the camera continuously pans over an entire apartment building, in and out of windows, before the killer breaks in and the diegetic source of the soundtrack is disclosed. The art of murder (fetishisation of violence and aestheticisation of death) is also elevated to new baroque, albeit self-conscious heights, as when a female victim's hacked-off arm spurts out blood and paints an unexpected fresco on a white wall.

Foregoing the lush Technicolor, Expressionistic extravaganza of *Suspiria* or *Inferno*, as well as the classical antiquities of 'Eternal Rome', Argento adopted here a new visual aesthetic influenced by Andrej Zulawski's *Possession* (1981). Alternating starkly lit, monochromatic interiors with open urban spaces and ultra-modern structures washed in bright sunlight, it not only ironically contrasts with the titular darkness (which is thus to be construed as primarily mental), but obliquely resonates with a bleak *Zeitgeist* (renewed violence in the latter half of the infamous Lead Years) generally absent from the director's previous efforts.

Last but not least, gender politics is even more pronounced than is customary for an Argento *giallo*, from the volatile lesbian couple (one of the women ferociously reviling the misogyny of Neal's books, while the other defiantly experiments with a caricature of heterosexuality in the guise of a muscular pinball player) to the almost camply effete figure cut by Christiano Berti and, most prominently, the mysterious woman wearing red shoes, played by a transsexual and obsessively featured in seemingly non-diegetic inserts that viewers gradually come to identify as flashbacks to an original trauma.   PM

Dir: Dario Argento; **Prod**: Claudio Argento, Salvatore Argento; **Original Music**: Goblins, Massimo Morante, Fabio Pignatelli, Claudio Simonetti; **Wr**: Dario Argento; **Cinematography**: Luciano Tovoli; **Editing**: Franco Fraticelli.

Thesis (*Tesis*)
Spain, 1996 – 125 mins
Alejandro Amenábar

Written and directed by Alejandro Amenábar, *Thesis* is a constantly intriguing example of self-reflexive horror. It reflects on itself, and on its own construction, by examining themes that characterise the horror genre: spectatorship and voyeurism; the desire to see shocking, violent and repulsive media images; the assumed pathology of horror audiences. Tackling such themes helped *Thesis* win international acclaim outside its Spanish production context, and launch Amenábar's career. Following *Thesis*, the auteur film-maker made his Hollywood début with *The Others* (2001), and went on to win a Best Foreign Language Film Academy Award for *The Sea Inside* (2004).

    Thesis's focus on so-called 'snuff' movies which claim to depict actual deaths doesn't pull any punches. Opening with a sequence which confronts the viewer with their assumed interest in seeing a gory incident

The science of snuff: Alejandro Amenábar's *Thesis*

– but then withholding any visual 'pay-off' – *Thesis* marks out its intent to challenge audiences from the word go. This is self-reflexive Euro-horror for the media-literate film-school generation and, as such, is set in a University School of Mass Communications. Its characters are film students or professors; some are even horror fans. Ángela Márquez (Ana Torent) is writing her dissertation on 'audiovisual violence', and she's aided by the geeky horror connoisseur Chema (Fele Martínez), who lends her movies from his collection. However, at the same time that Angela is studying snuff, students are mysteriously going missing from the university and somebody is making their own snuff films.

Following in the realist, self-reflexive footsteps of Michael Powell's British shocker *Peeping Tom* (1960), '*Thesis* has some pretensions to being taken seriously . . . [It] has a thesis'.[14] The film argues that stereotyping horror fans as weird is sheer hypocrisy because the desire to witness media violence is far more socially widespread. Its narrative ends with a snuff movie being broadcast and TV presenters warning viewers that they may be shocked. Angela and Chema – and by implication the horror fan audience – are positioned as highly moral observers who can see the hypocrisy and desire of the slack-jawed mass audience surrounding them. By contrast, it is Chema and Angela who have bravely sought to put an end to the snuff movie-maker's grim work. Even here, the writer–director of *Thesis* places himself within the frame, once again challenging viewers to consider their own complicity and voyeurism: 'Angela uses an electrical store's database to ascertain who might have bought the camera she believes was used to create the snuff video – one of the names on the list is Alejandro Amenábar.'[15]   MH

Dir: Alejandro Amenábar; **Prod**: Alejandro Amenábar, Hans Burman, Wolfgang Burmann, José Luis Cuerda, Júlio Madurga, Emiliano Otegui, María Elena Sáinz de Rozas; **Original Music**: Alejandro Amenábar, Mariano Marín; **Wr**: Alejandro Amenábar, Mateo Gil; **Cinematography**: Hans Burman; **Editing**: María Elena Sáinz de Rozas.

Tombs of the Blind Dead (*La noche del terror ciego*, aka *Crypt of the Blind Dead*, aka *Night of the Blind Dead*)
Spain/Portugal, 1972 – 101 mins
Amando de Ossorio

Following the success of George Romero's *Night of the Living Dead* (1968), it was inevitable that Spain would develop its own series of zombie films with its own unique mythology. Of the four *Blind Dead* directed by Amando de Ossorio, *Tombs of the Blind Dead* is clearly the best, as it introduces the undead Templar Knights to an unsuspecting populace.

Tombs focuses on three travellers in Lisbon and their misadventures: Virginia White (Elena Arpon), her old roommate Betty Turner (Lone Fleming) and Virginia's beau Roger Whelan (Cesar Burner). When Roger starts to take an interest in Betty, Virginia decides to do some exploring of her own in an abandoned monastery. Unfortunately, when night falls, blind zombies rise from their tombs and bite Virginia to death. Betty and Roger slowly uncover the history behind the monastery. Apparently, the ancient Templar Knights resided there and performed satanic rituals in their quest to become immortal. The townspeople decided to take the law into their own hands and hanged the knights from trees, allowing the crows to pluck out their eyes. Fearing that the Templar Knights will continue their blood sacrifices to the devil, Betty and Roger return to the monastery and encounter the monsters. Roger dies protecting Betty and the girl manages to escape the same fate by boarding a train. Unfortunately, the zombies have followed her and subsequently kill all the passengers, leaving her in a hysterical state as the credits roll.

One can detect similarities between *Tombs of the Blind Dead* and *Night of the Living Dead*, including the principal heroine being driven mad, the zombies' bites making dead humans into the undead (e.g., the 'reactivated' Virginia) and fire being one of the ways of destroying these creatures. However, Ossorio should be credited for making his zombies far more interesting than Romero's. While blind, they can target their victims by hearing their heartbeats. And they ride undead horses that allow them to move about the countryside very quickly. The religious themes should not be overlooked in *Tombs* either. Gregorian chants are played as the Templar Knights make their entrance; further, hoods cover up their skeletal faces, reminding viewers they were once monks who turned to the dark side.

The three sequels, *Return of the Blind Dead* (1973), *Ghost Galleon* (1975) and *Night of the Seagulls* (1976), take liberties with the origins of the Blind Dead. For instance, in *Return of the Blind Dead*, the villagers burn out the eyes of the Templar Knights before torching them to death. While the pace might be quicker in these sequels, the original *Tombs of the Blind Dead* remains the superior film in building the suspense as these creatures slowly rise from their graves to prey upon the living. For zombie aficionados, *Tombs* is a must-see film. JI

Dir: Amando de Ossorio; **Prod**: José Antonio Pérez Giner, Salvadore Romero; **Original Music**: Antón García Abril; **Wr**: Amando de Ossorio, Jesús Navarro Carrión (additional dialogue); **Cinematography**: Pablo Ripoll; **Editing**: José Antonio Rojo.

Torso (aka *I corpi presentano tracce di violenza carnale* [*Bodies Bear Traces of Carnal Violence*], aka *Carnal Violence*)

Italy, 1973 – 90 mins
Sergio Martino

Sergio Martino's 1973 *giallo Torso* is a significant departure from his earlier cycle of city-set paranoid *gialli* that made his name. Nearly all featuring the actress Edwige Fenech, these preceding films were associated with the cosmopolitan and stylistic excesses that Fenech brought to the movies through her star persona. Paring down the excess of his Fenech vehicles, like Mario Bava two years before him in *Twitch of the Death Nerve*, *Torso* is the closest the *giallo* comes to being a prototype for the American slasher movie. *Torso*'s deployment of the point-of-view shot and the ferocity and frequency of the effects-driven murders confirm the *giallo*'s predating of its US relative. The brevity of *Torso*'s plot doesn't require much description here, as there are few events on which to sketch out its series of languid erotic encounters and grisly sexual murders.

Set in the Italian medieval university town of Perugia, the educational hub for international students, *Torso* opens with an unexplained softcore *ménage à trois* that sets the scene for the film's predilection for the perverse – only for the scene to be punctuated by an educational voice-over narration explaining Perugino's painting of Saint Sebastian, a potent icon of erotic and masochistic male suffering. As the professor (John Richardson) is introduced in the next scene, his conversation with an American student, Carol (Suzy Kendall), sets up a provocative question that challenges her to consider whether Perugino was himself 'a painter or a butcher'. No coincidence then, that this snippet of dialogue should be so reflexive in nature as to beg a key question about Martino and the *giallo* genre. Reframed, this question is literally asking us to consider the genre as either 'art' or 'exploitation'. The answer, of course, is both. While *Torso* flirts with several heavy doses of softcore titillation, in its

final half-hour the film cranks up the mechanics of suspense and violence in an elongated sequence where Carol becomes trapped in a hilltop villa in a cat-and-mouse game with the killer – who turns out to be the professor. This sequence of prolonged entrapment and bodily dismemberment is itself echoed in later European horrors such as *High Tension* (2003), where a similar suspenseful set-up on the staircase and retreat into the bedroom wardrobe ensues.

What *Torso* lacks in *giallo*-logic ratiocination, it makes up for through its pervasive air of threatening sexual menace. *Torso* recasts rural Italy as a hot-bed of libidinously perverse males, whose every gesture is aimed at the female student populace along with Martino's openly voyeuristic camera. The killer's denouement reveals that he was originally being blackmailed by his female students after partaking in a threesome, triggering a traumatic childhood event where he witnessed a childhood friend falling to his death over a cliff while trying to rescue a doll. Unable to distinguish between women and dolls, the killer perceives both to be threatening to the security of his male ego – and therefore they must be destroyed. In true *giallo* fashion, it has no real psychoanalytic basis, but makes for yet another madcap explanation for the genre's parade of damaged male psychopaths.   GN

Dir: Sergio Martino; **Prod**: Antonio Levesi Cervi, Carlo Ponti; **Original Music**: Guido De Angelis, Maurizio De Angelis; **Wr**: Lewis E. Ciannelli (English dialogue), Ernesto Gastaldi, Sergio Martino; **Cinematography**: Giancarlo Ferrando; **Editing**: Eugenio Alabiso.

(Opposite page) A shocking discovery in Sergio Martino's *Torso*

Trouble Every Day
France/Germany/Japan, 2001 – 101 mins
Claire Denis

Despite the absence of a genre-driven horror film tradition in French cinema, every so often a French shocker comes along that breaks with both national and genre conventions. In this case, Claire Denis – not only a rare example of a woman directing a European horror film, but also a prominent art-cinema auteur certainly not associated with the bloody Grand Guignol excesses of this rethinking of vampire mythology. *Trouble Every Day* also fits neatly into recent French film-making trends – dubbed as a 'cinema of the margins' – that have given birth to such noteworthy productions as *Irreversible* (2002), *High Tension* (2003) and *In My Skin* (2002).

Trouble Every Day's art film credentials might leave genre fans with numerous unanswered questions about the real origin of Denis's bloodsuckers – possibly the victims of pharmaceutical experiments. Denis's trademark elliptical narrative structures, dangling causes in the narrative, decentred camerawork and aesthetic over-investment in abstractions of the human body (with notable cinematographer Agnès Godard) elevate the contemporary vampire film from the Gothic trappings and alternative music subcultures towards an intellectual and formal sophistication more akin to the art-cinema sensibility.

Trouble Every Day recounts how two individuals separated by the Atlantic suffer from an identical illness defined as an uncontrollable sexual bloodlust: an American scientist, Shane Brown (played with compelling unease by Vincent Gallo), and a French doctor's wife, Coré (Béatrice Dalle, whose non-verbal performance of animalistic sexual terror quotes her *Betty Blue* [1986] persona and takes it to a new level of psychotic excess). Doctor Sémenau (Alex Descas) connects both figures, as husband to Coré and professional peer to Brown; however, the plot reveals little of why these characters are connected and what drives them to a sexual desire only satisfied through blood and cannibalism.

Far from rendering her two monsters as human, existing outside the confines of the horror genre, Denis cleverly reworks the key characters of vampire mythology – the count and the succubus – giving them a modern twist not only through the clever casting of the eccentric Gallo, and of course Béatrice Dalle, but by elaborating on the sexual nature of vampirisim itself, an aspect that has usually been repressed in more conventional vampire films. Gallo's American in Paris has to masturbate in order to repress his vampiric urges; the film also features that other taboo body fluid in a simulated cum-shot, until his need to feed results in his attack on the hotel chambermaid where cunnilingus quickly turns to cannibalism.

Even more frenzied and explicit is the film's bloody centrepiece, where Dalle seduces a young house burglar with the lure of her naked body, only to pin him to the bed as she chews off parts of his neck and lip. The latter sequence is a real *tour de force* of abject body horror as blood clots and fingers slide under flaps of torn skin and Dalle licks away at the bloodied swollen face of her male victim. It is probably the shocking explicitness of this central sequence as much as the film's unexpected place in Denis's filmography that led to *Trouble Every Day* being the *enfant terrible of* the 2001 Cannes Film Festival – giving both Cronenberg and Gasper Noé the year off.   GN

Dir: Claire Denis; **Prod**: Georges Benayoun, Françoise Guglielmi, Philippe Liégeois, Kazuko Mio, Jean-Michel Rey, Seiichi Tsukada; **Original Music**: Tindersticks; **Wr**: Claire Denis, Jean-Pol Fargeau; **Cinematography**: Agnès Godard; **Editing**: Nelly Quettier.

Twitch of the Death Nerve (aka *Reazione a catena* [*Chain Reaction*], aka *A Bay of Blood*, aka *Antefatto, Before the Fact – Ecology of a Crime*, aka *Bloodbath Bay of Death*, aka *Carnage*, aka *Last House on the Left Part II*, aka *New House on the Left*, aka *The Ecology of a Crime*)

Italy, 1971 – 90 mins
Mario Bava

It has been suggested that the slasher film of the late 1970s and early 1980s owed a debt of gratitude to Mario Bava's *Twitch of the Death Nerve*, particularly the first two *Friday the 13th* films (1980, 1981). While it is certainly true, like the *Friday*s, that Bava's film is set against the backdrop of a lakeside wilderness, and two of Bava's victims are impaled with a spear while making love (a murder which appears in *Friday the 13th Part II*), that *Twitch* is known *only* for this connection is unfair, as it needs to be appreciated on its own merits.

Like most Italian *giallo* films, *Twitch of the Death Nerve* is narratively complex, yet the story is ultimately irrelevant. For the first twenty minutes or so, we see a variety of murders by an unseen killer. We are given very little narrative in which to contextualise these victims. For example, we are introduced to four teenagers who arrive at a lakeside villa, break in, make love and are then killed. Their introduction implies they will become the film's protagonists, or at least that one might survive – but that is not the case, as they are quickly killed off. After twenty minutes or so of these random killings, Bava gives us a 'story' – if anyone watching the film is actually interested in a story: Renata (Claudine Auger) and Albert (Luigi Pistilli) want to inherit a substantive amount of lakeside property in order to develop the region for their own benefit, and are murdering anyone who might hinder this.

Twitch clusters its narrative explanations in the middle of the picture, thereby enabling the original Italian audience in the *terza visione* cinemas

– third-class cinemas in rural and working-class neighbourhoods – to talk among themselves and wander about the cinema as the cultural context warranted. Bava then calls the audience's attention back to the screen for the final twenty minutes, as Alberto and Renata kill anyone else left alive who stands in their way.

The film ends with one of Bava's most remarkable moments: with nothing to stop them owning the entire lakeland region, Renata and Albert, at their final moment of victory, are accidentally shot by their own children playing with a shotgun. This moment is one of horror cinema's most ironic moments – a burning-of-Rosebud from *Citizen Kane* (1941) for horror movies. And yet, this ending is fully in keeping with the film's themes, reflected by the original Italian title, *Reazione a catena* (literally 'chain reaction'): each death/murder has a reaction which, like falling dominoes, affects the next narrative moment. The accidental deaths of Albert and Renata are merely the final (that *we* see) reaction within this chain.

From the very beginning of the film, Bava – who more or less invented the *giallo* – plays with the genre's conventions: the opening sequence, of a wheelchair-bound countess being stalked and then hanged by a black-gloved killer, is a typical *giallo* opening. Bava undercuts this formula, however, by revealing that it was the count himself who murdered his wife, and is immediately killed himself by persons unknown. *Twitch* assumes its audience knows the genre's conventions, and Bava plays with them. *Twitch of the Death Nerve*, in the final analysis, can almost be considered an anti-*giallo*.   MJK

Dir: Mario Bava; **Prod**: Giuseppe Zaccariello; **Original Music**: Stelvio Cipriani; **Wr**: Franco Barberi, Mario Bava, Filippo Ottoni, Dardano Sacchetti, Giuseppe Zaccariello; **Cinematography**: Mario Bava; **Editing**: Carlo Reali.

Valerie and Her Week of Wonders (*Valerie a tyden divu*)
Czechoslovakia, 1970 – 77 mins
Jaromil Jires

A distinctly Czech horror-fantasy, Jaromil Jires' *Valerie and Her Week of Wonders* takes as its central theme the sexual awakening of the eponymous Valerie (fourteen-year-old Jaroslava Schallerová). Her initiation into adult sexuality is expressed through the nexus of three overlapping generic formations: horror, sexual fantasy and fairytale. This concoction produces a form of surrealism at once whimsical and disturbing, where nothing is what it seems and everything appears ambiguously over-determined.

As with many horror films, *Valerie* seeks to express the otherness of the sexual body, the family and desire, filtered through the psychoanalytic concepts of the unconscious and the Oedipus complex. As a tale of sexual initiation it also bears a resemblance to contemporary European softcore films focused on rites of passage into female sexuality, such as *Emmanuelle* (1974), *Bilitis* (1977) and *The Story of O* (1975). Like in these films, sexual initiation is located in the register of fairytale, taking place in a space that is marked clearly as 'fantasy', signified not just by the impossibility of events and the non-linear, elliptical organisation of space and time, but also through the presence of symbolic imagery. In evoking a 'fantasy' modality, wherein a magic circle is drawn around events, *Valerie* prompts viewers to suspend disbelief and accept what unfolds, no matter how irrational or impossible. The generic mix and the film's main themes create a heady brew tailored to the invocation of Valerie's subjective landscape and the mysteries and enigmas associated with the awakening of sexuality, which often change the way the world and other people are regarded.

Couched in a time-defying blend of medieval and Victorian iconography, Valerie's world becomes full of sensuous wonders and, like a heroine from a 'feminist' fairytale, she faces all with boldness and wide-eyed curiosity. Events circulate around a pair of earrings that have magical properties, given to her at the point she experiences her first period. Following the gift of the earrings, she enters into a convoluted family romance where various relatives either desire her sexually or try to destroy her through jealousy. She sees her grandmother have sex with a priest, her father returns as a Nosferatu-style vampire and she is nearly burned as a witch. As in a dream, these family figures transform in the blink of an eye. Events unfold around images of a medieval carnival; concealment and revelation express the duplicity and convoluted nature of desire. Mutation and transformation provide the film's stylistic and thematic core, as fathers and grandmothers turn into monsters and innocence gives way to experience.

The film can be read as the precursor of a particular type of horror that has emerged in the past few years to attract a predominantly female audience. As well as significant overlaps with Neil Jordan's *The Company of Wolves* (1984) – based on a story by Angela Carter, who herself saw *Valerie* and was deeply impressed by it – more recent magic-based popular media, exemplified by the *Ginger Snaps* trilogy (2000–4) and *Buffy the Vampire Slayer* (1999–2003), also deploy fairytale/horror milieux for expressing the transgressive, transformatory and titillating aspects of becoming a woman. However, none of these capture the poetic and seductive dark charms of *Valerie and Her Week of Wonders*.   TK

Dir: Jaromil Jires; **Prod**: Jirí Becka; **Original Music**: Lubos Fiser, Jan Klusák; **Wr**: Vitezslav Nezval (novel), Jaromil Jires, Ester Krumbachová, Jirí Musil; **Cinematography**: Jan Curík; **Editing**: Josef Valusiak.

(Next page) Coming of age in a world of wonder: *Valerie and Her Week of Wonders*

Vampyr (aka Vampyr – Der Traum des Allan Grey, aka The Strange Adventure of David Gray)
France/Germany, 1932 – 75 mins
Carl Theodor Dreyer

The Danish film-maker Carl Theodor Dreyer directed only fourteen feature films in a forty-two-year period. Three of these films could be classified as horror, but *Vampyr* is undoubtedly Dreyer's greatest genre achievement and a recognised classic of 1930s' cinema. However, when the film was premiered, in Berlin in May 1932, it was poorly received, and Dreyer was not to make another movie until *The Day of Wrath* (1943), a story of witchcraft.

Vampyr is marked by Dreyer's poetic style, used in this production to create a daydream effect, leaving the viewer uncertain and hesitating as to the nature of events: a narrative mode defined by Tzvetan Todorov as the 'fantastic'. In the film, which is loosely based on Joseph Sheridan Le Fanu's classic vampire story *Carmilla*, David Gray (or Allan Grey, played by Julian West) travels to a remote castle to the aid of two sisters who appear to have been infected by a blood-sucking vampire, an old woman who is later staked. Almost all the cast were non-professional actors, their expressive and haunting facial features enhancing the hypnotic feel of a film that is cloaked in a hazy and abstract style.

Vampyr is unlike its contemporaries, the Hollywood horrors *Doctor X* (1931), *Frankenstein* (1931) and *Freaks* (1932), which were dominating early sound horror production of the time. It eschews the obvious chiaroscuro effects and heavy shadows of those films for diffuse lighting and a floating camera style that slowly tracks and pans through a series of grey, misty-looking, ghostly images. The feeling of disassociated shots created by a deliberately disjointed editing style adds to the film's illusion of an other-worldly realm and, when contrasted with the scenes that are long and uninterrupted, it leaves the viewer distinctly unsettled.

As an early sound film, Dreyer employs dialogue sparingly (and even then words are spoken quietly), allowing both passages of silence and a soundtrack of strange noises to establish the atmosphere. The images are equally surreal: a one-legged man who climbs a ladder and whose shadow has independent movement; the death of the doctor (Jan Hieronimko) amid a cloud of white powder at a plaster mill; and the famous shot (partly a point-of-view) of Gray, conscious, lying in a coffin helpless as a windowed coffin lid is screwed down above him.

Vampyr's hallucinatory passages, mixing realism and fantasy, partly recall F. W. Murnau's *Nosferatu* (1922), with aspects observed in American genre classics such as *White Zombie* (1932) and *I Walked with a Zombie* (1943). The lyrical nature of *Vampyr*, with its long periods without dialogue and its manipulation of sound, is present too in the surrealist vampire films of French exploitation film-maker Jean Rollin, most notably *Requiem for a Vampire* (1971) and *Fascination* (1979), as well as the dark experimental films of David Lynch, in particular *Eraserhead* (1976). IC

Dir: Carl Theodor Dreyer; **Prod**: Carl Theodor Dreyer, Julian West; **Original Music**: Wolfgang Zeller; **Wr**: Joseph Sheridan Le Fanu (novel), Carl Theodor Dreyer, Christen Jul; **Cinematography**: Rudolph Maté, Louis Née; **Editing**: Paul Falkenberg.

The Vanishing (*Spoorloos*)
Netherlands/France, 1988 – 106 mins
George Sluizer

A highly praised and extremely disturbing exercise in psychological horror, *The Vanishing* is based on the novel *The Golden Egg* by Tim Krabbé, published in the Netherlands in 1984. The story revolves around the disappearance of a young woman, Saskia (Johanna ter Steege), who, during a vacation in France with her boyfriend Rex (Gene Bervoets), goes to get soft drinks at a petrol station and never returns. Three years later a seemingly mild-mannered French chemistry teacher, Raymond Lemorne (Bernard-Pierre Donnadieu), approaches Rex, who is still obsessed with Saskia's disappearance. Raymond admits to kidnapping, but not to killing Saskia, and promises to show Rex what happened to her – only if Rex agrees to accompany him to France and undergo the exact same experience. Rex hesitates, but finally takes the sedative offered by Raymond, and the film ends with the shocking twist of Rex waking up buried alive in a cramped coffin.

Critics have often noted the debt *The Vanishing* owes to the work of Alfred Hitchcock. Like Hitchcock's films, *The Vanishing* both surprises and frightens. The film opens with Saskia's disappearance, but this is immediately followed by a series of flashbacks that reveal the identity of the abductor. The story is told both from the point of view of Rex and the point of view of Raymond. As a result, *The Vanishing* invites viewers to ponder *how* and *why* Saskia disappeared, rather than who abducted her. The film builds suspense by letting the audience play God.

Furthermore, like Hitchcock's films, *The Vanishing* cultivates the kind of character involvement in which the viewer is 'lured' into identifying with a sympathetic character and feeling concerned about what might happen to him. We are driven by the same curiosity that drives Rex. At one point, Raymond explains that his only motivation for randomly kidnapping Saskia was because he was fascinated with the idea of tempting fate and the possibility of committing an act of pure evil.

The lady vanishes: George Sluizer's *The Vanishing*

Raymond challenges Rex to participate in an experiment according to which he is capable of profiting only if he puts himself in Raymond's hands, out of his own free will. Tormented by Saskia's fate, Rex agrees, and the viewer appreciates his decision. But Rex is a rather dull and uninspiring person, while Raymond is imaginative and out of the ordinary, a textbook example of perverse allegiance.

   The film arouses dual tensions by crosscutting between Rex and Raymond at a square in Nîmes where Raymond has – under a false name – agreed to meet Rex. Raymond observes Rex first on the balcony of his home opening into the square, and later in the café where Rex is waiting, unaware that he is being observed. The viewer, who now knows that Raymond has something to do with Saskia's disappearance, monitors the scene like a privileged witness, seeing the disparity in the two characters, and this contributes to the feeling of suspense throughout the film's dynamic narrative. This is a clever, suspenseful and complex tale of obsession and psychological motivation told in an unassuming and distanced manner, which creates a tension that is all the more disturbing because of it.   TJ

Dir: George Sluizer; **Prod**: Anne Lordon, George Sluizer; **Original Music**: Henny Vrienten; **Wr**: Tim Krabbé (also novel), George Sluizer; **Cinematography**: Toni Kuhn; **Editing**: Lin Friedman, George Sluizer.

Viy
Russia, 1967 – 80 mins
Georgi Kropachyov, Konstantin Yershov

Based on a short story by the legendary Russian satirist Nikolai Gogol, this singular horror masterpiece bills itself as an unembellished dramatisation of an old Cossack folk tale but could easily be hyped with more modern references: 'Spring Break Madness!' 'Seminarians go wild!'

The opening reel plays like the set-up to a joke: three theologians get lost in the woods and spend the night on a farm. One of them, a sort of medieval frat boy called Khoma Brutus (Leonid Kuravlyov), settles in for a night in the barn when the farmer's wife, a gnarly old hag, tries to seduce him. Disgusted, he resists – so she crawls on his back and starts riding him like a horse. When that bizarre activity gives way to her riding him more like, say, a kite, he starts to realise, oh, she's a witch. In the spirit of 'Thou shalt not suffer a witch to live', Khoma clubs the old crone to death. Only then does he discover that the battered corpse at his feet is actually that of the local aristocrat's daughter.

Kuravlyov looks a bit like Mickey Dolenz of the Monkees, with a loose-limbed goofy charm reminiscent of early Jackie Chan. His comic performance, and the light-hearted tone of these early scenes, can be misleading: co-directors Konstantin Yershov and Georgi Kropachyov plan on sucker-punching the audience by letting this gentle farce descend into total nightmare.

Khoma is now obliged to sit with the girl's corpse for three successive nights, reading scripture to her departing soul. It's a creepy enough assignment even without his guilty secret, but Khoma's problems are only just beginning. During the night, he is bedevilled by jaw-dropping visions of terror courtesy of special effects maestro Aleksander Ptushko. As dawn breaks and the spooks retreat back into hiding, the bleary-eyed theologian faces the most horrifying thing of all: *one down, two more to go*.

Up until this point, Khoma has been a pretty dismal ambassador of Christ. The locals deferentially call him 'philosopher', but the guy thinks his theological education is little more than an excuse for whoring and drinking. Asked what he's learned at the seminary, he answers with a pub trick. Now his own soul is at stake and his only defence is a Bible he barely knows and a religion he disdains. When the witch brings out her army of ghouls, it's hardly a fair fight.

And that's the kicker that sends the movie into overdrive. The suspense comes from Khoma's (and by extension, our) realisation that each successive scare is guaranteed to be more outrageous than the last. And Ptushko does not disappoint. By the final reel, all memories of the silly first part have given way to full-bore horror. The cinematic imagination on display during this awe-inspiring finale is truly shocking. These are images that owe nothing to earlier horror movies, and were never copied by followers. Indeed, the story had earlier been adapted as a silent film (Mario Bava's 1960 Italian classic, *The Mask of Satan*, is also loosely inspired by Gogol's tale), but no one could hope to replicate the delicate and masterful grace with which *Viy*'s makers balance humour and horror, each one fuelling the other.   DK

Dir: Georgi Kropachyov, Konstantin Yershov; **Original Music**: Karen Khachaturyan;
Wr: Nikolai Gogol (story), Georgi Kropachyov, Aleksander Ptushko, Konstantin Yershov;
Cinematography: Viktor Pishchalnikov, Fyodor Provorov; **Editing**: R. Pesetskaya, Tamara Zubova.

What Have You Done to Solange? (Cosa avete fatto a Solange?, aka *Terror in the Woods*, aka *Solange*, aka *Who Killed Solange?*, aka *Who's Next?*)

Italy/Germany, 1972 – 112 mins
Massimo Dallamano

At an all-girl Catholic school in London, an Italian teacher, Enrico (Fabio Testi), is engaged in an affair with a student, Elizabeth (Cristina Galbó). During a trip down the Thames on a rowing boat, Elizabeth becomes convinced that she has witnessed a brutal stabbing. After her suspicions are confirmed, terror mounts as the victim is revealed to be a pupil at the school. With Enrico a prime suspect, other student murders follow, all marked by the same grotesque signature – a knife in the vagina. Soon it transpires that each victim has a connection to a mysterious former pupil called Solange.

Based on the Edgar Wallace story 'The Clue of the New Pin', this *giallo* murder mystery jettisons the baroque visual styling familiar from entries by the likes of Mario Bava and Dario Argento. Nevertheless, many traditional or iconic elements of the *giallo* remain, not least a string of murders that have a traumatic past event at their root. Like Dallamano's own *What Have They Done to Your Daughters?* (1974) and *Rings of Fear* (1978), the action revolves around a group of teenage girls, a highly exploitable element which the film struggles to balance with its more thoughtful passages.

What sets this apart from many other *gialli* is the perverse ambience that pervades the film on several levels, including the killer's modus operandi and the terrible event that is revealed as the primary motive for the murders. Steeped in sexual betrayal and Catholic angst, the mystery elements are often secondary to character relationships which serve to dramatise the film's own play upon themes of voyeurism, repression and guilt.

The overarching character opposition is between a group of schoolgirls and various elder patriarchs (comprising teachers, policemen, priests and literal fathers). Within this dynamic, generational and gender differences engender moral indiscretion and, ultimately, transgression. Dallamano's greatest difficulty is in extricating himself fully from the titillating aspects of teenage female sexuality. Thus, there is an uncomfortable balance drawn between the leering full frontal nudity of group shower sequences and the brief but brutal visual charge of the murders. While the film does not graphically portray genital mutilation, the use of an X-ray image, in which the murder weapon is shown deeply embedded, serves as a stark, clinical visual metaphor for sexual punishment.

Solange does play with the perverse blurring of sex and mutilation. This is particularly effective in the jump-cut from the thrust of a knife to the close-up of Elizabeth's seemingly orgasmic face, which is then revealed to be her horrified reaction to a waking nightmare. Elizabeth's role as witness to the initial killing also marks another departure point for the film – instead of going on to solve the mystery (as in many *giallo* thrillers), she is brutally drowned in a bathtub.

The most contentious aspect of the film is the motivational basis provided for the killer. Given the moral confusion that runs through *Solange*, the notion of a father righting the wrongs of a botched, makeshift abortion allows him to be read as a righteous (if deeply misguided) avenger. In a film full of the flagrant display of teenage female flesh, the denouement – with its delirious images of the title character being violated by a witch-like abortionist – leaves a particularly bitter taste. This is compounded by Solange's utter isolation in the final image.

The film was shot by Aristide Massaccesi, a prolific figure in Italian exploitation cinema. Also of note is the presence of Camille Keaton, who would later find infamy as the female avenger of *I Spit on Your Grave* (1978). Viewed today, her presence adds a retrospective iconicism to her role here as violated child.   NJ

Dir: Massimo Dallamano; **Prod**: Fulvio Lucisano, Leo Pescarolo, Horst Wendlandt; **Original Music**: Ennio Morricone; **Wr**: Bruno Di Geronimo, Massimo Dallamano, Peter M. Thouet, Edgar Wallace (novel); **Cinematography**: Aristide Massaccesi; **Editing**: Clarissa Ambach, Antonio Siciliano.

The Whip and the Body (*La frusta et il corpo*, aka *What*, aka *Son of Satan*)
Italy, 1963 – 88 mins
Mario Bava

Kurt Menliff (Christopher Lee) returns home to inherit the family estate to find that, in his absence, his father has arranged a marriage between his younger brother Christian (Tony Kendall) and Kurt's cousin and former lover, Nevenka (Daliah Lavi). Furious, Kurt sets about seducing Nevenka, only too content to develop a sado-masochistic relationship where love-making must be preceded by Kurt flogging her. Then, the night after a particularly graphic sequence on the beach, Kurt is stabbed to death in his room.

Nevenka's sleep is now disturbed by visions where Kurt returns from the dead to continue their relationship. The father's murder, in an identical fashion, only contributes to the further disintegration of the

Christopher Lee meets Mario Bava: *The Whip and the Body*

family unit, Kurt's cousin Katia (Ida Galli) openly expressing her love for Christian. In an attempt to exorcise Kurt's supernatural influence, Christian and the servant Losat (Luciano Pigozzi) burn his remains. As they do so, however, they glimpse a figure dressed like Kurt running to the castle. They discover it is none other than Nevenka who killed Kurt but immediately regretted the act. Driven by guilt and desire, she has brought him back to life in her imagination and killed the father whom she held responsible for Kurt's leaving. Now completely insane and convinced Kurt is still alive and with her, Nevenka returns to the crypt and stabs herself in the belief that she is killing him.

The Whip and the Body effectively condenses the themes of the Gothic and its iconography, notably in its use of Lee who erupts into the salon like Count Dracula returning from the grave. The themes of sado-masochism, necrophilia and *amour fou* inscribe this Mario Bava film into a tradition that embraces Poe, Gautier, Buñuel, Corman and fellow Italian directors Mario Caiano, Riccardo Freda and Antonio Margheriti. The concept of patriarchy and its attendant family secrets, central to Bava's *The Mask of Satan* (1960), structures the entire film.

The key to understanding *The Whip and the Body* lies in the beach sequence where we see Nevenka sitting brooding on the sand, staring out to sea or doodling with her whip. Suddenly Kurt's boot intrudes into the frame: is he there or is Nevenka conjuring him up? Bava's use of point-of-view shots here, as in the sequences where Nevenka is visited during the night, makes both interpretations feasible. In this way the masochistic dimension of her sexuality can be interpreted in gender terms. The woman cannot be open about her sexuality, bound as she is by the repressive conventions of patriarchy. When she determines to overcome this barrier, the dead weight of unconscious guilt overwhelms her.

Nevenka feels constrained to be punished, which takes the form of being flogged by Kurt *and* of flogging herself. That she should finally die by stabbing suggests an unconscious identification with a feminine position, explicitly diagnosed as that of the hapless victim of male desire and power, that of the daughter of the servant Georgia (Harriet Medin), who committed suicide when abandoned by Kurt. Thus, Nevenka's *amour fou* is a proto-feminist gesture of solidarity and a refusal to give up on her desire, however criminal a form it takes.   RH

Dir: Mario Bava; **Prod**: Ferdinando Baldi, Elio Scardamaglia, Federico Magnaghi; **Original Music**: Carlo Rustichelli; **Wr**: Ernesto Gastaldi, Ugo Guerra, Luciano Martino; **Cinematography**: Ubaldo Terzano, Mario Bava (uncredited); **Editing**: Renato Cinquini.

The White Reindeer (*Valkoinen peura*)
Finland, 1952 – 75 mins
Erik Blomberg

Erik Blomberg's *The White Reindeer* centres on Pirita (Mirjami Kuosmanen), a witch's daughter in Lapland, orphaned as an infant and raised by foster parents. She grows up to be an exceptionally lively and independent femme fatale, abandoning the traditional role of a reindeer-herder's housewife and embracing her mystical roots. A local witch doctor eventually provides the means to satisfy Pirita's libido: by transforming into a white reindeer, she becomes a rare and irresistible prize to any herder who crosses her path. As an animal, she lures the unsuspecting herders into a desolate gorge, where the tables are effectively turned; the unfortunate men meet their doom in the arms of a beautiful woman.

Structurally, *The White Reindeer* is indebted to traditional lycanthrope stories for, after killing off the supernatural threat, the male protagonist realises the slain beast was his beloved, a woman in animal form. In Finland, the parallel myth is of a white reindeer; men lost in the snowy plains are often said to have fallen prey to a witch in disguise. Blomberg and his spouse Kuosmanen, who served as his co-writer in addition to playing the female lead, also make use of the Laplanders' shamanistic beliefs. The power of transformation is gained by sacrificing a white reindeer fawn to the Stone God, represented in the wilderness by a religious shrine.

The White Reindeer's visual style is reminiscent of F. W. Murnau's classic vampire film, *Nosferatu* (1922), as Blomberg – formerly a full-time cinematographer – uses similar methods to achieve an unassuming, dreamlike quality. When hunted, the reindeer moves in slightly slowed motion, as if teasing its pursuers. The Stone God's blessing is shown via superimposed hallucinations, along with a negative image of a white

(*Opposite page*) Lycanthropy on ice: Erik Blomberg's *The White Reindeer*

reindeer in the dark plains. Lapland's great, snowy terrain illustrates Pirita's estrangement from her family, as she hears the calling of the witch inside her, stirred up by violent winds.

Jacques Tourneur's *Cat People* (1942) can be seen as a kissing cousin to *The White Reindeer*, with its similar story of a woman gaining sexual independence through her supernatural kinship with an animal. Whereas Tourneur only used paganistic aspects as a backdrop, however, Blomberg and Kuosmanen embrace them by creating an unambiguous succubus, the sensual result of a fertility magic spell.

The White Reindeer débuted theatrically during the 1952 Helsinki Summer Olympics, resulting in near-vacant screenings. A re-run some weeks later, however, garnered larger audiences and favourable reviews. While the picture eventually won a Grand Prix at Cannes and the Critics' Award at Karlovy Vary, the climate in the domestic film industry was changing, as television had started gaining a foothold. In 1957, when *The White Reindeer* was awarded the Golden Globe at the dawn of its North American premiere, the gears in Finland had already shifted. In the years immediately following, domestic studios would cut back on their productions, relying increasingly on government support.

While Blomberg refused to sell English-language remake rights to *The White Reindeer*, he also found himself unable to mount another fantasy film production at home. The door to the other-wordly had effectively been closed. *The White Reindeer* would thus be considered a curiosity in Finnish cinema, albeit a beautiful and haunting one.   LL

Dir: Erik Blomberg; **Prod**: Aarne Tarkas; **Original Music**: Einar Englund; **Wr**: Erik Blomberg Mirjami Kuosmanen; **Cinematography**: Erik Blomberg; **Editing**: Erik Blomberg (uncredited).

Who Saw Her Die? (*Chi l'ha vista morire?*, aka *The Child*)
Italy, 1972 – 90 mins
Aldo Lado

The groundbreaking inventiveness of the Italian *giallo* films directed by Mario Bava and Dario Argento has sometimes meant that interesting work from other directors in the same format has been overlooked. *Who Saw Her Die?* is a good example of that other work. It offers a level of achievement that might not match the sustained brilliance of Bava or Argento at their best, but which is still worthy of note.

Sometimes seen as a precursor to *Don't Look Now* (1973) with its Venetian setting and in its theme of mourning for a dead child, *Who Saw Her Die?* actually has its own distinctive character. Typically for a *giallo*, its plot manages to be both overwrought and obscure. Two little girls are stalked and killed by a figure clad in a black dress and veil. The father of one of the victims (played by a post-James Bond George Lazenby) discovers a conspiracy involving prominent Venetian citizens seeking to conceal their involvement in a sex scandal, while the killer turns out to be a cross-dressing priest who, at the film's conclusion, is accidentally set on fire and plunges to his death. It is never explained why the priest is into cross-dressing, although his garbled explanation of his crimes – he kills children to protect them from sin – makes a kind of deranged sense and, incidentally, aligns him with a similarly motivated priest-killer in Lucio Fulci's *Don't Torture a Duckling* (1972) (although a last-minute plot twist revealing that the killer in *Who Saw Her Die?* is only pretending to be a priest suggests a more general propensity for dressing up).

The atmosphere of civic corruption conjured up by the film can also be found in other Italian movies of the period, arguably reflecting the troubled political situation of the times. Despite this, the film's plot is not particularly coherent, with the audience often left wondering how the various story elements connect.

As is often the case with the *giallo*, what cohesion there is lies primarily in the film's stylistic properties. The director Aldo Lado, who also made the *giallo Short Night of the Glass Dolls* (1972), has a good eye for striking details: for example, an image of a man feeding some birds manages to be both picturesque and quietly disturbing as the birds become a formless shape engulfing the human figure. However, the film's most accomplished sequence is as dependent on Ennio Morricone's impressive score as it is on the visuals. Having a chorus of children's voices as the main theme for a film about child murder is a provocation in its own right, but a yet more audacious use of music occurs in the sequence leading up to the death of the hero's daughter. This intercuts scenes of children playing in the street and point-of-view shots from the killer's veiled perspective as he approaches a sex scene between the father and his girlfriend. The children are singing the film's theme – a song that by now we associate with death – and on the soundtrack we can also hear the more discordant children's chorus that is the killer's theme. Morricone's music bestows rhythm and shape on what would otherwise have been a fragmented sequence, with the final note in the killer's theme withheld until the climactic moment when the girl looks up into his face.

Here *Who Saw Her Die?* achieves a focus that its rambling plot is unable to sustain on its own. The juxtaposition of childish innocence and sexual knowledge, with the song of children gradually corrupted into a more knowing adult theme, is powerfully done, and the cutting away to the father also underlines the general absence of adults (save for the killer) from the scene of the child's death. Who saw her die? According to the film, no one, and this sense of adult failure, manifested in the inadequacy not just of the hero but also of civic society in general, is perhaps the main impression one takes from this flawed but fascinating picture. PH

Dir: Aldo Lado; **Prod**: Ovidio G. Assonitis, Enzo Doria, Giorgio Carlo Rossi, Pietro Sagliocco; **Original Music**: Ennio Morricone; **Wr**: Francesco Barilli, Massimo D'Avak, Aldo Lado, Ruediger von Spiess; **Cinematography**: Franco Di Giacomo; **Editing**: Angelo Curi.

Zeder (aka Zeder: Voices from the Darkness, aka Zeder: Voices from the Beyond)
Italy, 1983 – 96 mins
Pupi Avati

A struggling writer, Stefano (Gabriele Lavia), discovers a series of mysterious words ('The boundaries of Death will finally be destroyed . . .') imprinted on the ribbon of an old typewriter. Convinced he's found the plot for his new novel, he sets out to locate the typewriter's previous owner, only to stumble upon an international conspiracy and a thirty-year-old, well-financed project to bring the dead back to life. Even worse, one by one his closest friends and acquaintances turn out to be among the conspirators. Unable to stop his obsessive search for the corpse of a defrocked priest who had himself buried in one of the 'K-zones' from which the dead are thought to be able to return, Stefano selfishly keeps putting his innocent girlfriend in harm's way, until she finally becomes the conspirators' latest victim. Distraught and guilt-ridden, he buries her in the 'K-zone' with his bare hands, setting the stage for the film's strikingly chilling final image.

Pupi Avati is that rare mainstream director who, in a long and distinguished career spanning over thirty-five years and encompassing more than thirty feature films (plus a couple of very successful Italian TV series in the late 1970s), has been able to add to his usual output of quiet, bittersweet comedies set in the provincial towns of Emilia-Romagna three highly-rated horror films, two of which must in fact rank among the most powerful and highly original examples of the genre.

Zeder is set for the most part in and around Rimini (Fellini's birthplace and the setting for his 1953 masterpiece, I Vitelloni) and, like Avati's other horror masterpiece, House with the Laughing Windows (1976), makes extraordinary use of that region's countryside. The recurring shots of a massive, unfinished hospital uncannily rising from the flatlands at dusk and deeply threatening in its deserted stillness, must rank among the most powerfully Expressionistic images seen since the Caligari years.

In *Zeder*, the preposterous plot and absurdly stilted dialogue, rather than distancing viewers from the narrative, sets the tone for a series of profoundly disturbing, semi-hallucinatory sequences in which Avati avoids going for the shock and gore which, given the subject matter of the film, would be expected from a director like Lucio Fulci, choosing instead to slowly build a sense of impending doom. An early sequence in a swimming pool at night – as clear an homage to Jacques Tourneur's 1942 *Cat People* as any seen on European screens – establishes the film's constant visual opposition between light and darkness. Here credit must be given to cinematographer Franco Delli Colli, Avati's usual collaborator, who manages throughout to create extreme contrast between dark and light areas in the colour film stock.

Another of the director's regular collaborators, Riz Ortolani, composed the simple yet effective rock/synthesised pulsating chords, notably derived from Goblins' soundtrack for Dario Argento's *Deep Red* (1975). And indeed Avati's two horror masterpieces are splendid examples of that combination of *giallo* (Italian narratives of thrills and detection) and horror best embodied in Argento's celebrated film.   CU

Dir: Pupi Avati; **Prod**: Antonio Avati, Enea Ferrario, Giuseppe Minervini; **Original Music**: Riz Ortolani; **Wr**: Antonio Avati, Pupi Avati, Maurizio Costanzo; **Cinematography**: Franco Delli Colli; **Editing**: Amedeo Salfa.

Zombie (aka Zombi 2, aka Island of the Flesh-Eaters, aka Island of the Living Dead)
Italy, 1979 – 91 mins
Lucio Fulci

Lucio Fulci's *Zombie* opens with a derelict, fly-infested sailboat adrift in New York Harbor and boarded by two Harbor Patrol officers. When one of them is fatally bitten by the sailboat's sole occupant, the surviving officer shoots the attacker, who falls overboard and is lost. The dead officer's body is taken to the morgue and, unseen by the business-as-usual doctors in attendance, begins to twitch under its sheet. Meanwhile, the daughter of the boat's owner, Anne Bowles (Tisa Farrow), sneaks aboard the impounded vessel at night to discover a British reporter, Peter West (Ian McCulloch), has also come aboard to investigate the mystery. They discover a letter from Anne's father, a doctor. The letter explains that he is suffering from an unknown disease on the remote Caribbean island of Matou. Peter and Anne fly to the region and hire a couple on

A feast of flesh: Lucio Fulci's *Zombie*

vacation to take them to the island. Upon reaching Matou, they find that the island's medical staff, Dr Menard (Richard Johnson) and his nurse, are fighting off an infestation of the living dead that the island's natives insist is caused by voodoo.

From that point forward, the film's pace accelerates to a series of confrontations between the island's living inhabitants and the marauding zombies. One such particularly effective scene takes place in an old Spanish graveyard, where the bodies of rotting conquistadors rise from beneath the ground. Eventually, the only survivors to escape the island are Anne and Peter. Peter argues to Anne that they must take one of the reanimated corpses back to New York with them as proof of their incredible story, but this discussion is rendered moot when the boat's radio brings them the news that zombies have overrun New York City. The film's apocalyptic last shot shows a horde of zombies advancing over a bridge into the bedlam of the panicked city.

Later Fulci horror films will show a decidedly surrealistic turn; *Zombie*, however, is very linear and simple in its storyline. This quality probably played no small part in the film's financial success. Even *Zombie*'s most implausible and/or gore-heavy set pieces – two of the most famous being an underwater fight to the death between a zombie and a tiger shark, and a woman's eye being skewered on a long wooden splinter during a zombie attack – are in context at least related to scenes that have gone before and are staged and photographed with dogged realism. For those viewers who appreciate traditional conventions of storytelling, this film is one of Fulci's most accessible. But the film is deceptively simple. Its political subtext is that European colonialism is in some way being punished for its past abuses; the living dead are from the ranks of the old West Indian slave trade and the Spanish exploiters and conquerors of the Caribbean.

The film poses no pat answer as to what is causing the dead to rise and eat the living. Voodoo is mentioned as a possible explanation, and certainly the mysterious voodoo drums that beat softly but incessantly in the background suggest a connection to the plague and may be why both the former victims and agents of colonialism are now returning.

But the connection is not proven or even explored in any depth. Dr Menard cannot isolate a scientific reason, try though he might to experiment on natives and examine his own blood for signs of viral infection. Nor do Fulci's zombies possess the rudimentary cognitive functioning and memory retention of George Romero's zombies. Fulci's are unstoppable and incomprehensible forces. Their victory is inevitable. The islanders' losing battle against the zombies, in which the few survivors can only cut and run, is just the beginning of the rout of humanity, as the film's last shot of besieged New York illustrates. Thus, Fulci's film has a philosophical core of fatalism.

Zombie was initially perceived by many critics as derivative, or even a rip-off, of Romero's 1978 zombie film, *Dawn of the Dead*, re-edited by famed horror director Dario Argento – which had just been released in Italy as *Zombi* to great financial success. Fulci titled his living-dead film *Zombi 2* to capitalise on *Zombi*'s success, but in no obvious way is the film's plot related to the events depicted in Romero's movie. As Fulci himself has noted, cinematic zombies predate the Romero/Argento interpretation by decades and originate in Caribbean culture. *Zombie*, with its tropical setting and overt references to voodoo, belongs as much within the subgenre of voodoo zombie movies, such as Val Lewton's *I Walked with a Zombie* (1943), as it does to Romero's gory cannibalistic-zombie-as-political-metaphor films.

Regardless of the negative critical reaction, *Zombie* made over $30 million in Italy and went on to become a worldwide hit, in spite – or perhaps *because* – of the gruesome scenes that led to its being banned in Britain. Regardless, following *Zombie*, Fulci's career took off as an international horror auteur. PLS

Dir: Lucio Fulci; **Prod**: Fabrizio De Angelis, Ugo Tucci, Gianfranco Couyoumdjian (uncredited); **Original Music**: Giorgio Cascio, Fabio Frizzi, Adriano Giordanella (uncredited), Maurizio Guarini (uncredited); **Wr**: Elisa Briganti, Dardano Sacchetti; **Cinematography**: Sergio Salvati; **Editing**: Vincenzo Tomassi.

Notes

1. Raiford Guins, 'Blood and Black Gloves on Shiny Discs: New Media, Old Tastes, and the Remediation of Italian Horror Films in the US', Tony Williams and Steven Jay Schneider (eds), *Horror International* (Detroit, IL: Wayne State University Press, 2005), p. 11.

2. 'Dario Argento', *Filmbug.com*, (1998–2006), 15 April 2006, <www.filmbug.com/db/3183>.

3. Jodey Castricano, 'For the Love of Smoke and Mirrors', *Kinoeye: New Perspectives on European Film* vol. 2 no. 11, June 2002, <www.kinoeye.org/index_02_11.php>.

4. K. H. Brown. 'The Bird with the Crystal Plumage', *Kinocite*, 12 April 2006, <www.kinocite.co.uk/0/68.php>.

5. Martin Rubin, *Thrillers* (Cambridge: Cambridge University Press, 1999), p. 120.

6. David Kalat, 'French Revolution: The Secret History of Gallic Horror Movies', in Steven Jay Schneider (ed.), *Fear Without Frontiers* (Surrey: FAB Press, 2003).

7. David Kalat, 'French Revolution', p. 272.

8. Ernest Mandel, *Delightful Murder: A Social History of the Crime Story* (London: Pluto Press, 1984), p. 88.

9. See Jean Douchet, 'Hitch and his Audience', in Jim Hillier (ed.), *Cahiers du cinéma 1960–1968*, (Cambridge, MA: Harvard University Press, 1986 [1960]), p. 151.

10. Robert E. Kapsis, *Hitchcock: The Making of a Reputation* (Chicago, IL: University of Chicago Press, 1992), pp. 54, 100.

11. Brian Lindsey, 'Eccentric Cinema Reviews: *Inferno*', <www.eccentric-cinema.com/cult_movies/inferno.htm>.

12. Maitland McDonagh, *Broken Mirrors/Broken Minds: The Dark Dreams of Dario Argento* (London: Sun Tavern Fields, 1991), pp. 21–2.

13. Eve Kosofsky Sedgwick, *The Coherence of Gothic Conventions* (North Stratford, NH: Ayer, 1999), p. 40.

14. Marguerite La Caze, 'The Violence of the Spectacle', in *Kinoeye* vol. 3 no. 5, 10 May 2003, <www.kinoeye.org/03/05/lacaze05.php>.

15. Neil Jackson, 'The Cultural Construction of Snuff', *Kinoeye* vol. 3 no. 5, 10 May 2003, <www.kinoeye.org/03/05/jackson05.php>.

Index

Page numbers in **bold** denote the principal entry for a selected film; those in *italic* denote illustrations

List of Illustrations

While considerable effort has been made to correctly identify the copyright holders this has not been possible in all cases. We apologise for any apparent negligence and any omissions or corrections brought to our attention will be remedied in future editions.

The Beast, Argos Films; *Blood and Black Lace*, Emmepi Cinematografica/Productions Georges de Beauregard/Top-Film; *Blood and Roses*, Films E.G.E./Documento Film; *Brotherhood of the Wolf*, © Davis Films/© Studio Canal+/© TF1 Films Productions; *The Cabinet of Dr Caligari*, Decla Filmgesellschaft; *City of the Living Dead*, Dania Film/Medusa Distribuzione/National Cinematografica; *Daughters of Darkness*, Showking Film/Ciné-Vog/Maya Film/Roxy-Film/Mediterranea, Cannes-Lux; *Deep Red*, Seda Spettacoli S.p.A./Rizzoli Editore; *The Ear*, Svabik-Prochazka/Filmové Studio Barrandov; *Eyes Without a Face*, Champs-Elysées Productions/Lux Film; *The Fourth Man*, Verenigde Nederlandsche Filmcompagnie; *Funny Games*, Wega-Film; *The Golem: How He Came into the World*, Ufa; *Häxan: Witchcraft Through the Ages*, Svensk Filmindustri; *Hour of the Wolf*, Svensk Filmindustri; *I Vampiri*, Athena Cinematografica/Titanus; *Kill, Baby . . . Kill!*, F.U.L. Film; *The Lift*, Sigma Films; *Malpertuis*, S.O.F.I.D.O.C., Brussels/Société d'Expansion du Spectacle/Artemis Filmgesellschaft; *The Mask of Satan*, Galatea Film/Jolly Film; *Nightwatch*, Thura Film/Danmarks Radio-TV Fiktion; *Nosferatu: A Symphony of Horror*, Prana-Film; *The Stendhal Syndrome*, Cine 2000/Medusa Film; *Succubus*, Aquila Film; *The Tenant*, Marianne Productions; *Thesis*, Producciones del Escorpión S.L.; *Torso*, Compagnia Cinematografica Champion; *Valerie and Her Week of Wonders*, Filmové Studio Barrandov; *The Vanishing*, Golden Egg Films/Ingrid Productions/MGS Film; *The Whip and the Body*, Leone Film/Vox Film/Francinor/P.I.P; *The White Reindeer*, Erik Blomberg; *Zombie*, Variety Film.